412 DAYS

ISBN-13: 978-1-952484-04-9

Published by
The Last Reformation books
The Last Reformation, Inc.
6671 W. Indiantown Road, Suite 50-346 Jupiter, FL 33458
Email: Mail@TheLastReformation.com

412 DAYS

PERSECUTED FOR CHRIST
It's coming. Are you ready?

TORBEN SONDERGAARD

Foreword

Roughly ten years ago, I began to hear about a Danish Christian named Torben Søndergaard, leader of a worldwide movement called The Last Reformation. What was this movement about?

From what I could tell, Torben had been a somewhat traditional Christian who began reading the Bible through new eyes, as if the things that happened in the days of Jesus and the apostles could happen again today. And they did!

This created no small stir in his native country of Denmark, where much of the church frowned on the idea that followers of Jesus could drive out demons in His name or bring healing to the sick. Yet these were the very signs that marked The Last Reformation movement. After being dogged by controversy in Denmark, he made his way to America with his family to escape what he called religious persecution, and that is how we came to meet.

Some of my ministry school graduates had met Torben and were doing gospel outreaches with him here in the States. They assured me he was a solid believer who preached a true gospel, and they encouraged me to get to know him if I could. When he came to my area on July 7, 2019, we were able to meet together for two hours, sharing our love for the Lord and our passion to see this world encounter the real Jesus, then getting on our knees and praying together. As I journaled that day, "a delightful meeting with Torben from (The) Last Reformation at the office."

The next time I saw Torben was December 13, 2022, but this time it was by Zoom as he sat in a courtroom as a prisoner of the state.

What on earth had happened? I had been brought in to testify before the court on religious attitudes in Denmark, especially as it concerned views on Pentecostals and Charismatics, since Torben was seeking asylum in America due to religious persecution. I saw Torben on my computer screen as he walked into the courtroom wearing his prison outfit, shackled hands. As I wrote in my journal, "It's heart-wrenching to see him in handcuffs and in the orange jumpsuit, and he looks to be skin and bones."

How did all this happen? Why was he incarcerated in an American prison? Was he guilty of some nefarious crimes, as his critics claimed? Or was he a modern-day Paul, suffering persecution for the gospel?

When he came to the States, I encouraged him to get to know the pastors here, telling him he would find many of like heart (far more than he did in his small, home country of Denmark), encouraging him not to be isolated from the churches. In the months that followed, we were in occasional contact, as he shared with me some of the great things he saw the Lord doing. The next thing I heard he was arrested, charged with smuggling weapons into America from Mexico. Seriously!

It would have been one thing if his critics disagreed with his style of preaching. But that would not land him in prison. And if it was an immigration issue and he had overstayed his visa, he could simply be sent back to Denmark. But shackled as a criminal and put in prison? For what? Something was clearly amiss.

Torben actually called my radio show from prison on January 10, 2023, and it was a moving, powerful time. By then, he had already spent more than half a year in prison, and when I asked him why he was arrested and being held, he didn't have a clue. He told me that the ridiculous weapons accusations immediately disappeared, but he was being treated like a criminal, handcuffed, shackled, put in solitary confinement, then housed with other inmates who had committed all kinds of crimes, including murder.

But that was only part of the story. After battling some depression the first two months, he realized that this was his mission field for the moment, praying and reading the Bible day and night, leading prisoners to Jesus, seeing them healed and set free, to the point that, at one time 20 out of 25 inmates were doing Bible study with him. Yet why was he still languishing in prison?

On what basis was he being held? Why this seemingly cruel and unusual punishment, completely separated from his wife and children?

Some of these questions are still being answered, with members of Congress now involved, demanding serious responses from our government. But that is not the focus of this book. Instead, this is Torben's gripping, first-hand, brutally honest account of his 412 days in prison in America (yes, more than one year!), as he shares the ups and downs, the highlights and lowlights, the glory and the pain. It will all unfold in the pages that follow.

Speaking of his harsh imprisonment in the Russian gulag, Alexander Solzhenitsyn said, "I nourished my soul there, and I say without hesitation, 'Bless you prison, for having been in my life!'" Torben can now speak similar words, having encountered the living God in a profound and deep way alone in his cell. They are words of hope for those who suffer unjustly, for those who have been imprisoned by the circumstances of life, for those who are rejected and misunderstood, for those who are determined to follow Jesus no matter the cost or consequences.

Read this book and be riveted. Read it and be challenged. Read it and be changed.

- Dr. Michael L. Brown, host of the Line of Fire broadcast,
author of Revival or We Die

Preface

From its very beginning, America has always held high the banner of religious freedom. The Pilgrims and Founding Fathers alike knew that freedom of religion is humanity's most important and fundamental liberty. Indeed, all other freedoms depend on it.

Yet, freedom of religion is increasingly under attack, not only around the world, but even in the United States. In these perilous times, the story of Torben Søndergaard stands as a beacon of hope and an urgent call to action. As a lawyer and pastor committed to defending religious liberty, I find Torben's journey profoundly compelling - a testament to the unyielding power of faith in the face of seemingly insurmountable odds.

When forced to flee Denmark due to religious persecution, Torben exemplified extraordinary courage and faith.

Torben's arrival in America should have marked the beginning of safety and new opportunities. Instead, it unveiled another layer of persecution.

Despite these trials, Torben's faith never wavered. He continued to inspire and gather believers, even from the confines of a jail cell, mirroring the apostolic zeal of early church leaders.

His time in detention revealed the transformative power of faith. Stripped of his freedom, Torben turned a jail into a sanctuary. He initiated daily church meetings, witnessing a revival among inmates. Through prayer and the sharing of God's Word, he brought hope and light into a place of despair. His story illustrates that true freedom is found not in our circumstances but in our unwavering commitment to Christ.

Torben's experiences underscore the necessity of protecting our religious freedoms. His journey is a clarion call to the Church to wake up and prepare for increasing persecution. We must stand firm in our faith, trust in God's provision, and actively defend our rights. The erosion of religious liberty in one nation sets a dangerous precedent for others. It is our duty to guard this precious freedom, not just for ourselves but for believers worldwide.

Torben Søndergaard's story is an inspiration to us all. It challenges us to deepen our faith, embrace our calling, and trust in God's unfailing love and provision. His journey is a vivid illustration of the power of faith and the imperative to defend our religious freedoms against any threat. As you read these pages, may you be stirred to action, emboldened to speak out, and strengthened in your resolve to stand for truth and liberty.

May it inspire us all to live with a Kingdom mindset, ready to defend our faith and our freedoms, confident in the promise of hearing our Lord say, "Well done, good and faithful servant."

- Richard Harris, Executive Director of Truth and Liberty and Director of the Practical Government School, Charis Bible College.

Endorsements

"In my over 40 years as a journalist, I have never encountered a Christian leader treated so harshly and unfairly by 'democratic' governments as Torben Sondergaard was. Yet amidst all the terrible things he was forced to endure, watching what looked like the destruction of his life and ministry, Torben's choice to believe God turned terrible persecution into an extraordinary explosion of God's goodness and Holy Spirit power. The English evangelist Henry Varley said, 'The world has yet to see what God can do through a man who is totally yielded to Him.' As I read this book, I felt I was seeing that man. 412 Days is a must-read for all believers who very soon could face the same persecution."

- Dale Hurd, senior CBN News reporter

"412 Days is a 'must read' for skeptics and believers alike. It reads like an epistle from a modern-day Paul. Sondergaard describes both natural and supernatural experiences with such verifiable detail that the reader is left no doubt as to their credibility. Those experiences and the author's love for the Bible establish a foundation for the sound doctrine the author offers, drawn both from a life of obedience to Jesus and the wicked persecution Sondergaard has experienced in both Europe and America alike. The beauty of this work are the many God-given revelations the author shares and his ultimate conclusions regarding the cost of suffering and his compelling encouragement that the treasure of proximity to God, born from hardship, makes it all worthwhile. This amazing book evidences the good that God can do with the evil intended and represents a critical wake-up call to a slumbering Body of Christ about what more of its members are sure to experience in this evil age and the fruit to be born therefrom."

- Jim Boatman, Esq., managing shareholder,

Boatman Ricci Law Firm

"I have known Torben for several years now, and I've had the privilege of working alongside him in various training schools, tent meetings, kickstarts, and other ministry projects. We've shared both incredible moments and some really tough times. Over these past years, I've heard him repeatedly speak about the coming persecution to America. This book truly reflects the genuine heart of Torben's life and the deep burden he carries for the body of Christ. So, when I was asked to work on the book cover, I was really excited. The cover had already been designed, so my job was to step in and refine it. The first concept effectively drew the reader into the environment Torben was experiencing—depicting the prison cells, the bunks, and the building itself. But the more I looked at it, the more it felt like there was too much going on visually and it seemed to be missing that emotional connection that the story really needed to convey. So, I started over. Given the nature of the book, I felt that focusing on Torben's face would create a stronger impact. However, finding the right image was challenging. I reviewed one of his interviews where he discussed key moments from his time in prison. There was this one moment where he was in the middle of sharing his story, and it just clicked. That moment perfectly captured the emotion and essence of what the book is all about. With this shot of Torben on the cover, I aimed to do more than just show the author—I wanted to communicate the heart, the struggle, and the eventual sense of freedom that readers will discover in the pages of the book. The feedback has been overwhelmingly positive, with one person commenting, 'They say you can't read a book by its cover, yet I feel you can read so much from this!' It's true, you can't judge a book by its cover, but this cover tells a story all on its own. I believe this cover sets the tone before a single page is turned. It's a powerful story that's definitely worth reading, as it reveals both the brokenness of our world and the steadfastness of God's faithfulness."

- Ever Calamaco, Graphic Designer,
Founder & Contributor at One Way Gospel
EverCalamaco.com

"I'm so glad that you have picked up this book because you are about to get to know a different Torben Søndergaard than the one that has been portrayed in the news, on YouTube, and social media. This book will show you the real Torben Søndergaard—a compassionate father, a loving husband, a caring friend, and a spiritual father to thousands of people around the world. I'm proud to call him my friend and brother. I have lived and ministered in the States for 18 years, but I am Danish like Torben and have known him for almost 25 years. Torben and I did some ministry together in Denmark, but we were never really close. We lost contact after I moved to the United States to work for Matt Sorger Ministries and later as a pastor in a local church here on Long Island, New York. We reconnected when Torben and his family moved to the States in 2019. I attended some of his meetings, and I became hungry for the life he lived as a true disciple of Christ. I wanted it but felt stuck in my 9-5 job as a pastor, mainly doing administrative work. Three years ago, I received a divine phone call from Torben where God truly spoke to me that it was time. I took the biggest and greatest step of faith in my life; I quit my pastor job and started my own ministry. Since then, God has done amazing things in my life, and I have seen people being transformed like never before, making true disciples who obey our Lord. During Torben's time in jail, I often spoke with him over the phone. When his wife Lene got sick, I was asked to take over the daily communication with Torben. This was like an action-thriller. It was a difficult and stressful time, and I have never experienced anything like it before. Torben would often ask me how I was doing, and my problems seemed small compared to his life in jail. I felt convicted—would I be able to follow Jesus to the end? One day, I realized that Torben had invited me deeper into the book of Acts life. We were experiencing and living out the book of Acts. Torben was in jail like Paul the Apostle, "writing letters" to his disciples outside while they were busy baptizing, healing the sick, casting out demons, and establishing Jesus Fellowships around the world. I felt like Tychicus, entrusted with delivering letters and providing updates about Torben's circumstances. It has been life-transforming to be so close to the events as they happened, even though the waiting was extremely hard. I will never forget the morning on August 16 when I was on the phone with Torben, and he suddenly said, 'Kim, Kim, they are calling my name.... I'm going home.' It was the moment we had prayed and talked about for so long—the joy and emotions were so overwhelming that we both began to cry. They tried to discourage and destroy Torben by locking him up, but I saw him become freer and freer. I will never be the same again, and I thank God for the unique opportunity and time I had with one of His Kingdom servants. I know you will be challenged and changed by reading this book. Let the Holy Spirit do a new thing in you so you can be ready for what's coming soon."

- Kim Nielsen, The Kingdom Encounter

"When I first met Torben Sondergaard, I not only met him, but I also met God. After that day, my life has never been the same. I was healed, filled, and completely set on fire for God. Not long after that, I joined The Last Reformation training school and eventually ended up in leadership of the ministry, TLR. Over the years, Torben has mentored me and helped me grow into a strong Christian man. Sometime later, we started to travel. About a year into our travels, Torben reached out to me and said he was coming to Florida because he had received a letter from Homeland Security telling him to come to a meeting about his Asylum case. I was in Florida at the time, so I agreed to take him to the meeting. I dropped him off and went to get some food. He was supposed to text me when he was done for me to pick him up, but I never received a text. Two hours later, I went to pick him up, but the parking lot was empty, and he was not there. At that time, I texted his wife Lene to ask what was going on, and she called me to inform me that they had locked him up. I called my wife in shock and couldn't understand how or why they had done this. About three months later, I had a very strong feeling that I needed to go help Lene, who was in California while we were on the East Coast. I started praying about it, and about three days into praying, Torben called me and asked me to come to California to help the family. We arrived in California and went to check on Lene, who was not in good shape due to the stress of the lawyers, life, and missing her husband. We stayed for almost four months, and it was one of the biggest spiritual battles we had ever been in. The enemy was trying to attack Lene and everyone close to her and Torben in every possible way. This was one of the hardest battles we've ever been in, and we've been in a lot of battles. We were also there driving with Lene and the girls back across the US as she felt she should come to Florida to be closer to the jail where Torben was. Throughout it all, I've never seen a man keep his faith, stay strong, stay positive, and stay focused on God like Torben did. What an inspiration. Through this whole ordeal, I have been strengthened in my walk. I don't understand how a man like Torben could be beaten down and separated from his family for so long and still know that God is good. I don't ever want to go through anything like this again, but I'm so glad that God chose me to be there for him and his family during their time of need. We all need to love each other and learn to be one body. Read this book and let God transform your life as he has done with me and my family.

- **Dewayne Smith, pastor and full-time missionary,**
Sent by Two Ministries

"Four years ago, our lives changed forever! In January 2020, we discovered Torben Søndergaard and The Last Reformation on YouTube. God used this man to bring truth into our lives and a real understanding of the gospel. My wife and I ended up attending the Luke 10 School run by the ministry that year in North Carolina. We then stayed on to help with the next four schools and their tent revival meetings where we saw many people healed, set free, and baptized to Jesus Christ. We not only learned how to live like what we see in the book of Acts but also got to live it out. The gospel became part of our DNA, and there is no other way we would want to live. We are forever grateful to Torben and Lene and their obedience to Jesus Christ. Months after Torben was incarcerated, my wife and I had the privilege of washing the feet of God's disciples. You see, Torben's wife and daughters were led by God to come from California to Florida to be closer to the jail where Torben was locked up. This resulted in them living in an RV right next to us for three months. We witnessed first-hand the emotional and physical pain they went through during this time of testing and persecution. But what we witnessed there was their unwavering faith and reliance on God! They didn't let their circumstances define who they were, no matter how difficult it was. On the contrary, we saw Lene fighting her faith battle, holding on to God's faithfulness with everything she had, even though there was not much left at times. While she did that, Torben continued preaching the gospel, healing the sick, casting out demons, and baptizing people in Jesus's name. This book not only details what Torben and his family went through, but it is also here to prepare every one of us to be ready for the difficult and challenging times ahead."

- Andrew Nakhla, missionary and business owner

"When Torben went to jail, I was blessed and privileged to be able to help him write out this book from voice recordings he made in jail. Having worked beside him for several years, seeing the truth and authenticity he walks in, and the integrity he strives to apply to every situation, it was overwhelming to hear such ridiculous accusations against him. I cried alongside him when he cried, but also felt the victory and strength as the Holy Spirit spoke strong truth through him in the midst of this incredible injustice. Torben came to America to warn us of the coming persecution, and then he became a living, breathing example of this truth. Through Torben's shining example of steadfast faith and obedience throughout this ordeal, God is calling His people to Himself! We would do well to heed His call! He alone is worthy! Walking with Torben through this process was an incredible blessing, and it's very exciting to see this book ready for publishing. I pray anyone who reads it will hear what God is saying through this surrendered servant of Jesus Christ, and that it will prompt complete, unconditional surrender to God for each one!"

- Sandra Mancine, worship facilitator

"I had met Torben shortly after he was released from his horrific 412 days in jail ordeal and I was naturally curious to look into his eyes after such a long time. I will always remember our first engagement when he came to our house to preach the gospel to us. He was a tall, youthful and charismatic man whose Holy Spirit filled appearance would trigger every dark spot within us to be revealed. It was a life-changing weekend in which me and my household were changed eternally. Now seven years later, a skinny bearded man stood in front of me. He seemed to have been broken but not broken down, his softened voice and mild gaze told the story of a servant of Christ who had suffered and endured because of unrighteous persecution like none of us could imagine. Torben 2.0 is still the Torben who had radically and beautifully led our household to be born again but he seems to have become a new creation through suffering in obedience while remaining faithful to the end. This book is a must read for anyone who cannot comprehend that the promised persecution of Christians worldwide will come home sooner than most imagine. Rejoice like Torben—Matthew 5:11-12: 'Blessed are you when people insult you, persecute you and falsely say all kinds of evil against you because of me. Rejoice and be glad, because great is your reward in heaven, for in the same way they persecuted the prophets who were before you.'"

- Lou Bega, Grammy-nominated musician and singer-song-writer best known for his hit single "Mambo No. 5."

"The problem with Torben Søndergaard is that he is 100 percent committed to the gospel of Jesus Christ, and he doesn't care what others think. That's why he often suffers persecution. He is similar to a modern-day Apostle Paul. After his release from prison, he moved to Mexico. Through a mutual friend, I reached out and invited him to join me in Colombia, where we aimed to win 8 percent of Barranquilla for Christ. I needed someone to help train hundreds of pastors and thousands of people for this monumental task. What struck me about Torben was his humility and passion for souls. Used to working more independently, he humbled himself for the first time post-prison to support another man's vision in a new way. We evangelized together in malls, witnessing people collapsing and demons being cast out, which even led to Torben being kicked out of the mall. This made me understand why he keeps getting expelled from countries; he genuinely loves people but also walks with the power of God, which the enemy resents. Torben fearlessly ventured into the dangerous city of Malambo, where 70 churches united with their congregations. He preached with all his heart in the toughest neighborhoods. In Barranquilla, we had about 2,500 people from approximately 100 different churches. I asked Torben to pray over each person lined up against the wall. Despite never having done it exactly like that before, he humbled himself and did it, resulting in people falling, demons being cast out, and others speaking in tongues. Beyond teaching and ministering, Torben trains leaders. He trained my team and me. As we cast out demons, I sought his guidance, and he coached me, emphasizing the use of more authority by faith in Jesus' name. His message on baptism impacted me so deeply that, despite my 25 years in ministry, I asked him to baptize me again the right way as not like last time many years ago when my heart was not in it. Torben is one of the top evangelists in the world today. He is raw, real, and 100 percent committed to the Great Commission. This book offers a compelling and challenging read as it documents the real-life persecutions faced by a modern-day missionary. As 2 Timothy 3:12 states, 'Indeed, all who desire to live a godly life in Christ Jesus will be persecuted.' Reading this book will challenge you to ask yourself: In what ways am I suffering for the cause of Christ?"

- Steven Koko, president of Cities for Christ, co-founder of Nations for Christ, and TV personality, Mission Extreme Christian reality show

"Few people have impacted my life like Torben Søndergaard has. Especially in the relatively little amount of time I've had the privilege of knowing him. Still, fully surrendered disciples of Christ tend to have a deep impact quickly on those they cross paths with. From the moment we met, I sensed a powerful yet tender presence of God cascading over me while we talked. I knew this man was different. He carried something extraordinary on his life that intrigued me, particularly his commitment to making disciples. We built a friendship and I had no idea how much I would need a friend like him for the journey God had me on. Our entwined journeys exposed me to a vulnerable yet valiant man. I watched him face unprecedented challenges laid out in this book, 412 Days, step by step and yet his faith never wavered. Shockingly more so, he found ways to encourage so many others; including myself from some of the lowest points of his life. Like Jesus hearing that his cousin John the Baptist had just been beheaded and He desired to be alone. He laid his emotions aside and tended to the crowds who were desperate to receive a touch from Him. So, Jesus—moved with compassion, healed the sick and ministered to all who were hurting. He put the needs of others before His own. Torben lives his life like this. His posture reminded me that of Paul when he wrote, 'We are hard-pressed on every side, yet not crushed; we are perplexed, but not in despair; persecuted, but not forsaken; struck down, but not destroyed—always carrying about in the body the dying of the Lord Jesus, that the life of Jesus also may be manifested in our body' (2 Corinthians 4:8-10). As iron sharpens iron, Torben proved he was teachable. He wasn't some YouTube star, full of ego and pride. He was humble to receive suggestions and wisdom from those who had accomplished far less than himself. Clearly, this is a quality needed far more in the church today. His heart for the Local Church has only strengthened. As someone who owes a great debt of gratitude to the Local Church for its influence on my life, I'm so grateful for this. His desire to partner with those in the Body of Christ who perhaps don't agree with every point of peripheral doctrine has blessed me personally and countless others. Torben's strategies are effective. His passion is unparalleled. His commitment is unwavering. His sacrifice is noteworthy. His fruit is immeasurable. His devotion to his family is an example. He is a gift to both the Body of Christ and those who don't yet know Jesus Christ as their personal Lord and Savior. Above all, I'm proud to call him my friend. Devour this book, I believe it will change your life."

- Josiah Elias, lead pastor, Faith Chapel, San Diego

Table of Contents

Introduction
From Cell N, Pod B6

Welcome to this extraordinary book. I have authored several books before, but nothing like this. I am writing on paper with a security pen (one that can bend so I cannot hurt anyone) while sitting in my lower bunk bed in Cell N, Pod B6, in Baker County Detention Center in Macclenny, Florida.

As of right now, I have been locked up for more than nine months, exactly two hundred and seventy-eight days. My cell is eight by thirteen feet, with a bunk bed on the wall, a metal toilet with a sink on one side, and a shower on the other. It is also my source of lukewarm water for my coffee and where I wash my clothes. I spend nearly twenty-two hours per day in my cell, like right now, as I am writing this to you.

I have no idea what will happen to me or when I will get out.

A few days ago, my ICE (U.S. Immigration and Customs Enforcement) officer told me they needed my passport so they could deport me if necessary. Yes, according to him, he believes I will be here several more months, and then I will be deported back to Denmark. But we'll see what will happen.

According to my legal team, I have an excellent asylum case, but they have also never seen anything like this before, with all the lies and the amount of energy the enemy has spent to put me and keep me here.

"Torben, the enemy really hates you," a legal team member said a few days ago.

So, my situation is unique in so many ways. No, it is unprecedented.

My enemy wants to see me destroyed. He wants to see me stop sharing the gospel and is doing everything he can to put an end to my ministry. But I know God is in control, and even though I am suffering, God's hand is all over everything that is happening. Like Jesus, who suffered on the cross at the hands of the enemy, God was still in control. The enemy thought he had won the victory, but it resulted in his defeat.

I believe the same thing will happen here.

My faith doesn't rest in what my ICE officer, legal team, or the enemy says. My faith rests in God because He always has the final say.

This has been the most demanding season I've ever been in. Yet, at the same time, it has also been the most transforming. Even though it has been brutal at times, I've had some of the most beautiful moments ever.

I have fasted for forty days at various times in my life. All of you who have tried a long fast know how hard it is, but at the same time, how amazing and fruitful it can be. Being here is like a long fast. I am now on my two hundred-and-seventy-eighth-day of this fast, and I don't know when it will end.

Fasting is challenging; I've often dropped the fasts I've attempted in the past. I would start fasting, thinking I would go forty days, but then I would change my mind. I would only go for twenty or thirty days—sometimes only a few days—because it was just too hard, and the temptation was just too big. Imprisoned here, I understand that I did not have the character and fortitude I needed to finish those fasts.

But this time is different: I don't have the option to drop out.

During the last nine months, the pressure has often been too much for me. I have often told friends over the phone that if I could dial my way out of here, I would have picked up the phone and said, "Let's drop it, let's stop it right now, I give up."

But as the weeks have passed and slowly turned into months, I can see God's hand in it and His transformation in my life. Things are falling into place, and I know God is in control. This has allowed me to keep running the race in front of me.

I have received prophetic words from outside this prison that have helped me. Someone from outside said they had a powerful dream about me after I had been here for one and a half months, which gave me a great deal of hope during my stay here.

A little over a month later, another solid prophetic word came to me in a dark time. When I initially read it, I did not fully understand it. But as the weeks and months went by, more of the prophetic word fell into place, and it came true piece by piece. As each event unfolded, I started to see how much God's hand is all over everything, how He sent me here, and how He's the One who will release me when He has done what He needs to do in my life. Yes, this is much bigger than just me, and I know God has a perfect plan for everything.

Being here, seeing God's hand at work, is teaching me a lot of things about faith, hope, suffering, and endurance. Even though the pressure is intense at times, especially when my family struggles and my wife is under significant attack, I am thankful to God for sending me here. I know that He's in control. So here I am, in many ways, a different person than I was nine months ago.

God has revealed so much truth to me in His Word, and I have had amazing experiences in which the lives of my fellow inmates have been changed by being set free and baptized in Christ. Just a few days ago, a Muslim came into my cell and looked at me.

"Torben, what is it with you?" he asked.

"You are shining. I see glory all over your face," he said with a hint of the fear of God in his voice.

I hesitated, unsure how to respond. Before I got the chance to say anything, he continued, saying: "I don't know what it is. You have been with God."

He knew where the glory came from; he saw it all over me. He understood that it was from my time being in here alone with God.

The day after, he returned and said: "Torben, why are you so happy? You should not be happy with everything that is happening to you. Why are you so happy?"

Before I got the chance to answer him, he continued: "Yes, I know why. You are reading God's holy words," pointing to the Bible on my bed. I asked if he wanted to read it, but he said, "No thanks." But then he came back the next day and got one of my Bibles to read.

This is the reality: I have been with God in a way I have never been with Him before, and God is working in so many ways in here.

When a person spends this much time alone in their cell in the Word of God, with God in prayer, it changes them. One-third of the New Testament was written in prison, and when you sit in prison reading it, it comes alive in a way it never has been before.

After reading, studying, and being in the Word like never before, God spoke and gave me a new teaching series about the Kingdom of God. As I write this, I have finished twenty-four lessons, which will come out as soon as I am released. It begins in Eden in the book of Genesis and ends in Eden in the last chapters of the book of Revelation with the New Heaven and New Earth.

This new teaching will bless many people, set them free, and prepare them for what is coming. As soon as I finished the teaching, I asked, "God, what now?"

And then He told me, "Now, you start writing a book."

It was a surprise to me. I did not see that coming, but I got very excited, so here I am, writing to all of you.

I don't know how long this book will be; I'm not sure what to write, so I will start with one chapter at a time.

I also don't know what will happen to me or when I will be released.

Whether I write a few chapters here in my cell, get released, and write the rest outside the walls of this jail, doesn't matter to me. If God has more for me to do here before I'm released, I am submitted to His plan. I don't know many things, but I know that God is in control. I need to write this book and know that God will use it to transform many people worldwide.

Truthfully, I am more than ready to leave this place. Every day, I dream of getting out and being with my family. But God knows better. I was prepared to leave this place six months ago, but it did not happen. I have heard people out there talking about me and why I don't just forfeit my asylum claim. They have heard that if I do that, I will be free to leave right away.

I wish it were so simple, but it is not. First, if I forfeit my asylum case, I will be released but not today or tomorrow. It will still take several weeks or months if I do that, and then I will be banned for many years from entering the United States again. All this time, I have also always believed that I will be out sooner by standing firm on my rights, on the truth, and fighting rather than just giving in.

I know now, looking back, that if I had given up on day one, I probably could have been out by now. But I never felt that was an option, and again, I never thought I would be here for so long. It has always been, "Soon, very soon you will be free."

Another reason for not forfeiting is that I really don't know what is waiting for me out there. I don't see any option to return to Denmark and continue doing ministry there. Remember, there was a reason I came here to seek asylum, and now there are all those lies and the corruption I am also fighting against—things are very complicated.

I don't know who is behind all of this, and I therefore need to stay firm and fight to clear my name from all these false accusations against me. Yes, this is now about so much more than my asylum. Yes, this is also much bigger than "just" my life. I feel I am fighting for everyone else out there who will come after me, and therefore I cannot give up.

But the main reason I cannot just give up is of course God. If God wanted me to forfeit my case and stop here, my flesh would love that, as I so long for this to end. How nice would that be to leave and be with my family again. But that is not how it is. God has not given me that option to forfeit my asylum, and I need to fight for all of you out there who are coming after me.

God wants me to stand firm on the truth and not just give up—no matter how hard it often is. And as I have said before, I see God's hand all over this. I can truly see that today. I am forever thankful to God, that I did not get set free six months ago. I wanted to be released, but I see now I was not ready for it. I would have come out full of fear and anxiety. I would have said to all of God's children out there, "Be careful, don't go to jail! Be careful, don't let this happen to you!"

I would have only brought fear to everyone; it would not have helped anyone outside these walls.

God has taught me about suffering and many other things I needed to learn in a way that never would have happened otherwise. Now, I can invite you to join me on this journey to listen to the truth God has revealed to me. I pray it will do a deep work in your life and help prepare you for what is coming.

This book will be full of the Word of God. As beautiful as testimonies are, we need to build on the Word of God.

The Word of God is our firm foundation, and it is by the Word of God we stand.

It's the Word of God that grows our faith. And we need faith, together with hope and endurance, to finish the race in front of us, especially in the time we live in.

I hope and pray that this book will be an exciting read and give you deeper insights into my crazy journey so you may be strong and stand firm in the days of trials and tribulations, which the Bible says are coming all over the earth. I know God has called me as a pioneer to go in front and prepare a way for others—yes, to help make the way more manageable for the people who follow later.

Right now, the persecution is only being experienced by a few. However, God has shown us that soon, it will be for the many, and then for all who follow Christ as His disciples.

Right now, we see the harvest becoming mature. In Matthew 13, we read how wheat and tares grew side by side. Jesus said it would remain like this until the day of harvest when He would take the tares, throw them into the fire, and gather the wheat into the barn. This is what we are coming close to now.

"The kingdom of heaven is like a man who sowed good seed in his field. But while everyone was sleeping, his enemy came and sowed tares among the wheat, and went away. When the wheat sprouted and formed heads, then the tares also appeared. The owner's servants came to him and said, 'Sir, didn't you sow good seed in your field? Where did the tares come from?'

'An enemy did this,' he replied.

The servants asked him, 'Do you want us to go and pull them up?'

'No,' he answered, 'because while you are pulling the tares, you may also uproot the wheat with them. Let both grow together until the harvest. At that time I will tell the harvesters: First collect the tares and tie them in bundles to be burned; then gather the wheat and bring it into my barn.'" (Matthew 13:24-30 NIV)

The wheat and the tares are both becoming mature right now. They are becoming white, and we can see increasingly clearly the difference between lies and truth, good and evil, and the children of God and the children of Satan. I'm sure most of you have had your eyes opened these last few years with all the craziness going on around the world. This will just increase, and increase, and increase until the day of harvest when our Lord returns. I believe God has called me to prepare you and make you ready.

So, God bless you and welcome to this exciting journey, written here in my cell inside Baker County Detention Center.

- Torben Sondergaard,
a disciple of Jesus Christ

Chapter One
Make My People Ready

I'd like to start this journey back in Denmark, where I'm from.

I became a disciple of Jesus in 1995, married my fantastic wife Lene the next year, and from 1999 to today, I've been in full-time ministry, first with church planting in different cities around Denmark and then as an evangelist.

From 2002 to 2004, I was often on Denmark's national television network, preaching the gospel and praying for sick people. God did many beautiful things during that time, and many lives were changed.

But from 2005 to around 2011, God took us through our first significant desert period. It was a time of testing and suffering as well as a wonderful time with God, where He did a new work in our lives. The last nine months of being locked up here in America remind me of that time, but this is much harder now than it was then.

But as we see in the Bible, when David was facing a giant named Goliath, David believed he could kill him. Why? Because David had already won against a lion and a bear. And because he'd had those two victories before, David also had faith when facing this giant.

"But David said to Saul, 'Your servant has been keeping his father's sheep. When a lion or a bear came and carried off

*a sheep from the flock, I went after it, struck it and rescued
the sheep from its mouth. When it turned on me, I seized it
by its hair, struck it and killed it. Your servant has killed both
the lion and the bear; this uncircumcised Philistine will be
like one of them, because he has defied the armies of the living
God. The LORD who rescued me from the paw of the lion
and the paw of the bear will rescue me from the hand of this
Philistine."* (1 Samuel 17:34-37 NIV)

Those previous battles in our lives prepare us for the next great battle, which will also prepare us for even bigger battles. My wife and I, and many other believers, have repeatedly experienced this, and it's why we are standing and believing in God even now. A stronger relationship with God, a renewed mind, and a greater understanding of what it means to be a disciple of Christ will be the result. Yes, we believe we will learn a lot of truth in all of this.

Years ago, God did many new things in our lives during a tough time. One day, He told me, "Torben, we need pioneers. Start a pioneer school."

From this word came our free online Pioneer Training School, which has now been seen by tens of thousands of people and translated into many languages, and through it, thousands of lives have been changed.

Out of that Pioneer Training School, many new things started: we traveled around the world, held training weekends, and started training schools, and a movement was born that's still growing around the world today. For the last four years, while I have been in America and not able to travel outside the country, there have been Pioneer Training Schools in over thirty countries—Poland, Spain, Germany, and all over Europe, as well as Russia, Ukraine, Kazakhstan and other former Soviet bloc countries along with New Zealand and Argentina—yes, all over the world the movement is growing. Since 2016, we have also released three movies that have been seen by millions of people along with books that have been translated into over thirty languages.

God has been working; we have seen fantastic fruit through that crazy desert period. Many people worldwide have been set free to follow Christ and bear fruit daily. We honestly believe Jesus is the same yesterday, today, and forever. And if He is the same yesterday, today, and forever, then the Holy Spirit is the same today and forever. What we read in the book of Acts about the early church and their lives is the same today. It's the same Holy Spirit, the same power, the same gospel, the same fruit, and the same persecution. The truth God revealed during that time has kept me going.

In 2015, we established the Jesus Hotel in Denmark. A famous Danish soccer player named Peter Rasmussen had some years before came to faith in Jesus through our videos. He bought a mini hotel we could use as a training school, and at that time, things started to grow as we released our first movie, The Last Reformation: The Beginning. We had people from all over Europe and the world coming to us to be trained to live as disciples of Christ, which was beautiful.

As the hotel ministry was growing, Danish TV asked if they could follow me and do a program about repentance and how people can walk by faith and live the life we were living. As the Bible says, I should have been more alert because the world will hate us, as Jesus said, and we are called to be on guard. But then I'd only had positive experiences with Danish TV, so my guard was down, and I said yes. Over the next year and a half, they filmed what we were doing.

Everything exploded in a good way. The Jesus Hotel and training school was such a success that many came from all over the world, but with that came persecution.

The fire department came to check us out. The police came to check our passports because they heard that we had undocumented immigrants working there. The fire inspector, food control officials, and just so many people came to check us out because they thought there was something wrong. But all was as it should have been. But after a short time, the place became too small for us.

So, the soccer player, Rasmussen, found a more prominent place we could obtain: a sixty thousand square foot, old boarding school, and we moved there. We had people from over thirty-five nations at one time in our Bible schools. We simultaneously had two months of what we called "Luke 10 School" and a three-week Pioneer Training School.

It was then that persecution started to grow even more, and it became increasingly personal. At one point, government officials came and wanted to look at our kids and talk with them. It happened on the heels of a men's trip I led. One of our training schools took men on a trip where we walked ten miles into the forest and slept outside. While we camped out, we slaughtered the chickens we had brought and ate them for dinner. We spent time worshiping and being with God, slept, and went home again. It was a good survival men's trip focused on fellowship and Jesus.

But a few days later, two women from the principality came to our house and wanted to talk with my girls. Why? Because I had been on a men's trip and slaughtered a chicken.

"But there's nothing illegal with slaughtering a chicken," I told them,

"No, but we still need to talk with your girls."

"Yeah, but there's nothing wrong with slaughtering a chicken. It's not illegal to eat chickens."

"No, but we still need to talk with your girls."

"But our girls were not on the trip. It was only men. It was a man's trip," I said.

"Yeah, but we still need to talk to your girls."

Things didn't make sense, and we got nervous they might take our girls. One of the main reasons was our decision to homeschool our girls. This was not a widespread practice in Denmark. At the time, there were only around four hundred children in all of Denmark in homeschooling programs. So, because of the visit, we dropped the homeschooling and put our daughter in a private Christian school, hoping that would get the government to leave us alone.

Then, in January of 2019, everything exploded. Danish TV, following us for the last year and a half, came out with three programs.

This was a government-owned television station, the biggest one in Denmark, and now they were releasing three prime-time programs about us, which were quite bad. When this happened, it all exploded. I was not only on television those three times during that month, but I was on television over seventeen times during the next three weeks. Besides the programs they created, I was on the news repeatedly, and many other programs and newspapers also wrote about it.

The programs were evil and manipulative, designed to create fear in people and to attack me. After every program, politicians and government officials were interviewed and talked about how they needed to shut me down and how the country needed laws to stop me. It was so manipulative in so many ways. For example, they tried to tie us to other ministries in the programs that had done dreadful things.

One pastor had, years ago, been in jail for abuse, which was a big story when that happened. Another evangelist had some very evil affairs, which became a story in Denmark. And now they put me in with those guys on these programs, even though I had nothing to do with them.

After every program, hundreds of hate emails poured in. I received messages like: "Torben, you need to go to jail again," but I had never been in jail. "Torben, you need to stop abusing women," but it was other ministers who had done that.

People could not distinguish who was who on these programs.

A segment of the show highlighting demons and deliverance was edited to give a totally different picture of what really happens when people are getting free. They turned up the noise and made the deliverance look more terrible and horrendous than it was, never showing the absolute joy and freedom that followed the deliverance. Instead, they made it look like people were spiritually abused by the experience. I was branded as a child abuser through those deliverances.

Together with those programs and the news, they managed to change the mindset of the people in Denmark, making it terribly hard for us to minister. Talk of new laws they felt were needed to protect people from ministries like ours ramped up.

They also discussed giving more power to the child welfare organizations so they could go in and remove children from those families that are being hurt by our ministry's "practices."

It's challenging to explain how dark and evil it was, especially when they started to talk about removing the children. We were worried and nervous about them taking our children.

On January 9, 2019, the program that aired that night was so bad, and everything became dark for me when I saw it. I thought, "I am finished. I'm finished. It's over now. I can never do ministry again. No one would ever take me seriously."

Something broke down deep inside me, and I was distraught. I remember running into a field near our house, crying and shouting to God, "God, how can this happen?"

And there, something happened. God said to me, "Torben, look at Me."

And I was like, "What?"

"Look at Me. Yes, you have been put on national TV for everyone to see, in the worst light ever, but look at Me. I was hanging naked on the cross."

That evening, I experienced the worst thing I'd ever experienced, but it was nothing compared to Jesus nailed naked on the cross. That same evening, we had a fellowship where a friend shared about Jesus and suffering.

He said, "Torben, people relate stronger to each other in pain than in joy. For example, suppose a woman has lost a child. In that case, people around her can say, 'We understand, we follow you,' but then if she meets another woman who has also lost a child, those two can have a fellowship and relate to each other in a way none of us will ever be able to understand."

"Or people who have been in a war," he continued, "if a person has been in a war and they lost a friend in the war, and then later they meet another person who has been in a war and lost a friend, even if it's not the same war, they can still relate to each other in a way no one else can. Why? Because you relate better to someone in pain and suffering than you do in joy and good times."

This put it all in a new perspective. I saw in a new light what Jesus experienced and what it meant for Him when He died on the cross. Hebrews 12:2-3 (NIV) says, *"And let us run with perseverance the race marked out for us, fixing our eyes on Jesus, the pioneer and perfecter of our faith. For the joy set before Him, He endured the cross, scorning its shame, and sat down at the right hand of the throne of God. Consider Him who endured such opposition from sinners, so that you will not grow weary and lose heart."*

January 9th ended up being a special time with Jesus.

But on January 24th, everything changed when a friend called to tell me how serious things were for us. I knew immediately we needed to leave Denmark. So, in a span of two days, we said goodbye to some of the people closest to us and Lene's parents (my parents had passed a few years before this), and we left Denmark for America.

I was in shock when we entered the Amsterdam Airport Schiphol in the Netherlands. Everything had gone so fast. I could not understand how this could have happened. I had been so proud of being Danish. I'd been traveling in forty-five nations doing ministry for over twenty years and never had problems like this.

Yes, I'd experienced persecution like other people.

Yes, I'd had people against me, spreading lies.

But I had never experienced anything on this level, and I could not understand that it could come to this point.

If people had said to me just a few months before, "Torben, could you ever imagine that it could come to the point that you'd need to flee your country because of persecution for the gospel?"

I would have said, "No, not Denmark! Denmark is a good country. It will never happen here."

But it happened, and we were leaving Europe for America because of it.

While I was in shock and praying, God spoke to me again. (I'd like to add here that I'm not using the words, "God spoke to me," lightly, and it's not like I often hear the voice of God. This was not an audible voice, but I've learned to recognize His still, small voice, and sometimes you just know). He said, "I am sending you to America to make My people ready, for My people are not ready for what is coming. My people are not ready for what's coming to America, so I am sending you to help prepare them."

On January 26th, we arrived at the Hartsfield-Jackson Atlanta International Airport in Atlanta, Georgia. I still remember how nervous we were: we were in a new land and had not decided whether we would seek asylum in any way. We just needed to get away, and we hoped this thing would somehow simmer down so we could go home to Denmark.

Four years later, I'm sitting here in Baker County Detention Center, once again shocked and surprised, thinking, "How can all of this happen?"

The world is indeed changing, and I don't know what's coming. However, I want to say I'm okay with that. When they detained me, I had no idea how crazy this journey would be and that I would still be here. I'm happy I did not know all of this in many ways, as it would have been too much for me to bear knowing I would be here so long. But I know God is in control, and I must trust Him.

I've learned to take one day at a time, as Jesus said in Matthew 6:31-34 (NIV), *"So do not worry, saying, 'What shall we eat?' or 'What shall we drink?' or 'What shall we wear?' For the pagans run after all these things, and your heavenly Father knows that you need them. But seek first His kingdom and His righteousness, and all these things will be given to you as well. Therefore, do not worry about tomorrow, for tomorrow will worry about itself. Each day has enough trouble of its own."*

Yes, every day has enough trouble of its own. Therefore, we need to learn not to worry, but instead, we need to seek the Kingdom of God, stay strong in our faith, and learn that God is in control. This is not always easy. It means letting go and giving it all over to God daily.

While writing this to you, I heard some noise outside my cell door. I went out to see what was happening, and there was a fight. Usually, the fights here are not physical. It's mostly shouting and yelling. (I have been in three of those fights, not that I was screaming, yelling, and cursing like they were, but where people have gone crazy on me.) But today, I witnessed a physical fight.

It ended up with somebody hitting another guy on the head. Four officers came in, and we were all put into our cells on lockdown.

We were allowed to come out again six and a half hours later because there was dinner. But the lockdown continued a short time later due to another fight. I heard a noise. I went out, and one of my friends was bleeding from his head after another guy had jumped on him. So, they came in and shut us down for the rest of the day. So now, because of the fight, we are locked in for the rest of the day and couldn't come out of our cells. This just happened. What a life.

Now we are in lockdown and have no access to the pod to make calls or do other activities for the rest of the day. I have made a sketch where you can see where I am.

I am currently in a two-man cell pod in the B section of this jail, which is run by U.S. Immigration and Custom Enforcement (ICE) and deals with immigration cases. The jail has a total of five hundred and twelve beds, divided into A and B housing sections. Each section has eight pods with thirty-two beds in each, some with four-man cells and others with two-man cells. In my pod, there are sixteen, two-man cells, eight cells on each floor.

The pods are accessed through a central square in the building, where there is a security room on the first floor for staff to monitor us through cameras and windows. We usually do not interact with inmates from other pods, as everything happens within our own pods and the doors remain closed. I have labeled the pods in my drawing as B1, B2, B3, B4, B5, B6, B7, and B8.

When I first arrived, I was in isolation in B7, then moved to B8, and have been in B6 for the last six and a half months.

A television screen shines just outside my cell in the pod; I'm staring at it through my cell door window. I'll tell you more about that later, at another time, because that has been torture for me.

The area in our pod has four metal benches where people can play cards and two computers where you can make video calls. There are two vending machines when they are working. One of them is down now. One you can get candy and chips and one you can get toilet paper and a security toothbrush.

There are two phones and a computer on the wall that work as a small shop where you can order small items that they bring in two times a week. When we are not in isolation in our cells, the cell doors are open, and we can go out of our cells into the Pod. But in isolation, we're locked in the entire day, and we get food through a hole in our door. But more about this later

This is where I am. I want to say that this is very unreal to experience. I never expected anything like this. I have never had any problems with the law. Jesus transformed my life when I was a teenager.

But persecution is real. Suffering is real, and just as I learned in Denmark, I experienced fellowship with Christ through my suffering.

In America, I have experienced an even deeper fellowship with Christ through my suffering, not only with Him but also His Word.

As I said in the introduction, one-third of the New Testament was written in prison. When you read it in jail, it all makes sense in a unique way.

Chapter Two
Arriving in America

I'd been in America almost three and a half years when I suddenly got detained and put here, "as a national threat," as they see me, but more about that later.

While I'm writing this from my cell, we're still in lockdown after yesterday's fight. It was really bloody. I can still see, fresh in my mind, my friend with a large bump and gash on his neck, as well as blood streaming down his face onto the floor. This is just a different world here than what I am accustomed to. Usually, I like lockdowns. There's no television running, no shouting, no noise, just quiet time. I love it because, other times, it truly gets crazy.

In this chapter, I'd like to share what God has been doing in America over the last few years, which is truly unique. A lot is going on, so I'll try to keep it short and highlight the big things God is doing.

When we arrived in America, we stayed with some friends in Jupiter, Florida. After we left Denmark amid the persecution, everything shut down. There was nothing left. The media managed to destroy every good thing we had built up and created so much fear among the populace that we could no longer minister to people. At one time, different sports clubs rented our sports hall, which helped pay the bills. They all canceled when the programs went on the air.

We had people signed up for the next training school we were doing at our Jesus Center, but when everything happened, they all canceled. Everything shut down, and it quickly became apparent that we could not keep running the ministry center in Denmark because of everything that was happening.

So, we decided to close it down and those that were left there started to clean up the center and get ready to move on.

They started in our home. We had an apartment at the center we lived in. They did that a few weeks after we arrived in America. Some of our friends there walked around our house via Skype and asked us what we should do with our furniture and the things we had. Both of my parents had died a few months prior, and I had inherited a lot of things from my childhood home. But we decided to give everything away.

"What about your bed, Torben?" asked one of my friends.

"Yes, you can give it to," I said.

"What about this?"

"Give it to them."

"What about this picture, this painting, what about this, what about that?"

"Yes, all of it."

And there, over Skype, we gave everything away. This was hard, but we knew we would not be returning to Denmark to live.

I wept, and my wife, Lene, cried. We were in shock, wondering, "How can this happen? We are giving everything away—what now? We are here with no car, no home, and only a little money. We are staying in a room with some friends with nothing but eight suitcases and some clothes. What now?"

It was a moment we will never forget. We didn't lose faith, but we prayed and cried in faith, "God, we need You! What now? Help us!"

Five minutes later, something extraordinary happened. I got an email from somebody who asked, "Hey Torben, do you need any money to rent a house or something?" In the message, he listed his phone number.

I called this man and said, "Hi, do I know you?"

"No, we've never talked," he said. "But I got baptized at one of your meetings some time ago. I just felt I should write to you. Do you need any money for a house or something?"

"Yeah! Thank you!" I said. "Actually, as you probably know, we are in America."

"What?" he asked, confused. "Are you in America? No, I did not know!"

"Yes, we have left Denmark because of persecution."

"What?"

He knew nothing about it.

"No, I did not know. I just felt God wanted me to write to you. Do you need any money to rent a house or something?"

This confirmed that God was working even more: this was not somebody who heard about our troubles, felt sorry for us, and wanted to help.

"Yeah, we're actually in Florida," I said, but he interrupted.

"Are you in Florida?" he asked in shock.

"Yeah, but we are leaving now. We're going to Fort Lauderdale to fly to Dallas."

"I live in Fort Lauderdale, just five minutes from the airport!" he exclaimed.

"Well, we'll be there in forty-five minutes," I said.

"I will meet you at the airport," he said, "and will help you."

So, fifty minutes after we had given everything away, we stood at the airport, and a man approached me. I'd never seen him before.

"Torben, I cannot believe you are here!" He hugged me, put a piece of paper in my pocket, and left.

Stunned, I stood with my suitcases, wondering what he put in my pocket. I reached in and pulled out a check for fifty thousand dollars.

"Whoa!" I shouted.

Stop for a moment and consider what God just did: fifty thousand dollars from a man I'd never seen before while I was in line at an airport.

God was truly taking care of us.

Why did this happen there and to me? Jesus tells us in Mark 10:29-30 (NIV):

> "'Truly I tell you,' Jesus replied, 'No one who has left home or brothers or sisters or mother or father or children or fields for Me and the gospel will fail to receive a hundred times as much in this present age; homes, brothers, sisters, mothers, children and fields – along with persecutions – and in the age to come eternal life.'"

I believe this happened because we first had left everything for the gospel's sake, as we read in this verse. If we are unwilling to take the first step, we will not experience God taking the next step.

This answer came after only five minutes—this is not normal. But we have seen again and again God take care of us in miraculous ways. But as we read in the text in Mark 10, it comes with persecution. I have often thought, "God, why with persecution?"

Is it to humble us? Is it to teach us? Is it to test us? Is it to keep us dependent upon God?

Yes, it's all the above. There are many reasons, but Jesus has made it clear that persecution is part of our lives when we follow Him.

> "If the world hates you, keep in mind that it hated Me first. If you belonged to the world, it would love you as its own. As it is, you do not belong to the world, but I have chosen you out of the world. That is why the world hates you. Remember what I told you: 'A servant is not greater than his master. If they persecuted Me, they will persecute you also. If they obeyed My teaching, they will obey yours also'" (John 15:18-20 NIV).

Does the world hate you? I know some in this world hate me—I've experienced it. However, here's a comforting thought: if the world doesn't hate us, then there's something off.

When I started this life as a disciple of Christ years ago, I experienced hate, people lying about me, YouTube videos railing against me, conflicts, and pain. In the beginning, I felt sorry for myself. Sometimes I'd pray, "God, why? Why should this life be so hard? Why should I experience so much persecution, God?"

Then, I'd look down at my hands, and on one hand, I had all the persecution and all the hard things, and I said, "God, I don't like that." But then I looked at the other hand, where I had the fruit, the lives that were being changed, the testimonies of what God is doing, and the fellowship with Him, and I loved that.

Then I'd ask God, "Can I get that without the other?"

He did not answer because I knew the answer: "No, you cannot get the one without the other." I could not get a testimony like the fifty thousand dollars at the airport if I was not willing to go through what I went through to get it.

We need to be ready and willing to suffer for Christ for us to be able to come and live for Christ. I can say this with confidence because, after that check and many other miracles over three and half years in America, I was suddenly detained because I was seen as "a national threat" and put here, in this cell, all for the gospel's sake.

Chapter Three
Time to Wake Up

When we arrived in America, we were not sure what to do or if we should seek asylum. We spent untold hours with lawyers listening to our options, and we soon realized that seeking asylum was the last thing we wanted to do. It meant that we would not be able to go back to Denmark later and see our family and friends. This was not something we wanted, especially with Lene's parents still alive and not able to travel to us. Asylum meant never seeing them again.

In many ways, we hoped that all the trouble we faced in Denmark would fall to the ground. Now that we were out of Denmark, maybe it would somehow disappear, that they would forget all about us and move on. But the persecution did not stop when we left Denmark. The government in Denmark continued working on a new law meant to stop us. They spoke about me in the Danish Parliament even after I left, while they presented a new bill, L139, also known as the "psychological abuse" law. Find out more on the TorbenSondergaard.com/timeline.

Because of the continued issues flowing from Denmark, around the end of March 2019, we decided that seeking asylum was the only option. Shortly after, the bill was passed. This meant that casting out demons in front of children and disabled people could be defined as "mental violence." If I were to go back and continue doing what I'd been doing for years, praying for people and casting out demons, according to this new law, they could jail me for up to three years.

Some Christians might ask, "But Torben, why did you not just stay and fight in Denmark?"

There is a time and place when we should do that; in this case, I felt strongly that Jesus was reminding me of Matthew 10:23 (NIV):

"When you are persecuted in one place, flee to another. Truly I tell you, you will not finish going through the towns of Israel before the Son of Man comes."

People were persecuting us in one country, so we had to flee to the next. If Jesus had said, "Stay and fight," we would have stayed in our home country. But this time He said, shake the dust off your hands and feet and move on.

"When you enter a town and are welcomed, eat what is offered to you. Heal the sick who are there and tell them, 'The kingdom of God has come near to you.' But when you enter a town and are not welcomed, go into its streets and say, 'Even the dust of your town we wipe from our feet as a warning to you. Yet be sure of this: The kingdom of God has come near.' I tell you, it will be more bearable on that day for Sodom than for that town." (Luke 10:8-11 NIV)

We filled out our asylum papers, sent them in, and soon received the receipt we needed to be able to stay in America. We also got our Social Security number, driver's license, and bank account. Everything was set up. Now, we could stay here like everyone else, waiting for our asylum interview to decide if we would get asylum. This interview could take a long time before it took place, from one to five years. No one knew exactly when we would be interviewed; until then, we could live in America like everyone else and focus on what God wanted us to do here.

A few months later, I went to Virginia to do an interview on CBN (Christian Broadcasting Network). I was on a popular program called The 700 Club. They also did another interview with me about my asylum case. During this time at CBN, God showed us the next step in our lives here in America.

One morning, I was eating breakfast at the hotel located near the CBN studios in Virginia Beach, Virginia, and a woman recognized me and approached my table.

"Torben, I cannot believe you're here! I was just listening to your teaching this morning! I've been following you for years," this woman said.

She said they had a home fellowship and were meeting that evening if I wanted to join them.

But it was too far for me to go to their house, so they moved it to Panera Bread close to my hotel. That evening, my family and I went to Panera Bread where we met with the home fellowship group. It was a beautiful time! I did not know any of them, but the woman started to tell me how they all came together.

"Thank you, Torben," she said at one point. "We are all here because of you, of course, because of Jesus, but God has used you to start this fellowship! It started with one of us," and she pointed to a person there, "who went to your meeting, got baptized and set free, came home, told it to those people," and pointing at some of the others there, "who got set free." Then they went out on the street and met those people, and this way, she explained, is how they came together and how this fellowship started. I was just amazed, and it was beautiful. I did not know there was a fellowship like this in that city!

Two days later, I went to another city in Virginia to join a radio program. A guy offered his home so we could stay there, and my family and I stayed in his house.

While there, he said, "Hey Torben, we have a house fellowship here! We actually have a meeting tonight. Would you like to join?"

And I said, "Yes! Now we are here!"

That night, the living room was filled with about thirty people we neither knew nor had ever talked to.

"Can I say something?" one person asked. "Torben, I want to thank you and your family because we are all here because of you, no, of course, because of Jesus. But it started with one of us," this person continued and pointed to another person in the room. "He went to one of your meetings, got set free and baptized, went home, shared it with that person," pointing at another person," who got set free, who shared it with that person who came to God." He just kept telling me how they all came together one by one and how the fellowship got started this way. As I heard him tell the story, I was amazed. It was like hearing the story a few days before in another city. And I thought, 'Wow. How many places are there like this in America?" I have since seen this all over in city after city—how fellowships are starting because of what God is doing! So, the movement has grown in America, and it's incredible to see God's hand at work!

When I met with the people at those two home fellowships, I realized that with some slight adjustments they could grow bigger and healthier, and even multiply and bear more fruit.

I saw that they needed some help, but who should we send? Jesus' Word is true: *"The size of the harvest is bigger than you can imagine, but there are few workers"* (Matthew 9:27 CEB). I had no one I could send there to help them because most of the people we had trained were over in Europe. So that led me to the next step: the harvest is great, but we need more workers, and God led me to start a training school here in America.

To have more workers, we need to train more people. It would take time. But where and how?

We first thought of Florida, or maybe New Jersey, where many things were happening, but one day we went to Williamstown, Kentucky to the Ark Encounter, a large museum in the shape of Noah's Ark.

While there, my daughter Simone asked me, "Daddy, how did Noah bring the animals to the Ark?"

When she asked that, I said, "It was not Noah, but God who brought the animals to the Ark." Then something extraordinary happened.

As I spoke, the Holy Spirit powerfully came over me, and it was like, "Whoa! God brought the animals to the Ark!"

That line exploded in me in a way I had not experienced before. When I left that place, that line repeatedly ran in my head, "Whoa! God. You brought the animals to the Ark!"

I realized in a more profound way that God is in control! No human could do that, to bring one pair of the unclean and seven pairs of the clean, and male and female, and do it so that they don't eat each other along the way: no man can do that. But God did it!

On the way home from the Ark Encounter, driving back to Florida, we went by North Carolina, where somebody said there was a training center we should look at. We drove up in the mountains, but at that time, I was not sure if I wanted to be in a place that far away from the city.

So, I prayed, "God, why are we here? Why did we even go on this trip? I don't want to be in North Carolina; I want to be in Florida or New Jersey, where our friends are. And we don't have money to buy the center anyway, so why are we here? And why did I go on this trip?"

I thought the only thing I got from this trip was that God had brought the animals to the Ark.

A few minutes after I prayed, we arrived at the center. When we arrived, an elderly man greeted us with his arms lifted, saying, "Welcome to the Ark; you are the first animals God is sending to this place!"

I was blown away. Wow, what was happening?

"I am Noah," the older man said, "and this is the Ark. This building is shaped like the Ark in the Bible and that is why I call myself Noah. And I believe you are the first animals God is sending to this place!"

That was how he greeted us moments after I prayed in the car, "God, why did You send me on this trip? The only thing I got out of this trip was that You brought the animals to the Ark, and then this happened!"

It was so special!

This became our first training center in America; we rented it for over a year. It was a fantastic time with a lot of fruit. Hundreds of people were trained for ministry.

It was also a place of safety because it was during this time that the COVID-19 pandemic hit and the 2020 Presidential Election took place, shocking all of us. These two events became an eye-opener for many. I saw the same spirit I had seen in Denmark with the lies and manipulation.

I want to point out something about today's mainstream news media. A man said it so perfectly, "If you don't see the news, you are not informed. If you see the news, you are misinformed."

With today's media, it's hard to know what news to trust anymore.

COVID-19 and the 2020 Presidential Election opened many people's eyes to the times we are living in now. Since arriving in America, I've preached, "Wake up! Wake up! Persecution is coming to America! It's time to wake up!"

But most people have rejected it or thought, "Yeah, that's good. But this is America, God's own country, the land of the free, home of the brave. What you experienced in Denmark is not going to happen in America."

Then, suddenly, things changed, and people woke up.

"What happened to our freedom?" they asked. "Where are the brave people in America?"

It has become a wake-up call for all of us. Sadly, a lot of people are still sleeping. We are surprised how people can sleep through all the things happening in the world right now, but the truth is that most people are still sleeping.

Attuned to the need for people to wake up, a year after we visited the Ark Encounter, God told us, "Now it's time to go out, spread, and multiply."

From the beginning, we thought we should buy the place instead of renting it and would stay there for a long time. We didn't plan to leave precisely one year after the first school started, but the day we left, somebody reminded me, "Torben, are you aware that it's exactly one year since we started the first school today?"

And then I was reminded of Genesis 8:17 that when Noah and his family left the Ark to go out and multiply, they had been in the Ark precisely one year!

When we left the training center, we had a tremendous team of around seventy people ready to go out and multiply and train others.

In Ephesians 5:14-17 (NIV), we read:

> *"Wake up, sleeper, rise from the dead, and Christ will shine on you. Be very careful, then, how you live—not as unwise but as wise, making the most of every opportunity, because the days are evil. Therefore, do not be foolish, but understand what the Lord's will is."*

This is the time we are living in right now. It's time to wake up. Wake up, you sleepy Christian! Wake up and shine!

Why? Because the days are evil. Don't be a fool but understand what God's will is!

And sometimes His will is not what we expect. In our case, we never got an asylum interview. Instead, I was detained and put here in jail without knowing what was happening. At this point, I have been here for nine months, and my asylum case has never come before an asylum officer. Instead, it went directly to court.

Why? More about that later.

Chapter Four
A Full Life

We saw amazing things happen at our Ark, our new training center in North Carolina. It was a beautiful time when many lives were transformed. We also built up a dedicated team of disciples of Christ who were ready to go out, multiply, and cover the earth with the gospel's good news. After one year, we left the Ark, and many of us went mobile, spreading from place to place.

We had a big revival tent that could seat up to a thousand people. A large group of us went out with that tent, stopping first in Chicago. It was special in many ways: we knew this would cause some resistance because of the COVID-19 pandemic, but a few days before we arrived there, we received a strong word from God. It was through a powerful dream from someone connected to our team.

In the dream, she saw trains and railings, like train tracks. There were trains going in both directions. She saw a car driving on the rails to the left. She also saw a small village with a huge building and many homes. The houses were very old with ruined roofs, some even missing the roofing material—very old, probably one hundred- to two-hundred-year-old roofs. Then the police arrived and said we could not be there. They left but later returned, issuing us two fines.

When we arrived at the campground to set up the meeting, everyone was shocked: it was exactly like the dream. It was a one-hundred-and-fifty-year-old Methodist campground with old white houses, many with shutters due to the destroyed roofs. The rain was going inside the homes. There was also a big old hotel. Beside the camp was a place where trains were repaired, and there we saw trucks driving on the rails exactly as in the dream. Everything mirrored the dream.

As we began to set up, the police arrived, just as in the dream, and informed us that we could not be there without a special permit.

But because of the dream, we knew God was in control, and indeed He was. We managed to obtain the permit a few hours before the first meeting started, and it was an amazing week.

Everything went smoothly, and we had a fantastic week. We conducted teachings and trainings during the daytime and revival meetings in the evening. We witnessed many healings and deliverances, and many lives were transformed that week. Even today, years later, I hear about how this week changed many lives. It was the beginning for many to live fully for Jesus and start seeing fruit in their lives. I know of several missionaries in other countries who started their journeys that week. Not only did many experience healings and a new faith, but Christians were also challenged to prioritize Jesus and join the mission. The growth continued after we left and there are today many house fellowships there and they are still growing.

On the last day, I sat in the tent. We were talking about the dream, how God had spoken so clearly with so many details, and how the dream had given us the strength we needed to just move on even though we experienced resistance from the police in the beginning. They'd wanted to shut us down because we lacked some permits, and how we got the permit at the last moment.

Then, I said that the only thing still lacking from this dream was the police coming again, handing us two papers.

When I said this, somebody called, "Torben, the police are here, and they want to talk to you and the camp leader."

So, we went out, both of us spoke to the police officer, and he handed each of us a piece of paper—the two documents in the dream. Usually, we would be afraid if we received papers like that: they wanted to shut us down and fine us for having the meetings there. But God had prepared us through the dream. We knew God was in it and we had done nothing wrong. We knew it was about stopping the gospel's spread and nothing else. Therefore, we kept going, and everything ended well.

There were no issues, and we finished out a fantastic week. Many house fellowships started that week, and the fruit continues growing today. But this did not come without opposition.

From Chicago, we went to New Hampshire. We also experienced opposition this time as people did not like us having meetings and gathering due to the pandemic. Yes, there was a lot of fear, and many newspapers and TV stations were talking about us and how irresponsible we were, but we will not bow down to the spirit of fear that was everywhere. So, we kept going, and it went really well despite the resistance we experienced. But then somebody got word that we would experience a big attack, but the week went on, and we finished without a big attack.

Then that attack came. It is difficult to describe as this was the most insane thing I had ever experienced until then. Just as we had sent everyone home after the last meeting we had, and the whole team gathered in the tent where we were having a barbecue, suddenly the weather changed like we had never seen before.

A big, demonic storm struck the area. Usually, I don't use words like that to describe the weather, but I have seen nothing like it. It reminds us of Jesus and His disciples in Mark 4. Jesus said, "'Let's go to the other side.' Then He fell asleep in the boat. A storm rose up as they crossed. It was so bad that the disciples were afraid. 'We are going down, Lord! We are going down!'"

These were skilled fishermen who were used to the weather and storms, but this time, they were afraid. It appears that something supernatural happened.

"That day, when evening came, He said to His disciples, 'Let us go over to the other side.' Leaving the crowd behind, they took Him along, just as He was, in the boat. There were also other boats with Him. A furious squall came up, and the waves broke over the boat, so that it was nearly swamped. Jesus was in the stern, sleeping on a cushion. The disciples woke Him and said to Him, 'Teacher, don't you care if we drown?' He got up, rebuked the wind, and said to the waves, 'Quiet! Be still!' Then the wind died down, and it was completely calm. He said to His disciples, 'Why are you so afraid? Do you still have no faith?' They were terrified and asked each other, 'Who is this? Even the wind and the waves obey Him!'" (Mark 4:35-41 NIV)

This was what we experienced. Suddenly, a storm came up like nothing we had ever seen. The tent poles holding the big tent up started breaking. Stakes in the ground were torn out. The tent went down with us in it.

I have it on video; you can see how insane it was. The video is on TorbenSondergaard.com/412days: 'Went down with the tent—one of the craziest moments in my life'.

One guy was thrown into the air and then into our truck, smashing the window. Poles flew, and one went through our truck, making a big hole.

People were crying, some people had fainted, some people walked around with blood running down their heads. The sound of the people crying is hard to describe with words.

At one point, I could not find my wife and girls, and then I saw something under the tent, and I thought, "They are dead. My family is lying there, dead under the tent."

So, I ran to that place in the tent to try and lift it up, but it was too heavy. I had a friend with a knife, and we tried to cut through the tent to see who was lying under it. Thankfully, once we got through, we realized it was just bunched up and there was noone under the tent.

My family had run out of the tent and over to our school bus at the same moment it went down, so nothing happened to them. But many others got hurt one way or the other.

We took everyone to a big barn nearby, and it was like a war zone. Five or six ambulances came to the scene. The police and fire department came to help. The site of a revival meeting had changed into a war hospital. Five people went to the hospital.

After a brief time, I drove with a friend to one of the hospitals to find his wife, who was taken there, not knowing what had happened to her and not actually knowing which hospital she was in. When we arrived, she was not there; she was at another hospital. I cannot describe the emotions and feelings.

I was crying in the car, "Why God? Where were You? Why did this happen? Why didn't You stop it?"

But, as time passed, I saw that God was there. He saved us through this storm because many testimonies started showing how people were thrown to the ground and kept down while tent poles flew over them. Other people saw poles coming toward them, but then they suddenly moved, and it only grazed them. The person who was hurt the most was my friend Marcus. He received a fracture to his skull and a big black eye, and he ended up lying there in the hospital for several weeks.

I did a video call with Marcus from the jail here, and he was still so excited and thankful for everything because even though he got hurt, he had seen God's hand in all of it. It has opened the doors to spread the gospel to even more people, and today, over two years later, the Kingdom of God is still growing in New Hampshire, and disciples are still being made. Marcus was so thankful that we came. In the back of this book, I have a description where you can see how you can find this video on YouTube, where you can go and see it yourself.

The other day, I read 2 Timothy 3:10-11 (NIV), where Paul is talking about the suffering and persecution he experienced in Antioch, Iconium, and Lystra—and how the Lord rescued him out of them all:

*You, however, know all about my teaching, my way of life,
my purpose, faith, patience, love, endurance, persecutions,
sufferings—what kinds of things happened to me in Antioch,
Iconium and Lystra, the persecutions I endured. Yet the Lord
rescued me from all of them.*

When I read that, I thought, "What?" Antioch, Iconium, and Lystra. Paul, that was where people wanted to stone you. That was where you fled from place to place. You experienced a lot of persecution and suffering there and ended up getting stoned. And then you said, "Yet the Lord rescued me from all of them." How can you say that with everything that happened to you?

When we think about being "rescued" by the Lord, being "rescued" often infers in our minds that we will not experience any persecution or tough times. But this is not how God sees it. Psalm 34:19 (NIV) says, *"The righteous person may have many troubles, but the LORD delivers him from them all."*

The things we experienced in Chicago—the police wanting to shut us down and fine us—and in New Hampshire, the demonic storm where the tent went down, and people were hurt—the Lord rescued us out of it. Things could have been so much worse. Yes, we really saw God's hand in it all.

Jesus said, *"The thief does not come except to steal, and to kill, and to destroy. I have come that they may have life, and that they may have it more abundantly"* (John 10:10 NKJV).

What is an abundant life? What is a full life? If you look at Paul's description of himself in 2 Corinthians 11:23-25, it is like reading Paul's curriculum vitae. Here we get a small resume of his abundant and whole life.

He starts by saying, *"I have worked much harder (than anyone else), been in prison more frequently, been whipped more severely, and been exposed to death again and again."* And he continues, *"Five times I received from the Jews forty lashes minus one. Three times I was beaten with rods, once I was pelted with stones, three times I was shipwrecked,*

I spent a night and a day in the open sea, I have been constantly on the move" (2 Corinthians 11:24-25 NIV).

Paul continues speaking about how he had been in danger:

"I have been in danger from rivers, in danger from bandits, in danger from my fellow Jews, in danger from Gentiles; in danger in the city, in danger in the country, in danger at sea; and in danger from false believers. I have labored and toiled and have often gone without sleep.... I have known hunger and thirst and have often gone without food." (2 Corinthians 11:26-27 NIV)

When you read that, you think, "Paul, when have you not been in danger?"

Paul's life was hardships, persecution, prison, beatings, and danger everywhere he went. The reason he gives us this list is because he is boasting about his suffering. But Paul typically doesn't boast like that. Why is he doing it now? He is warning against those false apostles out there, those people who claim to be apostles but are not, showing that the true sign of apostles differs significantly from how we see it today.

Today, we often think that a sign of an apostle is a big church or a significant ministry, a big house or car, or a lot of money. But according to Paul, one true sign of an apostle is suffering. A few chapters before, Paul also talked about his hardships, how he is a servant of God in great endurance and troubles:

"Rather, as servants of God we commend ourselves in every way: in great endurance; in troubles, hardships and distresses; in beatings, imprisonments and riots; in hard work, sleepless nights and hunger; in purity, understanding, patience and kindness; in the Holy Spirit and in sincere love; in truthful speech and in the power of God; with weapons of righteousness in the right hand and in the left; through glory and dishonor, bad report and good report; genuine, yet regarded as impostors; known, yet

regarded as unknown; dying, and yet we live on; beaten, and yet not killed; sorrowful, yet always rejoicing; poor, yet making many rich; having nothing, and yet possessing everything." (2 Corinthians 6:4-10 NIV)

In verse ten, he is saying, "Sorrowful, yet always rejoicing; poor, yet making many (people) rich; having nothing, yet possessing everything." What a beautiful word.

This was Paul's life. I do not live anything like Paul, but he gives us an idea of what it means to follow Christ, not just as an apostle but as a servant of Jesus. Paul was not the only one who suffered for Christ. Suffering was a part of the early church, and many today bear the mark of true disciples. Everyone who wants to live a godly life will suffer for Christ.

I've experienced nothing like Paul, and my list is short compared to his. But Paul was persecuted in various places and fled. I've been persecuted in a country and fled. Paul, he went down with a ship. I can testify that I went down with a tent. And now, I can add one more thing to my list, that I've been in jail for Christ. So, this is the mark I am carrying in my life as a disciple of Christ.

Twenty years ago, when I was still in Denmark, I was a good Christian. I was a radical Christian in my own eyes and others, one who loved Jesus. I was sharing Jesus with others; in the church's eyes, I was living as a strong disciple of Christ. But when I looked at my life, it just felt empty. Something was missing. I was not living the whole life Jesus was talking about.

I began reading the book of Acts about the early disciples and the letters of how they were living and seeing how Paul lived his life: I was not living anything like that. I was not seeing the same energy flow out of me. I did not see the same fruit. I was not experiencing the same persecution as I read in the Bible. I was a good Christian, going to church and sharing Jesus here and there. Something needed to change. It was either go on as I was or submit to the Bible all the way.

I made a decision: my life would look like the Bible. I'm not here to change the Bible to fit my life. I am here to change my life to fit the Bible because the Bible is the truth and nothing else. This started a new journey in my life, where I, today, many years later, can add to the list, amongst many other amazing people around the world, that I have been put in jail for Christ.

I've shared this with you so you can pray and ask yourself: what marks do you carry for Christ? What does it look like to carry the cross in your life? I am honored to be here, and I know it's the beginning of many more things God has for me. When that is said, I think it is hard and really look forward to this time being over. Yes, I still have things to learn when it comes to suffering.

Chapter Five
A Shift is Coming

After the tent revival, we launched our first training school in Florida at a camp we rented. A few months in, the team was equipped to continue the training without me. This allowed my family and I to go on road trips across America, have meetings, and set up new house fellowships.

The first trip we took lasted forty-two days. After that, we went for thirty days, followed by our biggest mission trip: fifty-four days. Fifty-four days in the car, city to city, state to state, tens of thousands of miles all over America. We have been in forty-two states, and I can say how beautifully God is working to spread His Word everywhere.

For those who think the world is overpopulated, take a road trip across America. If you take a road trip, you will never again say that the world is overpopulated because there is so much space out there. Go into the northern United States, especially Montana, and you will see unique, beautiful places and wide-open areas and meet wonderful people while seeing what God is doing.

I am especially thinking of it now, as I'm sitting here in my jail cell with no windows or sun. I am only outside about one to two hours per week, where there is no grass under my feet, just a big fence with barbed wire. I can look through it and see the grass on the other side and some trees about three hundred feet away. When I get out of this detention center, I will first find a big tree and give it a big hug, as I genuinely miss nature. I am a man who typically hikes and rides bikes in the mountains, and I love it. I genuinely miss nature and the open spaces.

On one of the road trips, God began speaking to us about Mexico, South America and the Spanish-speaking countries, and that we needed to do more there. It was confirmed a brief time later when I talked to some of our teams from Europe: one of our leaders who lived in Holland had felt a call to move to Spain, where they are now doing training schools. When I called him, they had already started translating the books and movies into Spanish.

God moved us to go and start a training school in Mexico. But I did not have my papers here and could not travel outside of America; but God put Mexico and California in our hearts so we could start a school there too—one school in two locations combined.

One day, God reminded me of a man named Matthew. He was young with a long beard and came to our training school in Denmark a few years earlier. I remembered that he was living in Mexico. I knew God wanted me to connect with this guy.

So, I went on Gmail and Facebook and tried to find Matthew, the young man, but I could not find him. I knew God wanted me to connect with this guy but I could not find him. So, I started to pray for Matthew and that God would help me get in contact with him again.

A few days later, we were in California doing baptisms on the beach, and something amazing happened. I was standing in the water and had just baptized a woman who was filled with the Holy Spirit, and in that moment, I turned around and there stood a young man beside me. I just looked straight at him, pointed at his face, and said, "Who are you?"

I knew somehow that I knew this person, but I did not recall where I had met him.

Then he said, "It's me—Chris from Mexico!"

"Woah!" I said.

This was the man! His name was not Matthew, as I had remembered, but his name was Chris, which was why I did not find him on Facebook. That, and he did not have his long beard anymore. There he stood, the man God said I should contact, just in the water beside me. I was amazed and asked him what he was doing here, and he told me that he just felt he should come here that day, and there we stood in the water beside each other.

I love how the Holy Spirit leads us. It reminds me of Romans 8:14 (NIV):

> *"For those who are led by the Spirit of God are the children of God."*

To be led by the Holy Spirit is more than just "living a holy life." Yes, we are called to live a holy life. Yes, we are called to be holy because our Father is holy, but we are also called to live an active life—a life in obedience—as Ephesians 2:8-10 describes. We are created to do good works, which God created us to walk in. God has a plan for all our lives, and He wants us to serve Him.

> *"For it is by grace you have been saved, through faith - and this is not from yourselves, it is the gift of God - not by works, so that no one can boast. For we are God's handiwork, created in Christ Jesus to do good works, which God prepared in advance for us to do."* (Ephesians 2:8-10 NIV)

But there Chris stood, and a connection was made. He lived in Mexico, just over the border, close to San Diego. A brief time later, we moved to San Diego, as we could still not leave the United States as we were waiting for our papers. We then started one school in two locations. I was teaching students in California, and we streamed live to the students in Mexico as some of the staff were traveling from school to school. It was an amazing time.

God led us in unique ways. It was a beautiful time, and things blossomed in Mexico.

When school ended, I thought, "Let's do another one."

It is what I am used to doing, and we were witnessing fantastic fruit through our schools.

But God had other ideas.

"No," He said.

"What?" I asked.

"No," He said again. And then He spoke very clearly: "A shift is coming. A shift is coming. The people you need to train are already here. This is for the whole church."

I meditated on these words: "The people you need to train are already here."

Instead of having people come to us to join the schools, God wanted us to stay and train people in the churches where they live.

He then said a shift was coming to the whole church for the entire world. Several others in our team started to feel the same thing, and many things began to change.

Many of our leaders started to travel around and do mobile training schools where people were living, and we saw beautiful fruit out of that and saw how it was so much better to go to them and train them in their local environment instead of them coming to us. Besides that, it was much cheaper.

First, we met a woman who gotten healed in an immensely powerful way. She had had a very severe migraine headache for many years that had really paralyzed her in many ways, and she got set free and healed. We then came in contact with her friend and ended up going to her friend's house, where many new things happened as more people got healed and baptized into Christ.

House after house opened like this in our area in Southern California where we were.

At the same time, a local Pentecostal pastor in San Diego, Josiah, contacted me and said, "Let's meet and have dinner."

My wife and I went out to dinner with him and his wife. At the dinner, something happened that will be important for the future of America.

At one point during the meal, Josiah said, "The body of Christ, including the local church needs the kind of fruit that's coming from your ministry. I want to work with you."

"Yes," I said, pausing. Then, "But if you want this, I'm going to mess you up—yes, I'm going to mess you up in a good way because God has really taken us on a journey for many years and set us free from our church systems—our way of doing it is very different, but the fruit is beautiful."

He was willing as long as God was leading. From that place we built a friendship because he desired to see what linking arms would produce. For five evenings we went to him and trained his team, and the fruit was amazing! I did a video where we showed what God did and what I was sharing with them, and it was truly amazing. They experienced God in a new way, and at the same time, understood how they could go out and do this with others in a simple way. I called the video, "The Best Video Ever," because it was the best. This is something the whole church needs, including the local traditional church.

The week after, one of the guys in the leadership did something he had never done before as we experienced the first person set free, healed, and baptized in Christ. This was new for him, but as I shared in the teaching, he took it and just went for it. The first demon he ever cast out was from his own mother. Then he baptized his mom and sister the same day.

Another man there heard the testimony and wanted to experience the same thing. He understood that this is everyday Christian life for us. So, a few days later, he cast out his first demon, also from his mom. He saw his stepdad healed, and miracles happened, like powerful healings of people who were in pain for years—even long-term cancer sufferers.

This tiny group suddenly saw many lives healed, people set free and born again. I created the video, "The Next Best Video Ever," and it kept growing. The videos were to show how we, week after week, saw growth and the testimonials we got. It spread and we didn't need to wait for months and years to see that God is bringing people to faith around us. Yes, every week, it became stronger and stronger, and therefore, in "The Third Best Video Ever" at the end of this book, you can find a description of where you can find the videos. It was so simple yet powerful, and I knew then that this was what God wanted us to do in the future. He wanted us to take what He had shown us and bring it into the Church, into the body of Christ, in a new way.

One night, I was sitting at my fireplace at home, spending time with God, just talking about how amazing this has been, how simple it is, and how much the church needs this. As the church, we somehow do what we have always been doing, expecting different results. When will we stop just doing what we are doing and really dare to look at our fruit when it comes to making disciples that obey Jesus in their everyday lives, and ask ourselves, or better yet, ask God, "God, is there a better way we can do church? Is there a better way we can make strong disciples? Is there a better way we can prepare workers for the harvest?"

God started to put the church in my heart in a way I had not had in the years we had been busy planting and doing discipleship outside the church. But God now wanted us to go inside the church—to join the church in a new way, to see reformation happen there. God started a work in me—a work that He has continued to do in a big way these last nine months here in jail.

While here, I have often thought back to my evenings with God by the fireplace, where I cried out and said, "God, America needs it! We need to bring this to the church! People in the church don't see what you are doing here. It was so beautiful, and they all need it. It is so simple and yet so powerful. You need to help to get this out to the whole church."

I believe that because of that prayer, I am where I am today. Yes, because of these prayers and what God wants to do, I am in jail, as He has used this to prepare me and will use it in so many ways.

A few days after my prayer to God at the fireplace, some people from our Australian team sent me a powerful dream that one of them had had about me. This team has been exact when it comes to dreams and prophetic words, so when I got this word from them, I really listened, and at the same time, I felt it was from God in an extraordinary way. In the dream, they saw me enter an office and sit down. A person was sitting on the other side of a desk. Then the person picked up some papers and stamped them. They looked like some particularly important documents—government documents.

They then gave the papers to me. I looked at the documents, smiled, and loudly said, "This is good!"

Then, I looked into heaven and said, "This is good, Father! This is good!" The dream ended there.

The woman who had the dream felt that this had to do with my asylum papers. At that time, I had been waiting for the asylum interview for over three years and had heard nothing.

We were very excited about that dream. A few days after they shared the dream with me, I got a letter from the U.S. Department of Homeland Security saying that they wanted to see me on June 30, 2022 in Orlando to talk about my asylum case. I was so excited when I got that letter.

"Yes! It's happening now! Now we will have our asylum interview, an interview we've been waiting to get for several years!"

I showed it to my family, who were also excited.

Then, I shared the letter with my asylum lawyer, but she was not excited.

"No, Torben, this is not your asylum interview," she said. "This is something different, and there are red flags all over it."

She was apprehensive because it did not make sense that they wanted to talk to me. She wrote to them to learn more about what they wanted. She got a letter from the asylum officer, which was sent from an FBI task force email address. This made her nervous, and she suggested I bring a criminal lawyer with me, a friend she knew, but it would have cost five thousand dollars, and I did not have that money.

I thought, "But come on, nothing bad will happen because I've done nothing wrong. I have all my papers in order."

On top of that, I had just gotten this prophetic word, so I knew God was in control. So, I ended up going myself. I said goodbye to Lene, and said, "I'll see you in a few days."

And that was now more than nine months ago.

We have often cried over the telephone, talking about that goodbye and how that goodbye might have been if we'd known we would not see each other for over nine months. This is a special day as I'm writing this chapter. It is the 4th of April, and it's my wife's birthday. It has been hard for her not to have me around on a day like today.

I have been here in jail for my birthday, our wedding anniversary, Christmas, New Year, my youngest daughter's 18th birthday, and now my wife's birthday, and it's been hard. But as you can hear and see, God has been leading us through all these years, also here in America, so we believe this is also part of something much bigger than just us.

We genuinely believe a shift is coming for all of us

A shift is coming to the church.

A shift is coming to the country, and my being here is part of that shift.

Chapter Six
You are Detained!

When I arrived in Orlando, a few days before the meeting with the U.S. Department of Homeland Security, a friend and I had a meeting, and as always, it was terrific. We saw twelve to fifteen people baptized, healed, and set free, and God did extraordinary things.

It started in the afternoon while I was out driving. I was going out to a forest to play disc golf by myself. I'd been there many times before with my friends when we had a training school in the city. Now, I just wanted to go alone and spend some time with God and play a little at the same time.

On the way there, I decided to stop at a 7-Eleven to get some water. When I came out of the 7-Eleven, someone recognized me and called me over. She had just seen my video and was amazed I was there. I prayed for her outside her car at the 7-Eleven, and she fell down as she got set free and filled with the Holy Spirit. It was a powerful moment. It was clear I did not go there for the water but for her.

She came to the meeting that evening, and I started with this beautiful testimony. Yes, it was all a fantastic day, and I had no idea it was the last time in a long time I would be out doing a meeting like that or also just walking about in a beautiful forest like I did.

Yes, I had no idea it would be many months without experiencing nature again. I genuinely miss it all.

I recorded several testimonies from that night, from people who met God, got set free, or got baptized, not knowing that the Federal Bureau of Investigation and U.S. Department of Homeland Security the next day would take my phone, and I have not seen it since so the testimonies were never sent out to anyone. When I arrived at the Homeland Security building, I was not worried, to be honest, about being arrested, even though I knew something was not standard in all of this.

It was also because I knew my asylum case was good and I had not done anything wrong, so I went in there thinking everything would be good. Yes, I told a few friends there was a chance I would be arrested because my lawyer had said that, but I still did not believe it would happen.

When I entered the Homeland Security office, a manly officer greeted me and took me into a small room with another woman. They showed me an FBI badge and said, "Let's go to another place where we can talk without people around."

They took me to another room and there the man asked me many questions, first about my salary, how I get a salary and if I pay taxes. I said that we get paid by our organization and pay taxes as usual. He asked if I get checks or cash or how we receive funds. I told him I received funds by bank transfer and began feeling weird.

All the time, I was thinking, "What is happening here? What are they looking for?"

But I knew everything was in order, so I was not afraid. But I wondered what was going on here; it all seemed weird. Then they started to talk about weapons, and one of them said, "The reason you are here is because we've heard you've been smuggling weapons from Mexico to America."

When I heard that, I was in shock. "What?"

But to be honest, I also smiled a little because it was so insane to think I had anything to do with weapons smuggling; it was so crazy that when I heard it, I thought no one could ever believe something like that, and therefore nothing terrible would happen. It was a big misunderstanding, and I could easily prove I was not a weapons smuggler and had never even been to Mexico.

But he continued and said, "Therefore, you are not going home today. We will keep you here. You are detained."

Then they asked me to stand up and put my hands on the wall. Then they searched me and put handcuffs on me. It was like a movie playing out. I felt nothing because it seemed to be happening to someone else.

There was nothing like, "You are under arrest, you have the right to remain silent, you have the right to a lawyer," as I had seen in the movies. That was never said, and it still hasn't been said. They took me into an office in another room where people were working on computers, and then they said I could have a phone call if I needed to call anyone.

I called my asylum lawyer and told her what had just happened, but when Í said the words "weapons smuggling," she said, "I cannot talk to you about that. You need to talk to the other guy (a criminal lawyer she had told me she knows if I needed that)," and then she hung up on me.

That was weird to me; I did not understand her actions. I have since learned that since she is an asylum lawyer and not a criminal lawyer, she would be the one assigned to the case if she started giving me advice, which would not have been a good thing. I was not actually arrested on a criminal charge like she thought from what I told her, but she hung up on me.

And there I was.

They let me take some phone numbers out of my phone and write them on a piece of paper. Then they took my smartphone and put me in a holding room for a few hours. Afterward, they came and said they would take me to an Orange County jail for the night and then, the day after, take me to one of the immigration detention facilities.

Things had gone from surreal to a terrible movie. But I still didn't feel much, as it all was like a movie playing out, and I was just watching it happen. I couldn't really understand that this was really happening to me. Yes, it may be difficult to understand, but that was how it was.

When they moved me to the Orange County facility, I had to take my shoelaces off so I could not use them as a weapon. They then put chains around my ankles, chains around my hips, and handcuffs, and then they fastened the handcuffs to my hips. Then they dragged me out to a car. This is still one of my strongest memories from the last nine months.

That moment of walking out to the car and being transported to the jail with handcuffs on is difficult to describe. I could not lift my feet. My shoes were open because there were no laces, so I dragged my feet across the floor. There I was, as "a hardcore criminal," transported to jail.

I will never forget it.

I look back now, and remember Jesus' last words to Peter in John 21:18 (NIV):

> *"Very truly I tell you, when you were younger you dressed yourself and went where you wanted; but when you are old you will stretch out your hands, and someone else will dress you and lead you where you do not want to go."*

This was what I felt. Jesus was predicting Peter's death, and while I haven't died yet, the feeling of being taken away against your will is devastating.

They put me in a minivan that was modified to transport prisoners. There were three rows in the back, with a partition for the window, and I was chained to the vehicle, so there was no way out. Then they drove me to an Orange County jail. I'd never been in prison before, I'd never been arrested before, and this was a shock for me; it was all so unreal.

First, they took a mugshot of me, then I was told to sit and wait, first for around a half hour to an hour, and lastly, they took me into a room where I had to take all my clothes off. It was just like we hear about on television and in the movies, totally naked, "Squat down, turn around, cough," all of it.

I was humiliated. Then they gave me a suit to put on, and I sat in a chair again to wait. I sat there for eight hours.

All around me were drunks, people sleeping, and several were high on drugs—I was suddenly in a shockingly new world.

I couldn't cry outwardly because there were so many people around me, but inside, I cried, "What is happening here, God? Weapons smuggling! I have done nothing wrong, and what will happen? Weapons smuggling is a big deal!"

Thank God, there was a phone by the chairs with a long cable people could use, so I could call Lene while I sat there, and she encouraged me.

"Maybe it's because Jesus wants you to share the gospel with somebody there," she said.

She knows I feel alive when I share Jesus and that people here need the gospel.

The humiliation didn't stop at the stripping and squatting. At one time, I needed to go to the restroom, and there was a restroom just behind me. I was in a spacious room with people coming in and getting checked, people waiting to be taken to their cells, and officers working on computers. And there was the restroom. I went in, closed the door, and used the bathroom, but the door was locked when I wanted to go out, and you could not open it from inside. So, I knocked on the door, and after a brief time they heard me, and they came and opened the door.

An officer shouted, "What are you thinking, closing the door? This is a jail! You should never close the door!" He was so angry at me and yelled, "You should know!"

How could I know that? I have never been in a jail before.

After eight hours of waiting, they took me to a cell with twenty other people who had come into the jail the same day as me, and that was where we would sleep that night. There were ten bunk beds and three toilets in an open area, so there was no privacy when you needed to go.

That night, I lay in bed, trying to sleep. The mattress was so thin it hurt to lay on it. I wanted to double it, but it didn't work. It was extremely uncomfortable, and I couldn't help but feel that I was watching this happen to someone else.

But it was real, and I was there. While I tried to sleep, I heard somebody talk about the Bible, and I was like, "No, not now. I need to sleep; I am so tired."

But then I thought about Lene's words, "Maybe there's somebody there you should share Jesus with, and that's why you're there," so I ended up joining the conversation, and after a brief time, I got out of my bed and went to their bunk bed and sat down.

We ended up having an intense conversation that night, where I shared Jesus, and prayed for one of the guys.

When I was done, he said, with tears, "Thank you. I know that God sent you here for me."

He was thankful for what had just happened; God spoke to and touched him that night. This experience and his words really encouraged me, so I said to God, "God, You are in control even though I don't know what's happening right now."

And I went to bed.

Around 3-4 a.m., after sleeping only one or two hours that night, they took me back to the holding facility at the Homeland Security building.

I waited there for three or four hours before they needed to transport me to the next place. Again, I was chained around my feet, hips, and hands. Then, they took me to the Baker County Detention Center near Jacksonville. It was a three-hour drive. It was hard to sit in the back of a transporter vehicle with bars on the windows. Many thoughts were going through my head. I felt like a lamb that was being taken to slaughter. I was not in control of my life anymore. I was not in control over my decisions. What would happen to me? What was awaiting me in this new place?

There is so much to say about these last months. While writing these words, I am writing on an empty stomach because the food was not cooked when we got our lunch today. The meat was raw, so everyone in my Pod sent it back.

This is not the first time this has happened. There have been several times we have had to send the food back. Most times, it's because they put too much pepper in the food, and we are just unable to eat it. Yes, someone out there doesn't know how strong pepper is.

One time, we did not eat it because one person found a maggot in the food. It was very nasty, and none of us wanted to eat that meal.

There are so many stories to tell from the last nine months; again, I still do not know how long I will be in this place. Three days ago, there was another fight, and I saw blood running down a friend's face. What a different world it is here.

From the moment I entered the Homeland Security office until now, a lot has happened, and many emotions rise in me when I think of when I got detained and what has happened since then.

It is extraordinary to sit here in my cell, locked up after two hundred and eighty-eight days, still not knowing exactly why I am here or when I will get out.

Just as I have celebrated birthdays and anniversaries here, as I write this today it is April 5. Twenty-eight years ago, I gave my life to Christ on this very day. Twenty-eight years ago today, I repented, and the Holy Spirit came over me in a powerful way, and my new life started. Yes, twenty-eight years ago today, I said yes to following Jesus and have followed Him ever since. And I will always do that, no matter what. I think of April 5, 1995, as my spiritual birthday.

I've often, especially in these last months, thought a lot about my journey until now, being here alone with little to do but to think. If I had known, twenty-eight years ago, what this life would bring, I would have done it all over again, even though it has been a hard life in many ways.

I love Jesus, and I am thankful for my life. I am grateful for the life He has given me, and there is truly no other way than His way, and to follow Him, which means together with everything that follows. I will serve Him when life is easy and when it is hard and costs everything.

Chapter Seven
Isolation

I remember so clearly when I first arrived here at the Baker County Detention Center. It was 8 o'clock in the evening. It was terrifying because I did not know what to expect. I also want to add that it's one thing to be a criminal and go to jail because you have done something wrong. It's another thing for me as I did not understand anything because I had done nothing wrong.

Criminals often come from a different environment than I do, having surrounded themselves with other criminals. They are more used to this environment. They drink, curse, have tattoos all over their bodies, and many of them take drugs or know people who take drugs. And when they get arrested, they know what to expect.

But here I was, having never been in jail before, having only seen it on television. I've been a disciple of Jesus for twenty-eight years. Yeah, I had fought a few times in the past, but that was over twenty-eight years ago when I was a teenager. I don't drink. I don't smoke. I don't take drugs. And I don't hang out with people who choose to live in sin.

I had heard that there were two immigration centers in Florida, one in Miami and one in Baker County. I heard that the one in Miami was nice and different from a regular jail. It was an immigration center where people were locked up, but they could play pool and volleyball and move around, and you could buy a soda and get hot coffee and many other things.

Not here. Not in the Baker County Detention Center. This place is ancient and worn out. It is dirty.

When I arrived here, I was first waiting in a small cell for one to two hours before they checked me in and then took me to the isolation pod, B7, and put me in a cell there. There were sixteen cells in the pod, eight on the ground floor and eight upstairs. They put me into one of the cells and closed the door, and there I was. I asked if I could make a phone call, and they said I could do it in a very short time. So, I stood in my cell, and I just looked around, and to be honest, I was just in shock. I don't know how to describe it. I was in a small and very dirty cell. Fastened to the wall was a mirror, a toilet without a toilet seat, and then a shower, and it was just nasty. There was mold on the ceiling, underwear left in the shower, garbage left on the bunk bed, and leftover food, which was very dirty, nasty, and old. Somebody had also left a cup, but I was pleased about it because it became my cup for an extraordinarily long time and was the only thing I had to drink with.

I made my bed, sat down, looked around, and was more in shock than anything else. Then, I was allowed to make the phone call. I went down and called Lene, and just hearing her voice was so special, and I'm crying even now when I think of it. It has been a blessing every time I hear my wife's voice; it's just so special.

And she said, "People are praying for you. All over the world, people are praying for you. You are not alone. you are not alone."

She tried to encourage me, and it was so special. When we needed to hang up, as our time was over, those thirty minutes had gone so fast, and I went back to my cell.

When I first arrived here and they processed me, they gave me a red jump suit. A few days later, they switched it to an orange one. Red suits are for people who came from jail, signifying they are criminals with a physically violent past. Orange is for those charged with a misdemeanor, a minor offense, and not charged with any physical violence. Blue is minimal risk. Why they put me in a red suit in the beginning, I have no idea.

When I arrived here, they gave me a mattress, a pillow, and some clothes. It's tough to describe the bed and the pillow. They are plastic made of string-like material, joined together on a machine. It's all plastic and very uncomfortable to lay on. But you get used to it like so many other things in here.

The plastic bed has given me ideas for maintaining my health and the health of my cell. I had a problem with some of my teeth some months ago, where I started to experience a lot of pain because I had some holes; I really needed some dental floss to clean my teeth.

So, I made a quick call and asked them if I could get some dental floss, but they could not give me that because it's a security risk. So, what did I do? I took the plastic strings from the mattress and used them to clean my teeth.

I've also taken some of the plastic from the bed and used it to wash the toilet and the shower when it gets dirty.

In the Pod outside my cell there were two vending machines and a kiosk. The kiosk was a computer on the wall where you could set up an account and buy some things, like food, clothes, playing cards, etc. It was brought in two times a week. However, I did not use the kiosk while I was in isolation because no one showed me how to use it. I was just left in there without anyone showing me how things worked. I was only out of isolation a half-hour per day, and every second counted because I wanted to spend that time talking with Lene. We talked about what was happening outside, how people were praying for me, and sharing with others about my detention. Then, we talked about the case, lawyers, etc. So, a half hour went very fast.

The first night after talking to Lene, I remember how I went back to my cell, and they closed the door behind me, and there I was. I sat down on my bed, looked around, and then broke down. That was the first time I really broke down. It's very emotional to talk about it even today; there are tears in my eyes as I think about it. I cried like I've never cried before. It was so unreal. Was this really happening? I was there in the cell alone in jail. The door was closed behind me, and I could not come out. It was a moment where panic tried to grip me, but I was like, "No, don't panic, don't panic. Relax."

It was very, very scary.

In the evening, they turned off the lights, and I went to bed and tried to sleep. They woke me up the following day, very early. I found out later that it was around 4:30–5:00 a.m. that they woke us up. I was in a cell without any watch, phone, computer, newspaper, or communication with anyone, just a tiny window. I could look out to the Pod, but no one was walking outside in the Pod as it was isolation.

There were no windows you can look out of in the pod.

In the Pod, there was a television on the other side of my cell, and then there was a hole in the door under the window that they used to give me food.

That morning, they woke us up, gave us a breakfast bag, closed the small door under the window, and then moved on. I didn't know the program for the day—what time we would get food again, and how long would I be here in isolation without talking to anyone? No one told me anything.

I grew disoriented, not having a watch, programs, news, or anything. Those first days, I cried like never before. I had nothing to do, no books or papers, just a small cell nine feet by thirteen feet (2.7 meters by 3.9 meters).

The first day, I tried to clean up the cell, calm down, and relax, but I kept breaking down and crying.

At one point, I got a hold of myself.

"Okay, Torben, calm down. Go through the Bible. Let's get the Bible up from memory."

So, I sat on my bed and quoted Jesus' words, what I remembered, and tried to go through different verses from the Bible.

This helped, but I was all over the place. I was bewildered, and I remember one time, I really needed peace in my mind so I decided, "Okay, let's start in Acts 1, Acts 1:1. Let's just start there and then go through the book of Acts by memory" like I was reading it, but this time it was from memory.

So, I started in Acts 1 and had most of the chapter in my memory in the beginning, not word for word, but most of the stories. And I went through chapter one, chapter two, chapter three, chapter four, chapter five, and I started to feel calm.

Chapter six, chapter seven, and I came to chapter ten with the house of Cornelius. And then I felt blank. "Uh, what is chapter eleven? What is twelve? What is happening there?" I asked myself.

I jumped a little to chapter sixteen and chapter nineteen and some other places I remembered very well.

Food came again, and I just tried to go through Scripture, and I prayed. I was also waiting to hear when it was my time to call Lene. When my time came, I ran out the door, went down, and called Lene. To call her was the highlight of the entire day. It was what I looked forward to when I woke up. I often thought about her and my family.

It was also very, very cold in the cell. The air conditioner was blowing chilly air, and our blanket was very thin, so I slept in my jumpsuit every day. I tried to take two showers daily because it was a way to escape, spending time standing under the hot water But the water only ran for five seconds, and then I had to push the button again. But it was nice to stand there and feel the water, and it also helped warm my body.

I longed for a Bible, so I often prayed to God, "I need a Bible. I truly need a Bible. Can you send me a Bible?"

I had been locked up three days without a Bible, but I got a gift from heaven on the fourth day. An angel sent me the most beautiful gift I have ever received. The angel's name was Sheila Zilinsky from Canada. She is a woman who had a ministry, and I had been on her radio program a few times. She sent me a Bible—a small, black King James Version Bible, a block of paper, and a few pens to write with.

When an officer gave me the little Bible and a block of paper and pens, I could not describe how it felt. I hugged the Bible. I kissed the Bible. I was crying. It was a scene like you would see in YouTube videos of the underground church in China when the Chinese see a Bible for the first time. That was how I felt. Never in my life had I been so happy like this, to get the Bible. Even though it was a King James Version, and

I'm not good at reading English, especially the King James Version, I took it all in as I'd never taken the Bible in before.

Right away, I just started with Jesus' words. The Bible had Jesus' words in red. So, I began to read Jesus' words. I then read the book of Acts. I read the epistles. I just could not get enough.

I absorbed the Bible.

I took notes on my pieces of paper.

I wrote in the Bible, and it was just so different.

It was like a different book. It was like I got the Bible for the first time. It is difficult to describe. Plus, the hunger—I never had a desire like I had in that moment. I've never been as thankful for the Word as I was then.

In everyday life, I have two or three Bibles, Bibles on my computer, Bibles on my telephone, and Bibles all over the place. I've never been in a place in my life where I lacked the Word of God, and in many ways, I never genuinely appreciated the Word of God like I do now. Now that I had been without it and then got it, I loved it like I had never loved it before.

Now, when I read the New Testament, it is as though I am reading it with a different set of eyes. I was looking for different things in the Bible. I was looking for hope. I was looking for encouragement. I was looking to find peace in jail. And it's interesting when you think of it that one-third of the New Testament was written in prisons. I could see that now. I saw things I'd never seen before by being in jail and reading the Word.

At the same time, I started a diary to keep up with the days, how many days I was there, and what happened on different days. Initially, I did not write many things; it was just a few words or a line or two. But this helped me, knowing how many days I'd been there and knowing what happened on those days. And it has been a big blessing to me today as I write this book because I can go back. I often go back to see when things happened.

When I look at my diary, I write about how I arrived here on a Thursday evening and, how I broke down, and how Friday, Saturday, and Sunday were just very hard. I did not know what to do with myself. And when I got the Bible, everything changed. Time changed. I could go into the Bible and was suddenly away from this world. I was in another place. The Bible gave me so much. I understand Jesus' words now that we should not live by bread alone but by every word that goes out of God's mouth (Matthew 4:4). It gave me so much strength, and I will never see the Bible in the same light after that moment.

Out there, we have an abundance of Bibles—I know I have—on my phone, computer, and tablet. I have several Bible translations lying around in my bedroom and other places; we have so many Bibles. It's so easy to get to that point where we somehow lose respect for it and don't appreciate what we have been given. But now, I fell in love with the Bible in a new way because it was taken away from me, and I got it back.

I want to encourage you to have a paper Bible and not only read the Bible on your phone or tablet. I was so used to reading the Bible on my phone, but now my phone and computer were taken away from me, and I no longer have them. The only thing I had now was a paper Bible, and it really became good in a new way because the more I read, the more I truly started to understand the context of what I was reading—where things were on the page, what was on the other page, what book it was part of. And you see the context differently than reading it off a phone or a computer. You know what's on the page before and what's coming later. And then, when you turn the pages, it's simply different.

God used this to speak to me once, which became an extraordinary moment. I love the story about Joseph, and in every school where we've taught, one of the first sermons I do is about the life of Joseph, where we look at his life and how God was working in him. It's a sermon where we talk about fruit and roots and that there are times in our lives when God grows deep roots so we can bear more fruit in another season. There are fruit seasons, and there are root seasons.

I went in and read about Joseph as I have done many times. But this time something special happened. It was like God let me read it like it was the first time I read it. I have read it many times before and know the story and how it ends. But it was like God took me through the story, as if it was the first time. So, when I read Genesis 39, I read verses 11 through 18, and how Potiphar's wife tried to seduce Joseph repeatedly, and something struck me. At one point, she took hold of his cloak and asked him to come to bed with her, but he left his cloak in her hand and ran out of the house. And we read:

> "She called her household servants. 'Look,' she said to them, 'this Hebrew has been brought to us to make sport of us! He came in here to sleep with me, but I screamed. When he heard me scream for help, he left his cloak beside me and ran out of the house.' She kept his cloak beside her until his master came home. Then she told him this story: "That Hebrew slave you brought us came to me to make sport of me. But as soon as I screamed for help, he left his cloak beside me and ran out of the house."" (Genesis 39:14-18 NIV)

So, we read how Potiphar's wife was trying to seduce Joseph, day after day and how she ended up lying a very evil lie. Joseph did nothing wrong. He did what the Bible said: flee from sexual sin (1 Corinthians 6:18-20). So, when she wanted to seduce him, he fled, he ran away, and did nothing wrong. But there was this woman, lying, telling evil lies about Joseph, and the result of that was he was put in jail.

When I read that, something exploded inside of me. It was like a righteousness rose up in me like, this is evil! This is unfair! I remember almost shouting out very loud, "God, why did you allow this? Why didn't you stop this? Joseph did nothing wrong? She is evil, and this should not happen."

It just came out of me because it was like I read this for the first time, not knowing what would happen later, and it seemed too unfair. Then, as I continued reading the story, I turned the page and you can see why God allowed it. You see why God did not stop it. On the next page, you see God needed to do it in Joseph's life, to get him thrown into jail so he could later minister to the baker and the servant, for him later to be lifted up to the right hand of Pharaoh, and for him to fulfill the calling on his life to save his family and his people from hunger—fulfilling the call God had given him.

When I saw it in my Bible and turned the page, it was like God said, "This is where you are now Torben. You feel it's unfair, and you don't understand it. And you say, 'God, why did you not stop it? Why did you allow this to happen?' And the reason you don't understand it is because you haven't read the next page yet. But everything I do will make sense when the next page is turned in your life."

It became a powerful revelation to me, and it's essential for all of us.

We experience hard things in our lives: suffering and unfair times, and we can almost blame God.

"God, why did you allow this? Why didn't you stop it?"

The only reason we don't understand it all is because we are so limited. We don't see the future in front of us. We live here on one page at a time and don't know what the next page will bring. It became solid for me and gave me great comfort.

Now I'm sitting here, and I can just see it again, and again, and again. On so many occasions over these last few months have I wanted to say, "God, why not right now? I'm ready for it. Let me out of here."

But then He turned the next page, and I saw things I would have missed if God had let me out.

But it was a special time in isolation—a time I will never forget.

Chapter Eight
Apollos

The ten days in isolation impacted me deeply. Even though it was challenging on many levels, it was also a time when God did many things in my life. We humans are created to have fellowship with others. We are created to touch other people. And it's simply weird to go ten days without fellowship with people, touching anyone, or speaking with anyone. But it was a beautiful time in the end because I was alone with God there and spent a lot of time with Him, and I was in His Word all day long.

After ten days, they moved me to pod B8. It was the pod next-door filled with four-man cells, each with two bunk beds fastened to the wall. I walked in, and twenty-five people were staring at me—the new guy. It was frightening. Most of them were in red suits, and only a few were in orange, as was I after the color of my suit had been changed from red to orange. Most people here, if not everyone except me, had come from prisons where they had served time. Some had even been in prison twenty to twenty-five years for murder before they were sent here, waiting to get deported. Some were forever changed by the length of time in prison; in a way in which they had become crazy being in an environment like that for so many years.

"What is happening here? How do I survive this?" I wondered, gazing back at the other men.

I took my things into my cell and then went to call Lene to let her know they moved me out of isolation. I went to the pod phones, but other inmates were on the phones, so I stood waiting for one of them to be free. I waited and waited and waited. Finally, the guy on one of the phones was finished. I took the phone and started to dial Lene's number, and war broke loose in the pod. I had no idea what was happening.

People were yelling and shouting about me using the phone in the pod. I was in shock.

Some shouted, "What did he do?"

"You cannot call here!" others yelled.

"It's not your turn!" shouted someone else.

Another guy came up and said: "Relax, Relax! He's new. He doesn't know it."

Two groups—one Black and one Hispanic—started arguing: "This is a Black phone! He cannot use our phone! You can have him on your phone."

In the pod, there were two phones. There was a whole order and system in which people signed up to use the phones. One phone was for the Black people, and the other phone was for Hispanic people.

But as one phone has a long cable and the other has a short cable, they change the phone daily to avoid problems. So, one day, the phone with the short line was the Black phone, and the next day, the Black people had the long cable phone.

Standing there with the phone in my hand, and people shouting and yelling, I thought a fight was going to break out, I just wanted to go back to isolation again. "God, please, I beg you, take me back into isolation; I really don't want to be here," I prayed in my mind.

In this pod, there were two other white men. They came to me later and helped me sort out the rules.

One was an older gentleman in his late sixties with gray hair and a big beard. He had been in prison for five years for robbing a bank, and now he was waiting to be deported to England, his home country. He was genuinely nice. However, one of the first things he said was, "Sorry to say it, but you stink."

That was his greeting: "You stink."

The other white guy, a young man, also from England, covered in tattoos from head to toe, came to me, gave me some soap, and said, "Here, you can have my soap. You are really stinking so here is some soap."

I tried to explain, "But I've been taking a shower daily. It's not like I don't take a shower."

And then they said, "But you stink terribly; it's your clothes."

Then I remembered: it was so cold in isolation because the air conditioner ran all the time that I slept in my orange suit because the blanket we had could not keep me warm by itself. I suddenly realized I had been walking around in that suit for many days, not noticing that I was stinking. Yes, I could not smell it myself.

To be in B8 was like another world from being in isolation. I was now in a four-man cell with three other people, and only one of them spoke a little English. They had to explain how the toilet system worked: "If you do '#1' at night, you don't flush, but if you do a '#2,' you flush." They also told me about the rules regarding the shower as we now had four people using one toilet and shower. This made me miss isolation even more: at least I could go to the toilet there without people around me.

That night, when I went to bed, I was crying inside; yes, most people cry in here, if not outside, then inside when they first arrive at a place like this. I so wanted to get away from this place.

The day after was better because I discovered I could make a video call via two computers here and use them to call Lene. Yes, we had to pay for it, and I found most men didn't use it because of the cost. This gave me the freedom to call Lene whenever I wanted, without being in line for the telephone and being involved in violent discussions all the time. It was a hidden blessing for me.

I also learned to operate the kiosk. There was a computer on the wall where you could set up an account to buy food and candy, soap, and other things you needed.

You could buy a security toothbrush. It was a four-centimeter (1.6 inches) toothbrush, but it was still better than the one we got here, which you put on your finger. It was not easy to use.

You could also buy clothes. I bought blue shorts. I'm wearing them right now. So, I don't wear the orange suit anymore; only when I must leave my pod. If we go to the doctor or other places, we need to have the suit on and be handcuffed.

After several days in the new pod, an event like discovering fresh water in the desert happened. A man came to me and invited me to a cell. When I walked into the cell, seven other men were there, Bibles in hand.

"Woah! What is that?" I thought.

The man leading the meeting was Rico. He spoke okay English. He had been in jail for five years and was now waiting to be deported back to Mexico. He had been there in that pod waiting for over a year and had been there the longest. While in jail, he had met God, genuinely repented, and now led a Bible study in B8, teaching what he had learned.

And right there, he became my Apollos.

In Acts 18 we read about a Jew named Apollos who taught others the way of the Lord. He only knew about the baptism of John, but he spoke with boldness. When Aquila and Priscilla heard about him, they invited him to their home and explained the way of the Lord to him in a clearer way.

> *"Meanwhile, a Jew named Apollos, a native of Alexandria, came to Ephesus. He was a learned man with a thorough knowledge of the Scriptures. He had been instructed in the way of the Lord, and he spoke with great fervor and taught about Jesus accurately, though he knew only the baptism of John. He began to speak boldly in the synagogue. When Priscilla and Aquila heard him, they invited him to their home and explained to him the way of God more adequately."* (Acts 18:24-26 NIV)

That happened here, in B8 of the detention center. Rico had heard of the Lord's way and experienced true repentance, but he had never gotten baptized in water and with the Holy Spirit.

Over the following days, I spent quite a bit of time teaching Rico the way of the Lord, and he asked many good questions. He was hungry for the truth, and it was beautiful.

Five days later, he got baptized. On this special day, I baptized him in my cell. It was with a cup of water over his head; that was the only thing we had. I would never do it like this outside the prison because baptism means to immerse. But in a place like this, where I did not know how long he would still be here and where there was no option of immersing him in water, I knew God would bless what we had to do. And He did. It became a powerful evening.

Looking back, it is special to think that this was just a small taste of what was waiting for me later, as I saw men baptized and set free in powerful ways. But Rico was the first I baptized like that in jail and he will always stand out as someone special.

The day after, he asked if I could pray for one of his family members over the phone who had a lot of back pain. I prayed for the person over the phone and God healed her. It was very special for Rico to see. The next day, we had another meeting in the cell. Here, Rico shared with all the others what God had done in his life the last few days, how he got baptized and filled with the Holy Spirit, and how God had healed one of his family members over the phone, and it was all so beautiful.

I then took some time to pray for people, and we saw strong deliverances. A young man from Jamaica, whom I later became good friends with, got delivered that evening. He fell down between the toilet and the wall, almost laying over the toilet, and there he got delivered from some unclean spirit.

I have seen this many times, but it is one thing to see this happen in churches or homes, and it's just so different to experience this in a jail, with people wearing orange and red jumpsuits. At that moment, I felt like Paul or Peter: teaching the Word of God, praying for people, and seeing God move in the prison.

The day after, I shared communion with Rico/Apollos. We sat in our orange suits on the jail floor, worshipping Christ and taking part in His Body and Blood. You don't know what you have before it's taken away. It was the most beautiful communion I ever had, up to that moment, because I understood the importance of the fellowship of brothers. I hadn't seen any brother or sister in Christ since I was detained; I'd been alone. But now I had a disciple; I had a brother in Christ I could sit down with and share communion with; it gave me a new understanding of communion. I now understood how the early church was a church that was persecuted and how they looked at communion much differently than we do.

As beautiful as this moment was, a few days later, after more than one year in jail, Rico/Apollos was suddenly deported. To our surprise, he was gone. The meetings stopped because I didn't speak Spanish, and they didn't speak English, and there I was alone again, and I really missed Rico/Apollos.

As I said, you don't know what you have until it is taken away. Here, I finally had fellowship with a brother in the Lord, and then suddenly it was taken away from me, and I was all alone again, and it was hard. But I so appreciated the days I got with him. It was like fresh water in the desert and gave me so much. But now I am alone again, and I still don't know why I am here. I still expect to be released any day because this is all a misunderstanding. I did not smuggle weapons. I have not done anything criminal; I should get out soon.

But as you can understand, I still don't know when I will get out. Lene found a lawyer to represent me. Otherwise, there is no more information about why I'm here and what is happening.

Because of the new lawyer, I finally met an ICE (U.S. Immigration and Customs Enforcement) officer after being here for two to three weeks. It was a very shocking meeting.

The ICE officer came to my pod and gave me the papers.

"Here are your papers; this is about your court hearing that will be set in August, but it will be changed later," he said.

"No, no, I need to be out before August," I said, shocked at the news. "You know we have a lawyer, and I hope to come out on a bond."

The ICE officer looked at me and said, "No bond for you. You are going to be here many months, and then you're going to be deported. Get used to it."

Those words hit me so hard. "What is happening here? I cannot be here for many months. I cannot be deported. What is happening?"

Nothing made sense to me.

A few days later, I had another meeting with an officer again, and everything became even more unreal and crazy.

Another ICE officer gave me a piece of paper.

I looked at it and said, "What is this?"

And he looked at it and said, "Oh, this is because they've done a review that you will continue being here. You are not leaving."

I said, "What? Because of what?"

He looked at the paper and said, "Oh, because you have a chronic care condition," and he looked again; "you are obese."

He looked at me, eyeing me up and down like he was surprised.

"You are not obese," he said, giving me the paper and leaving.

The paper was a Notice of Custody Determination. It said that it had been determined that I should be kept in custody. It said I had a "chronic care condition" medical professionals had confirmed, and that condition was obesity, and therefore I should remain in custody because my condition places me within populations identified by the U.S. Centers for Disease Control as potentially at higher risk for serious illness from COVID-19. Like it was not a higher risk of becoming sick in a place like this with no fresh air or windows. Yes, it sounds crazy

When I read it, I was like "What? I'm not obese, and no professional has ever checked me. It's all lies."

Nothing made sense. This is so crazy; no one will ever look at me and think I am obese. And I have not been checked by any professional. It was both funny and scary at the same time. What is happening here? There is no one I can trust.

The paper also said that I had overstayed my visa, but I had not overstayed my visa. I did not stay longer than the ninety days I was allowed by my U.S. Department of Homeland Security ESTA (Electronic System for Travel Authorization) application when I came into the country. It was a lie, as I sent in my asylum papers before the ninety days were over and got a response saying I could stay in the United States as my case was being considered.

It was all lies and at the end on the document it said: "Based on this review a decision has been made to maintain custody."

It is difficult to put into words all the emotions that were going through me.

But here I was, and it did not look like I was going home. I often just spend hours in my cell, sitting on my bunk bed on a very thin mattress, studying the Bible, reading, spending most of the time alone. To give you an example of how much I was sitting, here is a little funny story. One night, I went to bed. Suddenly I felt something on my butt and thought, "Oh no, I've got a rash. Oh no, I'm sick."

On my butt, I had very weird skin I never had before, like tough skin.

So, I thought, "Oh no, I'm getting sick; what is happening?"

Then I checked the other side of my butt, and it was the same.

"Ah, it's not a rash. It's hard skin from sitting on my bed, studying the Bible."

Yes, I spent hours and hours just sitting on my bed, reading and reading and reading, and I got hard skin on my butt, something I have never had before.

I cried a lot after those ICE officers had been here. I didn't understand what was going on. But today, when I look back, I am so thankful He did not take me out then. I know today why. I know today that if I had come out at that time, I would have come out as a mess. I would have come out full of fear. I would have come out not ready and strong but broken and weak. And I would have come out where I would not be a blessing for the Body of Christ at all.

I would be the opposite. I would have said, "Be careful everyone, don't go there, keep away, stop doing what you're doing, don't take any chances, this is the worst thing that could ever happen to you."

This was why God did not take me out: there was a lot that I still needed to learn, and therefore, he kept me in here. There was freedom I needed in here before I could come out.

Philippians 4:13 (NIV) says, *"I can do all things through Him (Jesus Christ) who gives me strength."* Many people take this verse out of context and think, "Hey, I can be the best football player in the world, and I can be the best singer in the world; I can do everything if Jesus Christ strengthens me."

But if you read what Paul is saying in context, in the verse before that, he says, *"I know what it is to be in need, and I know what it is to have plenty. I have learned the secret of being content in any and every situation, whether well fed or hungry, whether living in plenty or in want"* (Philippians 4:12 NIV).

And then comes, "I can do all things through Him (Jesus Christ) who gives me strength."

Paul is saying that even if we go through tough times, even if we have nothing, even if it is challenging, we can do it because Jesus Christ gives us the strength to get through it.

This was what I needed to learn. And many people out there need to learn this, too.

I needed to learn this and so many other things were still waiting to be revealed and experienced. So, I am thankful I did not come out then and it shows God knew what He was doing. He still does.

Chapter Nine
The Dream

Sitting here in my B6 block cell, I look back at the time in B8. It was really one of the hardest times in my life. I, at one time, became very depressed and, in many ways, not prepared for what I experienced.

I was incredibly stressed about everything happening and did not understand any of it. So, in many ways, it was indeed the hardest time I've been through, and it still is, but I stand in another place today, mentally, spiritually, and with a greater understanding of suffering.

But it was back in B8 that God spoke to me, and it became a new beginning in my life, a fresh start I am now seeing the fruit of.

I now realize that it is often at the hardest points in life when God speaks and does something new. When we really get desperate and come to the point of surrendering everything, our life changes. Our best prayers often come out as deep, deep cries from the deepest part of our hearts and souls.

Even though God did not save me from it right away, as I wanted Him to, He spoke to me, and things slowly started to change inside me.

So often, in the current season of our life with God, He has given us just enough to keep running the race. His manna is for the moment. I have seen it repeatedly in the last few months. Lene and I call it our manna in the desert. When we were tired and could not continue anymore and just wanted to give up, God gave us manna in the form of a word, a dream, a prophecy, or an experience—something that just helped us to keep running a little further.

In B8, trials were immense, but Rico/Apollos was manna for me at the right moment. It was so beautiful to see the power of God and how he got baptized—the first inmate I have ever baptized in a cell. But then he left, and I was alone again, and it all became hard.

On the heels of Rico/Apollos leaving, my court hearing came up. This was an opportunity to get a bond, allowing me to finally get out. I was excited and ready to leave this terrible place. I had been praying for the day I would meet the judge, and I had a piece of paper where I'd written down some things I wanted to say to the judge.

"Dear, Your Honor," I wrote, "I really hope you give me this opportunity and grant me a bond so I can come out. I've been married for twenty-seven years to the same woman. I have never done anything criminal. I've never been jailed before," and so on.

I was ready and in prayer when they called my name over the loudspeaker. The door to my Pod opened, and I walked out into the next room where they put handcuffs on me and took me down the hall. We went into a small room where there was a TV screen in a small office. I could see the judge in the courthouse and some other people working with him on the screen.

Nothing went as I expected. The judge was not interested in hearing me. He said that a bond was not under consideration due to how ICE had detained me and something about my case. But more about that later. He said it was up to ICE if I should come out on a bond, but they had denied me that already.

The court hearing was only five minutes long, and the judge issued a new date for my full hearing: October 19, 2022. That was over two months away, and I will never forget that moment. I remember so clearly when he said the next date was October 19; I broke inside.

"What?" I thought. "October 19? This cannot happen. This is like the worst day ever. First, it is over two months from now, and it cannot be that day. Let it be the 20th, the 18th, or any other day. But not that day. October 19 is my wedding anniversary."

When the judge asked if I had something to add, I said no and looked down at my papers. Even though the papers I had with me contained everything I planned to say, I could not say anything. This was like a nightmare that just became ten times worse. This was worse than anything I could imagine. I was in shock. It seemed all dark, and I felt all hope had been taken from me. I left the hearing shattered. No bond and a hearing on my anniversary over two months from now.

They took me back to the cell, and I was like, "God, what is happening here? October 19, two more months in this place? It cannot be that day. Lene cannot see me like this in an orange suit with handcuffs on."

At that time, I did not know she would not see me, but I thought she would be at the court. I imagined her sitting there, seeing me like a hardcore criminal on our anniversary. No, that was terrible to think about. Words cannot describe the disappointment I felt. It could not have gone worse than this.

I will never forget that moment with the judge on the screen.

Sitting in my cell, I opened my Bible and read the book of Job. Job was the only one I could relate to at that moment. To add salt to the wounds, the following day was my birthday, and although I got a lot of greetings from people out there and was truly thankful for that, everything was hard and I felt so alone.

Psalm 13 (NIV) came to me:

"How long, LORD? Will You forget me forever?
How long will You hide Your face from me?
How long must I wrestle with my thoughts and day after day
have sorrow in my heart?
How long will my enemy triumph over me?
Look on me and answer, LORD my God.
Give light to my eyes, or I will sleep in death,
and my enemy will say, 'I have overcome him,'
and my foes will rejoice when I fall.
But I trust in Your unfailing love; my heart rejoices in Your
salvation.

I will sing the LORD's praise,
for He has been good to me."

This became my chapter. Everything seemed so far away.

However, even in Psalm 13, we see that though God does not answer the question, the Psalmist does by saying, "But I trust in Your unfailing love."

That was also the answer God gave me when I asked, "How long, God?" It was like He answered, "Just keep trusting in Me."

And things started to change.

"God, I truly need a breakthrough now. What to do? I am here, I feel depressed, I don't want to be here. It looks like I will be here for several more months." So, the only thing I thought of doing was, "Okay, I need to start fasting."

So, I started a water fast to seek God more intensely. The same day, I got a new legal team. I needed a different lawyer because the case had become more complicated. Later, they helped me find out many things about who was behind all of this.

But the day after I started my water fast, a new cellmate moved in with me, making everything much worse. This man was indeed a gift from Satan. It was the worst encounter I've ever had. I don't use these words lightly: he was like a child of the devil. He had been in jail for ten years for murdering a homeless guy.

When he told me the story, he was angry that they found out who the homeless guy was by a dental examination. He felt that was unfair because he would not have gone to jail for such a long time if they didn't know who he was. He showed no remorse, only anger.

This was a large man covered in tattoos, and he hated me. I felt his hatred, and he took over our four-man cell. He was now the leader. He brought food into the cell and invited others in to eat with him, and everyone but me was offered food. At one point, he bought fifteen to eighteen soup bowls at a time, made with chips and tuna. He shared with everyone but never offered me anything. He never looked at me, even though everything happened in my cell.

Now, I was fasting and would not eat anyway, but that was not why he didn't offer me anything to eat: he just didn't like me. The way he looked at me was very frightening.

I cried out inside, "God, what is happening here? I really need You!"

There were several times I was sure he would strike me. His friends were always in the cell, so I had no place to be alone or to feel safe.

A few days later, I received a message that changed everything. A man in Texas whom I had not met personally but had been at one of our meetings dreamed about me. He sent it to Lene, and she sent it to me so I could read it over the Pod computer.

"There is a very interesting dream here," she wrote in the email, "that you need to read."

In one of the lowest moments of my life, I read the dream, and the Holy Spirit came over me. I knew this was from God; He was speaking to me right then.

After a few lines, tears welled up in me, but I did not want to sit there and cry in front of everyone, so I closed my eyes, looked down, and just calmed down a little, crying inside and praying. After ten to fifteen seconds, I was able to read the next few lines. Then, I needed to stop again and take it all in: God was finally speaking clearly to me. He saw me and knew I needed to hear from Him. I was so excited but also afraid at the same time.

What will He say to me?

What will the next line say?

Will it say I will be here for a long time?

In the first part of the dream, the man said, "I saw you (Torben) in a large football stadium where a game was about to begin. My point of view was looking into the stadium, where I could see both sides of the bleachers with the football field in the middle. The field and the left side bleachers were completely empty, with no one at all.

"My focus went to the right side of the stadium, where I could see only a small handful of inmates spread out sporadically in separate groups across the bleachers. All the groups were casually talking amongst one another before the game.

"However, you were quietly sitting there all alone in the midst of all the other inmates in the middle toward the bottom. You had your head down with your hand on your head, and you were not talking to any of the other groups of inmates. You were just sitting there thinking. You were so depressed and lonely and couldn't believe how long you had been in prison. I could hear your thoughts and feel how downtrodden you had become. It seemed like depression dominated your thoughts and emotions. All you could think of was when you were (going) to get out. Then, it occurred to me as if you didn't realize a game was about to begin. No one there did. All the other inmates were also oblivious.

"You know, normally, the crowd is cheering loudly and going crazy before their team comes out to play. But this wasn't the case in this scene. It was as if everyone was passively talking like there wasn't a game about to start. No clapping. No cheering. No excitement. Nothing was happening that would lead you to believe a game would ever start. Everything was bleak and dull in color. The only emotion I felt at this point in time was the deep depression and loneliness that was overtaking you.

"But then, suddenly, the scene immediately shifted!

"Everything became bright and colorful. My view went to the left-side bleachers, and suddenly, I saw the entire stadium full of people. Everyone was on fire with excitement, clapping, and yelling! Cheering with everything inside of them! Their passion was unlike anything I had ever seen before! They all knew a great and marvelous game was coming! It was like they somehow knew the greatest game they would ever see was about to begin!

"Then in a single moment, as I heard everyone cheer— I started to feel what was in everyone's hearts—the word REJOICE immediately jolted into my spirit!

"REJOICE! REJOICE!! REJOICE!!!

"Tell him to REJOICE! Then I woke up!"

I was that guy, sitting there with my head in my hands, alone with no one to talk to, depressed, and could only think of when I would be released.

But through the dream, God spoke to me, and He said, "Stand up, Torben. Take responsibility for your life. Don't sit there and feel sorry for yourself; stand up!"

It became an immensely powerful moment. And the man who shared the dream continued later with a message from God to me:

> "Do not be afraid. Do not fear this light affliction. Lift up your head, my dear child. Do not be down any longer. Get up. Your current suffering will not overtake you. It is the answer to your prayers to know and partake of my suffering, cross, and resurrection.
>
> "Rejoice in your cell! Rejoice in the halls! Rejoice in the yard! Rejoice for what is to come! For I Am at work. Get in the game, My disciple! This is My game! Rejoice in it! Cause those around you to Rejoice! Let My fruit come out of you! Can you hear the abundance of rain that is coming? Hear the sound of My mighty Spirit pouring out over this prison, this region, this nation?! Let My Spirit move through you in that prison. Satan has bound My children for far too long! You should give them the true and Good News of My Kingdom! It is for you to bring My healing power to their broken hearts!
>
> "Awaken and cast your cares off to the side! Get all that weight off of you! That's not who you are."

I knew I needed to listen to this, even though it was hard as I was down still, and it was so difficult to understand at that moment. Two days later, I almost ended up on the verge of a fight with the guy in my cell: he seemed ready to jump on me at any moment. But instead, I was moved to another Pod, to B8, where I've now been writing this for seven and a half months.

That dream changed everything. From here, I have read this dream and the prophetic word he gave afterward almost every day, and it has become a part of me.

I also began taking responsibility for my life. I continued my fast, and after ten days of fasting on water, I started to feel sick in my body. The water was bad. I wanted to continue my fast, but I could not the way I was feeling, so I started to just eat a little bread in the morning and a little every time we ate, just enough to keep my body running.

I continued like that for forty days. I lost twenty pounds (nine kilos) in that time. Then, I just continued eating one meal daily and seeking God, which I continued for sixty-five days.

At the same time, I trained physically every day and found out how important it was. To be in jail and not move around a lot is not suitable for anyone. I started running up and down the stairs in my Pod daily. I did push-ups in my cell and other exercises to strengthen my body. When I entered the jail, I thought I could only do a few push-ups because I'd never really used my body like that. As I often run, I am strong in my legs, but I have never trained my upper body. But now I do around two hundred push-ups per day. I am stronger than ever before as training like this has become part of my daily routine.

But it was not only for the training. At the same time, I spend more time in prayer. I'm not able to shout in here, and sometimes you just want to get the frustration out of your body, so this is a way I can shout, not with my voice, but with my body. I spend a lot of time praying and listening to God, sitting on the floor and sweating doing my training. The floor is often wet with my sweat. I have had the best prayer moments this way. Adding all this to my deep reading of the Bible, I am being transformed in ways I never imagined.

Although I want to get out, I am here and don't want this time to be wasted. I want to grow both spiritually and physically. I want to see good fruit come out of this, as the dream said: "Stand up, Torben. Take responsibility for your life. Don't sit there and feel sorry for yourself; stand up! Let My fruit come out of you!"

I'm forty-six years old, and a funny thing, for the first time in my life, I can see a six-pack on my stomach. I've never seen my stomach muscles, and that just tells me it's never too late.

Please hear me: it's never too late to change our lives, but we need discipline. This is what God taught me during this time: I needed to control my mind, body, and life to survive and get something profitable out of this experience. The Father taught me the truth of 2 Timothy 1:7 (NIV): *"For the Spirit God gave us does not make us timid, but gives us power, love, and self-discipline."*

In I Corinthians 9:24-27 (NIV), Paul discusses the training we are in:

"Do you not know that in a race all the runners run, but only one gets the prize? Run in such a way as to get the prize. Everyone who competes in the games goes into strict training. They do it to get a crown that will not last, but we do it to get a crown that will last forever. Therefore, I do not run like someone running aimlessly; I do not fight like a boxer beating the air. No, I strike a blow to my body and make it my slave so that after I have preached to others, I myself will not be disqualified for the prize."

Everyone who runs goes into strict training to be able to run the race. I went into training, physically and in my studies, which brought me so much freedom. Today, the church desperately needs self-discipline, focus, and a lot of love and power from God. We need to be able to control ourselves, our thoughts, our minds, and our bodies because if we cannot control ourselves, we will not be able to finish the race in front of us.

Just three days ago, there was a fight here in the Pod. It started with a discussion, as it always does, over the TV, and this time, people were trying to hit each other, but it got stopped by other inmates. The guards came and shut us down and told everyone to get in our cells, and we were all shut down for a few hours.

Then they let us out again, saying, "You have to behave now, and if there are any more problems, you'll be locked down for the rest of the day."

Everything exploded again when we came out of our cells to eat a brief time later. While we were eating, another guy went to one of my friends and, from behind, hit him in the back of the head. Blood was running down his face and onto the floor. I saw blood all over the floor. Everyone was shouting; people were pushing each other. I called some guards, and they came in, and we all got shut down the rest of the day until noon the next day.

Why did that guy hit him? Because he lacked self-discipline.

What is the consequence of this? For him to hit somebody in the back of the head while waiting for answers to his case can have a significant impact—it can mean several more months here, and it could mean that he will lose his case.I saw him later, out in the yard, where he was in the doghouse. That is for people from isolation or more dangerous people who spend their time outside; they cannot be with others out there. All this and more because of a few seconds of lack of self-control. As I said, this will have a significant impact on his life.

This is what happens here if you do not have self-discipline. I've personally been in several "fights" since I came here. For me, it has not yet been physical, but shouting, yelling, and people getting furious and cursing me. It's hard to be in all of this, and I hate it. This is, in many ways, what I hate most here. And honestly, if you do not have self-discipline, you can quickly lose it in a place like this.

I've been learning a lot: fasting, physical exercise, and being in jail is great training to learn self-discipline and how to control your emotions. If any of you want to finish the race that Paul talked about, you need to have self-discipline and learn not to let your feelings dictate how you act. So, the dream really started a new beginning in my life.

Chapter Ten
Truth is Growing

As I've said, I am in B6. Seven and a half months have passed since I was detained initially. While B8 was a four-man cell, B6 is a two-man cell. This means I can often be alone, and I love it.

I have had cellmates, but often only for a brief time. Otherwise, I've been allowed to be alone, as nearly everyone else here speaks Spanish, making it difficult for me to share a cell. I cannot communicate with them. They also prefer to be with somebody they can talk to, and I therefore often can get people to move to other cells that are empty or where there is only one person in the cell.

In B8, red suits and orange suits are mixed. To remind you, red suits are people from prisons who have committed violent crimes. Orange suits often are people who have committed smaller crimes like drunk driving or nonviolent things.

Several men in B8 had, for example, committed murder; one was sentenced to twenty years for murder. Another man was doing twenty-five years for murder. There were some scary guys in there. To make matters worse, the population in B8 was half Black and half Hispanic, creating a lot of problems between the groups.Here in Pod B6, there are no red suits, and most people have only been in prison a few months before coming here to fight their case.

B6 is an easier place to be. The main problem I face here is that only a few people speak English. Most of everyone is from South America. I am often the only white guy here, and it is extraordinary when we stand in line to get food. I am also a head taller than everyone else. I'm white, very tall, and I don't speak the language, so I don't fit in here in so many ways.

Right now, there is only one or two who speak English that I am talking with. The television is always in Spanish. When they play cards, it is in Spanish. Everything is in Spanish, and I still don't speak Spanish.

People have said, "Then learn it, Torben. You're in jail, so it's a good opportunity. Why haven't you learned it yet?"

The answer is that I thought I would be out next week, and it has been like that since the day I got here. I will be out next week, I will be out next week, I will be out next week, I said to myself. Now, nine and a half months later, I still hope I will be out next week. You don't start to learn a language if you believe you will soon leave this place. Besides, I am currently busy writing this book, which is what I'm focused on now.

Since coming to B6, I've wanted to share Jesus with the people around me. So, I tried initially to talk with those who knew a little English to share Jesus, but only a few understood what I was saying, and those people didn't seem interested.

I tried several times, gave up, and kept to myself for a long time. I only come out of my cell when I need to go down and get food, change clothes, or do a video call, so I often spend twenty-two to twenty-three hours of the day alone in my cell.

At the same time, God is working within me, so I love spending time alone with Him. It is beautiful what God is doing here, but it is hard, and I deeply miss my family. They are in a new house, and I haven't seen the place. I am here and they are in my home I haven't been in or seen. I will come back to that new house later. But it is hard because it is because of me that they are suffering. They are suffering by not having me there. It has been an extra burden to them for me being locked up here.

Then there was the whole thing with the lawyer and the money we needed. That was a new world for us, and we did not understand why it cost so much. Then there were the YouTube videos and all the lies they were spreading about me. So many people had ideas or opinions as to what I'd done. There has been a lot of talk online, and even though I cannot see the videos, I hear a little about what is happening out there from others. Those things make it so much more complicated than if you were just in jail without all of that.

Not understanding why exactly I'm here is also an enormous burden, as it creates a sense of unrest in Lene and I about what will happen and the next thing they will do to me. Will they come out with some added charges against me? Will I spend many years like this? Yes, there is enough to worry about as it is.

When I entered detention, I was not like how I am now. I was not strong, and most people are the same in my situation. But I am just in a different place when it comes to God today. The truth of God's Word and His plan has also grown in me. The truth had started to slowly set me free. The fact is I am so free now. Yesterday, a friend on the outside recorded a phone call with me and sent it out as an update on my YouTube channel. The video I called, "Free Behind Bars." Even though everything around me is still something to get depressed over, and I'm still here behind bars, I'm free!

I see now that the state of being free behind bars began when I was first detained. It started with words from the Bible and words from books I read that Lene sent to me over a tablet—stories I've heard before that really started to grow in me. These stories were mainly about persecution, suffering, and endurance. I was doing a lot of studies, especially in the book of Acts, learning how the early church was persecuted and what Jesus and the Apostle Paul said about persecution.

Before, I wasn't looking at God as sovereign; not the same way I do today. God is sovereign, and He is in control. That is not something we talk a lot about in the circles I have been in. But when you go through things like this, you want to know how things work. God used this pain to show me that there is a reason for it and how God also works through this. I want to add here that I would never become a Calvinist, but I also don't see myself as an Armenian. If you are not aware of these terms, Calvinism focuses on God's sovereignty in salvation and emphasizes predestination, while Arminianism emphasizes the free will and believes in conditional election and the possibility of falling from faith or grace.

I am in the middle of it all. I just wanted to share it with those who think about it. But God is in control. Even I hold on to the fact that we have free will, and we cannot blame God for the evil that happens in this fallen world.But I was learning important things about many things. I was studying the Word, praying, and thinking about many things in my life and what God was saying in His Word. I still did not fully understand it all, at least not with my heart, but I started to understand some of it in my head. In the dream relayed to me from a person in Texas, there was a lot of truth. One of the things this prophetic word said is that God was the One who had put me here, and He had a plan, and this was why I was here. Even though the enemy had his hand in it; God was the One who was in control.

I started to think about many of the people in the Bible who walked with God, especially Joseph. If we look at him, along with many others in the Bible, we see how God was in control, even though it often did not look like that when evil things were happening to them. We see God's hand all over Joseph's life; we see God's hand all over Abraham's life, and we see God is all over many other people in the Bible. I, like most of you, see it and somehow know it, but for me, it still was mostly in my head.

Then I saw in the book of Acts how the early disciples were persecuted and went to jail. In Acts 5, we see how an angel of the Lord came and opened the prison door, and the apostles went out from the prison and began to preach again, as the angel told them to.

"They arrested the apostles and put them in the public jail.
But during the night, an angel of the Lord opened the doors of the

jail and brought them out. 'Go, stand in the temple courts,' he said,
'and tell the people all about this new life.'" (Acts 5:18-20 NIV)

Hallelujah! I wanted to see that.

In Acts 16, Paul and Silas are in jail, and suddenly, an earthquake occurs, and the chains fall off, and everything changes. Hallelujah! That is what I wanted to see. "Woah! God is really in control!"

But then you also read other places in the Bible where God did not come and set them free like that, but where they stayed in jail a long time.I ask many questions like: God, are You really in control? If so, why am I still here? Why have I not been supernaturally set free from jail, when so many thousands of people are praying for me worldwide? Why don't I see it like the Apostles in Acts 5 or Paul and Silas in Acts 16?

In Acts 5 and 16, for example, Paul spent years in jail or under house arrest. And we know that even Paul, Peter, Silas and the apostles, and many other people, got delivered from jail at one time and ended up in jail again later or ending up dying as martyrs. At that time, no angels were coming to set them free.

If we look at the twelve disciples, John was the only one who did not die as a martyr, but he still ended up on a prison island, and it did not seem at first like there was any angel from God coming to set him free.

As you can see, many questions were swirling around in my head: "Does God only help us sometimes? Does God really have a plan with all of it? Does it include a plan for suffering (something we don't really understand)? Where is God in all that is happening with me right now?"

From there, I started reading about the house church movement in China, the persecuted church, and especially a book I read several times before going to jail called The Heavenly Man: The Remarkable True Story of Chinese Christian Brother Yun. I've read it four or five times now, and when I got here, somebody sent most of the chapters to me, and my wife sent the rest, one chapter at a time. Then, there was another book Brother Yun wrote called Living Water: Powerful Teachings from the International Bestselling Author of The Heavenly

Man, which is mostly sermons, and it also got things started in my mind. In one of his books, Brother Yun wrote:

"When a child of God suffers, you need to understand it is only because the Lord has allowed it. He has not forgotten you! When I hear a house church Christian has been imprisoned for Christ in China, I don't advise people to pray for his or her release unless the Lord clearly reveals we should pray this way. Before a chicken is hatched, it is vital that it is kept in the warm protection of the shell for twenty-one days. If you take the chick out of that environment one day too early, it will die. Similarly, ducks need to remain confined in their shell for twenty-eight days before they are hatched. If you take a duck out on the twenty-seventh day, it will die."

Words like this made me sit up and say, "Whoa! It aligns with what I saw in Scripture and what I began to experience here. It lines up with the dream I received, but do I really trust that God is in control? If I do, the next question is, "Do I then trust that He is good? And what if He thinks I can manage this, but I really cannot?"

Brother Yun also wrote:

"There is always a purpose to why God allows His children to go to prison. Perhaps, it's so they can witness to the other prisoners, or perhaps God wants to develop more character in their lives. But if we use our own efforts to get people out of prison earlier than God intended, we can thwart His plans and the believer may come out not as fully formed as God wanted then to be"

All that I read in the Bible was working in me, but to be honest, I did not know what to believe. I saw it in Scripture—it makes sense, but I was still unsure. But today, nine and half months later, it is the truth.

I know it now, not only in my head but also in my heart. I feel it, and this is some of the truth, together with so much in the Bible, which has truly set me free.

Back then, it was still working within me. I was studying, and one day, I read a passage from Genesis 15:13-16 that shook my life. Abraham received a prophecy of what would happen for the next four hundred years. He would have children, and generations later, those children would be enslaved for four hundred years, and how God would then send somebody (and we know that somebody was Moses) to deliver them. We will read the text, and when we read this, know that this was before Abraham even had one child; God was prophesying about it all—about Isaac, Jacob, Joseph, about slavery for four hundred years, and about Moses and how they would be delivered with great power out of Egypt.

> *"Then the LORD said to him, 'Know for certain that for four hundred years your descendants will be strangers in a country not their own and that they will be enslaved and mistreated there. But I will punish the nation they serve as slaves, and afterward they will come out with great possessions. You, however, will go to your ancestors in peace and be buried at a good old age. In the fourth generation your descendants will come back here, for the sin of the Amorites has not yet reached its full measure.'"* (Genesis 15:13-16 NIV)

Before Abraham had one child, God knew. This truth was really working inside me. The truth grew in me: "Did God really put me here, like He did with Joseph? I know that Joseph needed to go to jail to fulfill God's plan. It was all part of God's calling on Joseph's life. Is it the same with me?"

And there were many things about how suffering was working in me.

If God did not allow Joseph to go to jail, then yes, He would not have fulfilled the prophecy He gave to Abraham several generations before. If God had not called Moses and let him go through the desert for those forty years before calling him, God would not have fulfilled the prophecy He gave Abraham four hundred years before. They were all part of a bigger story, like you and me. Yes, God has a plan with it all, even though we do not always see it right here and now.

Then I read the letter of 1 Peter:

> *"In all this you greatly rejoice, though now for a little while you may have had to suffer grief in all kinds of trials. These have come so that the proven genuineness of your faith—of greater worth than gold, which perishes even though refined by fire—may result in praise, glory and honor when Jesus Christ is revealed."* (I Peter 1:6-7 NIV)

Coupled with another quote from Brother Yun, and the reality of God's sovereignty took root and grew in my heart:

"We can grow to such a place in Christ where we laugh and rejoice when people slander us, because we know we are not of this world, and our security is in heaven. The more we are persecuted for his sake, the more reward we will receive in heaven. When people malign you, rejoice and be glad. When you walk through a painful experience, embrace it, and you will be free! When you learn these lessons, there is nothing left that the world can do to you."

Nine and a half months later, it is the truth. I'm free! There is nothing the world can do to me anymore. I have seen it in my own life, and it has become a revelation to me.

I want to end this chapter with one more powerful quote from Brother Yun's book Living Water.

"How we mature as Christians largely depends on the attitude we have when we're faced with suffering. Some try to avoid it and imagine it doesn't exist, but that only makes the situation worse. Others try to endure it grimly, hoping for relief. This is better but falls short of the full victory God wants to give each of His children. The Lord wants us to embrace suffering as a friend. We need a deep realization that when we are being persecuted for Christ's sake, this is an act of God blessing us."

Woah! I've gone through these three stages these last nine months. When I came in, in the beginning, I tried to avoid it and imagine that it did not exist. It was too difficult for me to understand what was going on, and I felt it should just stop right away, but as we see here, that just makes it all worse.

Then, I realized, "Okay, I am here. This is a reality, so I need to endure it."

I had a time when I really endured all the persecution, and the humility, and the fights, and the food, and the people, and the lockdowns, and all of it. I was doing it grimly, hoping that it would soon be better. It was better, but still, there was no full victory in all of it.Later, with the Holy Spirit's help, I embraced it as a friend. Those people who were after me, those who really irritated me with their noise, fights, and problems, instead of looking at them and becoming irritated, I started to see them as an instrument of God to humble me. I began to see this place as a friend because it was to make me look more like Jesus.

And for me, being here was an act of God blessing me. When this finally went from my head to my heart, everything changed, and therefore, I could do a YouTube update the other day called, "Free Behind Bars." I want to say to everyone here at the end of this chapter that you can be here in Baker County Detention Center and be free; you can also be out there and still be behind bars.

Jail is not the physical thing that happens around us; it is in our minds and spirits. For the first time, I can genuinely say that I'm thankful to God for sending me here, but it took months to come to that point. I hope this book and the teachings I'm coming out with will help you to receive this truth faster than I did.

"Blessed are you when people insult you, persecute you and falsely say all kinds of evil against you because of Me. Rejoice and be glad, because great is your reward in heaven, for in the same way they persecuted the prophets who were before you." (Matthew 5:11-12 NIV)

Chapter Eleven
God Poured Out His Spirit in the Jail

In the last chapter, I shared about the truth working in me as I came to B6. I had more questions than answers, but I was beginning to understand mostly with my head what was happening, but not with my heart. The worry and fear I felt showed that I did not truly grasp what I was reading because when the truth becomes reality in our lives, the truth sets our minds and hearts free. I could see in my life that I was still not free, but the truth worked in me like never before.

In isolation, I read about Joseph in Genesis 39, the story of how Potiphar's wife wanted to seduce Joseph. As I read the text, what she was doing to Joseph seemed so unfair. Joseph did nothing wrong, but she tried to seduce him, and finally, she took hold of his cloak, and Joseph fled. He fled out the door from sexual sin and left his cloak in her hand, and then she told evil lies about Joseph and told everyone he did things he had never done.

As I followed the text, I asked, "Why did you not stop it, God?" But then I turned the page and would see why: God had a plan.

I realized that my problem lay in the fact that I didn't see the next page. God does, but I don't. We all live one page at a time; therefore, we often don't understand what God is doing because we don't see ahead to the next pages of what is about to come.

At that point, I had now been in jail for over one hundred days, and it was still hard in so many ways. Lene and I often cried. I missed my family. They missed me. There are no windows on the Pod walls, but they have them in the ceiling; yet they are covered so that you cannot see the sun—just if it is light or dark outside.

I don't have my friends around me and not a lot of people to talk with. I was alone all day long. It was emotionally and mentally difficult. "Why God? Why is this happening? Can I get out soon? You know I'm innocent. Why haven't you set me free yet? How much longer?"

I knew many people around the world were praying for me to be released, but it seemed like nothing was happening, and I did not understand it at that time.

I'd received the stadium dream that spoke powerfully to me, in which God said, "Let My fruit come out of you. Can you hear the abundance of rain that's coming? Hear the sound of My mighty Spirit pouring out over the prison, the region, and the nation. Let My Spirit move through you in the prison, for Satan has brought my children away for too long; give them the truth."

But that word was something I just didn't see. Yes, I had faith for it to happen out there, but in here? No, imagining God's Spirit being poured out in this place was difficult.

"But God, I've tried. You see, I've really tried. I've tried to share You again and again with the people in here, but nothing is happening," I prayed.

I had tried to bring them Jesus, but they did not seem interested, and I had somehow given up. I still prayed and read the prophetic words daily, but I struggled every time I came to this part about the prison and God pouring out His Spirit—that it would start here. I had faith for America, but will it start here?

But then, one day, something extraordinary happened that I will never forget. It was one of those moments you know will be part of your life forever: God poured out His Spirit over the prison as the prophetic word said. It started with me sitting on my bed in my cell reading the Bible, and suddenly, I stopped and noticed something was different.

At first, I was unsure what it was, but then I noticed it was quiet outside. The TV is usually always on, and our TV is very loud. Being locked up, the TV has irritated me a lot. First, it was so loud there was no way to escape it. And then it's in Spanish, so I didn't understand a word of it. It has tortured me because there is no place you can go to be quiet if you need that, and you often do.

But on this day, it was suddenly quiet. I stood up and went out my cell door. My cell is on the second floor with a good view over the whole Pod. We have eight cells downstairs and eight cells upstairs. There I stood and looked over the entire Pod, and I saw the TV was mute because everyone was standing in a circle on the floor with their heads bowed, and two inmates in the middle of the circle. One was praying for the other.

"Woah! What is this, God?" I asked. "God, what is this? What is happening here?"

I'd been in this Pod for over fifty days at the time. I'd tried to share Jesus. I'd even tried to invite people to a church service they have every second Sunday, not because it's perfect, but because that is the only opportunity we have here. Usually, there are only three to five people from all the Pods who show up among one hundred and fifty to two hundred inmates. No one in my Pod has joined me for church.

Until now, I had not seen people praying to or talking about God. I had never seen them reading the Bible. But here they were, standing around two people, praying. It was an extraordinary and holy moment. I felt it. I felt God in it, and it was bigger than me.

But what was it?

I heard God whisper, "Now, Torben. Now, Torben is your moment. Take it."

"My moment?" I questioned. "No, God. You know I've tried. I've tried again and again. God, it's hard to be here, and you know how I have tried, and no one wants to listen. And I just want to leave this place and go home."

But God kept saying, "It's your moment, take it."

I stood still for ten to twenty seconds and then said, "Okay God." I took a deep breath and said, "God, not my will be done, but Yours."

I went down the stairs and joined the prayer circle. I approached one of the men who spoke a little English and asked quietly, "What is happening here?"

He told me that the mother of the guy in the middle had just died. Therefore, they were all praying for him. I knew this was my moment, and I needed to take hold of this.

But it was tough, and everything in me just wanted to return to my cell. I was so tired and wanted to leave this place and go home.

But I said, "Okay God, help me."

As soon as they stopped praying, I went into the middle of the circle, lifted my hand, and got everyone to stop and look at me.

"Everyone, listen here, I need somebody to translate for me." I found one who could translate. I said, "I have been in this Pod for over fifty days. I've been in jail for over a hundred days and have never seen anything like this before. Guys, this is very, very special. What's happening here is an extraordinary moment. Listen, when I came in here after one month, I was depressed. It was hard to be here, but God gave me a dream. And the dream really spoke to me about standing up, about not wasting my time here, and I stood up, took responsibility, and many things changed in my life."

I continued: "Guys, none of us want to be here, but this can be the best time in our lives because this can be when we find God. It is the time you find God and get your life transformed."

I then told them about how my mom got sick when I was fifteen years old and how it was a tough time in my life, but also the time I started to think about God and later how I found God and how Jesus transformed my life.

"Guys, don't waste your time here," I urged them. "Seek God. There is a reason He put you here and wants to speak to you if you seek Him. Don't waste this moment. I'm here for all of you, and if you need anything, let me know."

And that was it. I didn't feel I should say more at that moment, and I stopped and went back to my cell, shaking all over my body, knowing something very profound was happening there.

It didn't stop there; it was just the beginning of something I had never experienced. The day after, there was church, and I went there again as I sometimes do. I don't want to criticize the people because they're doing the best they know how, but it's very religious, and they sadly lack the power and the gospel in there. Thank God for them for what they do, but if we could get the power of God and the gospel, then it could be so much more beautiful.

I went as usual, and expected to be alone, but not this Sunday. Nothing was as it used to be this Sunday. This time, six others from my Pod went with me, and the message was the best I have heard. Even though many things were still missing, God was truly there using it. God's presence was there, and the two holding the service were as excited as they'd ever been before. They also said they had never had so many people in church before and felt something was happening.

One shared a strong testimony about his life and how he came to faith. Afterward he called people up, and four of those six from my Pod went up, tears running down their faces, calling out to God.

We were all shocked, like, "What's happening here?"

I don't think they had seen anything like this before, and God was truly moving.

When the service was over, we said goodbye to each other with much joy. Everyone was like small children, not knowing what leg to stand on. It was so unique and nothing like normal. Yes, everyone was hugging each other—something we haven't done before.

I then returned to my cell and asked, "God, what are You doing here? What is happening here? Something is changing."

Then I heard in my spirit the words again, "Stand up, Torben. Take responsibility."

I knew what I needed to do and did not want to. But I knew God was using this to teach me so many things.

So, shortly after I was back in my Pod, I gathered everyone in the Pod one more time. I found a translator and said to everyone, "Listen here. Yesterday was very special; today, some of us have been in church, and it was also extraordinary. God is really doing something in this place. I am a missionary. I am a pastor, and I've been to forty-five nations sharing Jesus. I'm used to teaching. I've seen many lives transformed all over the world. I have personally baptized over three thousand people. I know God has sent me here for you, and I would like to invite you all to church here with me every day at 5 p.m. from now on, starting tomorrow."

That is what I said, and I thought, "Okay, here we go."

I could already feel something had changed; a shift had already happened in how people responded to me. The following Monday at 5 p.m., I called out for church: "Iglesia en cinco minutos" (church in five minutes). Yes, I had just asked an inmate how to say church in five minutes, so I learned a few words in Spanish. But these were also words I used repeatedly over the next few months.

I did not know how many would join, but to my surprise, everyone came. There were around twenty-five people there. I shared the Word with someone translating, and we continued the next day, the next day, and the following day. I also prayed for a few people, but most still held a little back, reluctant to let me pray for them. But God was slowly softening their hard hearts.

At the same time, this was happening inside the jail; my wife, Lene, was really struggling outside. I was excited about what God was doing in my Pod, but at the same time, I was crying inside because it was so hard to see my family, especially my wife, Lene suffer as she did. There were a lot of emotions all over the place. On the one hand, I saw God was moving; on the other hand, my family was struggling, and I just wanted to come home, and I was so split between it all.

After four days, things really started to happen in my Pod. It began when I felt strongly that I should speak about something I hadn't spoken about before. I felt God wanted me to speak about dreams and how God wanted to speak to us through dreams. I had never spoken on that before, but that afternoon, I spoke about dreams and came up with examples of how God has been speaking to me through dreams and how He wants to speak to everyone here.

The day after, the first man came into my cell. He spoke very little English and told me how he, that same morning, had had the same nightmare three times one after another. He woke up with it, fell asleep again, woke up with the same nightmare, then slept again, and woke up the third time with the same nightmare. He said it was spiritual, even though he was not born again. He asked me if I could pray for him. So, we gathered together with my translator in my cell and I prayed for the guy with the dreams. He was staying in the cell right under me.

As soon as we started to pray, the Holy Spirit came powerfully over him, and he fell on the floor and got delivered, puking all over the floor and screaming. We were shouting, and everyone in the Pod heard that something was taking place inside my cell. After a fight, he finally got delivered. The Holy Spirit came over him with enormous peace. My translator and another guy who came in cried when they witnessed this, something they had never seen before. Vomit was all over the floor, and it was a mess, but we were all worshiping God and giving glory to Him for what we had just witnessed. He got set free! I have seen thousands set free before, but to experience this here in my cell was like nothing I had experienced before.

I have also never seen anyone vomit so much before being delivered. There was vomit all over the cell floor, and I used all my toilet paper to clean it up. I needed to get some toilet paper from some of the other inmates' cells as I had used my ration for that week. So I bought some of the others' ration of toilet paper with candy and chocolate I got from the vending machine, but that was a joy because of everything God had done.

From that day on, this man was free. Everyone saw that he was a different person.

The day after, he came to me saying, "Torben, I just feel amazing. I feel so happy. I feel so full of peace. I have slept so good like I haven't for a very, very long time."

He kept smiling, and from that day on, he worshipped God all day. Because he lived under me, I could hear the worship through the toilet and the air conditioner!

Afterward, another man approached me, saying, "Torben, I need to talk to you. I had a powerful dream last night but don't know what it meant. What was special was that I called my wife and talked with her about it, and she, the same night, had exactly the same dream I had. And none of us know what it means."

Then he told me about the dream and how, in the dream, a snake came toward him, and then he picked up a stone, threw it at the snake, and the stone crushed the head of the snake. This was his dream, and his wife dreamed the same thing that night.

From that dream, the door was wide opened to share who the snake was, and who the stone is—Jesus Christ. His life got transformed as he became a disciple of Jesus after this! God was moving in this place, calling people to Himself. As the prophecy had said, the abundance of rain was pouring out upon the prison, and this was just the beginning. I continued teaching for eighteen days. More people had dreams, and God was calling people!

We sometimes had two older gentlemen come into the Pod and ask if anyone wanted a Spanish Bible; this time, everyone wanted one. People were standing in line. Something extraordinary was happening here. At the same time, God was teaching me many things through all of this. I start to understand God's purpose.

Yes, I wanted to get out.

I was crying, "God let me out."

I was begging Him to release me, but no.

Thousands of people worldwide were praying for my release. Now, I started to see the purpose of my being here. If I had been released then, I would have missed this, and the lives that were going to be transformed would not have been transformed.

This was just a small beginning, but it was the next page in my life, in my story. I understood why God did what He did. The page was turning, and I could see God's plan and purpose with all of it. I started to put away my own feelings and my own ideas and surrendered to His plan. I learned how important it was that we do not walk by the flesh and what we feel, but that we let God work in our lives and walk by the Spirit.

This was just the beginning.

Chapter Twelve
Cell Groups

As I'm sitting here in my cell, writing about what God did in that time, I cannot stop smiling. It was extraordinary. And what I have been sharing was only the beginning of many exciting things God was doing, both in me and through me, and in my fellow inmates. In this chapter, I will continue with what happened when the revival, as I will call it, started to take off.

I was doing teachings daily for ten days when I felt more was needed: I wanted to get more men involved. So, I started what we call Bible Discovery Groups. These groups are a fantastic tool that we've used quite a bit. It's like a Bible study, but it's easier to get people involved unlike regular Bible studies. Essentially, we don't have somebody that is teaching, but we let the Bible teach itself as the group goes through different Bible verses, and then the group answers three questions:

1. What does this verse say about God?2. What does this verse say about man?3. Is there anything in this passage that we need to obey?

This tool has been used all over the world to significant effect. At the end of this book is a link to a video where I talk more about the Bible Discovery Groups. I encourage everyone to use this tool to start their own groups. It's so easy to start, and everyone can learn to lead a group quickly. This is what I've seen here.

In seven days, we went through:

- Discipleship (not just conversion)
- Repentance
- Faith
- Baptism in water
- Baptism of the Holy Spirit
- Resurrection from the dead and eternal judgement
- Fellowship with God

When we started, I called the groups Bible Discovery Groups. But then, as I talked with a friend over the phone and told him what God was doing here, he laughed and said, "Torben, what you have are cell groups."

I laughed with him: he was right. So, I just called it our cell groups in Pod B. The cell group was held every day at 5 p.m., and they replaced me teaching everyone. At that time, I had three people who spoke English, had met God, and were hungry for more. One of the guys was the man who was set free, delivered, and worshiped God all day in the cell under me. But all three have met God and were also the only ones who spoke good English here and became my main disciples. I met with three of them in my cell every day at 1 p.m. and gave them the Bible verses for the day. We went through them together and I discipled them. Then they met with people in their cells at 5 p.m.

Twenty-two of twenty-five people in the Pod were in the cell groups every afternoon. God was moving.During the cell groups, the entire Pod was silent. The television was put on mute, and everyone, for the next hour—sometimes an hour and a half—were in their cells, studying the Bible. A few didn't join the study but used the opportunity to relax.

Three Bible studies went on in the different cells. I walked around in the Pod praying, sometimes looking in through the cell window to see if all was good. I opened the door a few times and asked if everything was okay and if they had any questions.

But all was good; they just did it by themselves.

After five days of studying the foundation of the Bible in cell groups, my good friend and translator Enoch wanted to be baptized. The Word of God had gone deep into his life, and one night, the Holy Spirit touched his heart to repent of his sins and he was ready to surrender all to God. This happened in his cell as he was alone; God moved on him sovereignly. God's touch led to him asking me to baptize him into Christ. We met with two other men, and we baptized him in his cell.

To baptize him, we used a big cup of water and stood in his cell in the middle of the floor. I poured the water over his head and prayed for him. As I laid hands on his head, the Holy Spirit came over him, and he fell and was delivered: demons manifested and left him. He burst out crying. Finally, he got up off the floor, and we gave each other a big hug. He broke down again, and God healed his heart of unforgiveness and pain. He told us he felt fire when he cried: his tears burned. As they fell on his hands, he felt the heat. At one point, he said he thought blood was coming out of his eyes because it was warm like he had never experienced before. It was a beautiful day when Enoch got baptized. He took a shower afterward to get wet all over.

The Sunday after, we had church again. This time, nine people were from my Pod and a few from the other Pods. Enoch was sharing his testimony with everyone, how he got baptized and was set free, forgiven, and got a new life. He was also being used as a translator that day in the church as he was proficient in English. And from that day on, he grew in the Lord very fast.

The day after, I shared communion in my cell with three of the strongest disciples who were now born again and on fire for Jesus. Sitting there with three new disciples, sharing communion on the cell floor, was quite special; it is one of the most beautiful communions I've ever had. It's just something unique being in prison with other inmates, seeing the power of God, and the transformation of the Gospel. Then, to share communion and remember what Jesus did on the cross for all of us—it was profound. When we broke the bread, we all cried. It deeply touched us, and people's lives were even more changed.

Some of the men in my Pod are from religious backgrounds. Some are not. And those who are from a religious experience really don't know the Bible. When I said, "Let's go to Matthew 5," it was interesting to see everyone take the Bible, start in Genesis, and go through all the books to find where Matthew is in the Bible. They knew very little, even though many had been in church for years.

Enoch said a few days later, "Torben, I'm 26. I have been in church my whole life but have learned more this week than in those twenty-six years. I'm seeing now how the church is sleeping. I have heard and seen things I have never heard or seen before this week."

God was transforming lives in my Pod, and he was just one of them. Baptisms and deliverance began happening one after another. After someone met God, I gathered all the people in the Pod afterward and let the person who had just met God share his testimony. We did that several times a week. It was shaking the Pod up spiritually.

At this point, the names of two of them were Joseph and Enoch, which was easy to remember because they're good biblical names. The other names I can't pronounce. It began picking up pace as the testimonies were shared in the gatherings. The Word became flesh and was visible to everyone there.

One of the stories really sticks out to me now. The man in the cell beside me had been drawn by God, and now he was seeking and praying. He was older than me; he was the oldest man there.

One day, he was ready to repent to God and follow Christ. He and I sat down and went through a deep repentance talk, as we always do, to know that people are prepared and have understood what repentance is. We baptized him into Christ in his cell, and we let him stand in the middle of the floor in his underwear and a T-shirt. We prayed with him in faith and baptized him by taking a big cup of water and pouring it over his head. Out there, I would never do it like this. Baptism is immersion. I would rather drive two or three hours to find water than do what I did here. But when you cannot drive to find water and have no other options, this is the best thing we could do.

When I poured the water over his head, baptized him into Christ, and put my hand on him, he just broke down. He fell and was crying with deep, deep sobbing. Then he manifested and was set free, filled with the Holy Spirit, and spoke in tongues. It was really a beautiful moment.

I was a little surprised. I did not expect it to happen this way, not with him. But God did a deep work in him, and his testimony became very powerful.

After I baptized him, he went into the shower, and when he came out, he was very excited. He said that as he took the shower and washed himself, he felt his sins washing away. God reminded him of sins in his life, which were washed away one by one. He had never felt so clean and free before in his life.

It reminded me of Ananias in the Bible, when he baptized Paul and said to him, *"And now why are you waiting? Arise and be baptized, and wash away your sins, calling on the name of the Lord"* (Acts 22:16 NIV).

Just as we did with everyone else, we went out, gathered everyone in the Pod, and then he shared his testimony. This led to the next conversion and baptism, and one by one, their lives were transformed by the power of the Gospel.

At the same time, God was working in my heart. I've seen many people's lives transformed, and I love it! I've baptized thousands of people, and I love every one of them. It never becomes old to see somebody repent of their sins, get baptized into Christ, see them filled with the Holy Spirit, and receive a completely new life. It never gets old. But this was different in so many ways.

First, it was in a cell, so I felt like Paul or Peter and the early disciples we read about in the Bible. I felt like I was living the book of Acts all over again. Secondly, it was because of the dream and everything God spoke in my life at the same time as this happened. I was learning so much. When I got that dream, I believed it could happen, but I almost gave up. After waiting a long time, God did it most powerfully.

Thirdly, it was happening to people who could not leave. Some came to the Bible studies not because they wanted to read the Bible, especially not in the beginning, but because there was nothing else to do. Others were hungry. I saw how the Word still came into many people over time, broke them, and they surrendered.

But after a few weeks, opposition arose. I felt it, and people talked: they were irritated at me and all the activities that were going on in the Pod. If it was out there in the "real world," I would have said, "Let's go to another place and continue with those people we have here who are hungry." But we could not go to any other place this time. It was behind prison walls, so we couldn't move things. The opposition was unavoidable. I learned a lot about people, the Bible Discovery Groups, and how I loved this tool so much more now than ever. It's a fantastic tool to help people grow in the Word quickly and start new groups with new people. It is something the church really needs. Even if you do it with people who are not ready to surrender, the Word will be sown into their hearts, transforming them as they receive it. One by one, they will come to faith.

Yes, the Word of God is indeed the seed. How often do we hope for a harvest without sowing a seed? Here, many seeds were sown. Some fell on the side road, and so on. But many also began to fall on the good ground, as Matthew 13 talks about; those seeds produced a lot of fruit. But the Word needed time to go deep, and we needed to keep watering it by the Holy Spirit. This all happened as we saw the power of the Gospel of Christ transform these people from the inside out. They became new creations.

But as I said, the opposition started to rise, and I started sensing it. I will share more with you about that in the next chapter.

Chapter Thirteen
Persecution Begins

When I was detained nine months ago, I did various Bible studies. First, I read through the whole Bible. Then I read the letters. Then, I studied different letters and went deeper in my research than ever before. After that, I started doing different studies of people in the Bible. I learned much from that and developed a deep love for Abraham, David, and Moses.

With David, I read the Psalms at the same time while I was looking at his life. Since I came here, I have read the Psalms three times, which has done great work in my life. I deeply love the Psalms now, and I understand why David was a man after God's own heart, even though he was not perfect.

At one point, I went back and did an extensive study of the book of Acts again. I thought I knew the book of Acts because it's a book I've read many times. But this time, I studied like never before. I wanted to know who the people in the book of Acts were. Where did they come from? And how did they work as a church? How did they work together? What kind of persecution did they experience in the different places they went?

My eyes were opened to so many things. I spent one and a half months alone in the book of Acts and recognized why we are experiencing persecution. One reason goes back to the Garden of Eden. In Genesis 3:15, we read that God put enmity between the snake and the seed of the snake and the woman and the seed of the woman.

> "And I will put enmity between you and the woman, and between your offspring and hers; He will crush your head, and you will strike His heel." (Genesis 3:15 NIV)

The world was cursed because of the sin of Adam and Eve, and we can still see enmity between the children of God and the children of Satan today. One of the reasons people hate us is because we are not of this world, as we read here:

> "Do not be surprised, my brothers and sisters, if the world hates you. We know that we have passed from death to life, because we love each other. Anyone who does not love remains in death." (1 John 3:13-14 NIV)

Another reason many people hate us and persecute us is jealousy. Yes, jealousy is one of the things we see again and again as a cause of the persecution the disciples experienced. You see it throughout the book of Acts. Sometimes it was jealousy from the Jews. Other times jealousy from the Gentiles. Before we look at some places in Acts where we see this clearly, we will read a verse about how evil jealousy is.

Proverbs 27:4 (NRSV) says, "Wrath is cruel, and anger overwhelming, but who is able to stand before jealousy?" In Song of Solomon 8:6 (NASB), Solomon says, "Jealousy is as severe as Sheol; its flames are flames of fire, the flame of the Lord."

Jealousy is something we really need to be aware of. A jealous person is more dangerous than an angry person, and I can testify that this is true. I have experienced that repeatedly in my life, and I have discovered that jealousy is the main reason why I'm locked up here today, but more about that later.

I saw in Acts how the disciples went to a place and started to preach the gospel. Very often, they started in the synagogues, and some people were very positive in the beginning and loved them. Beautiful things were happening, but we see almost every time that there is a "but": a few people filled with jealousy turned against them, got others on their side, and suddenly, the disciples saw a change transpiring and persecution became very severe. The disciples often had to flee to the next town because of this, or they were put in jail.

It was no different for me. God was on the move; however, nothing good from God happens without our enemy trying to stop it. Before I get into what happened in my case, let's look at times in the book of Acts when persecution arose. In Acts 5:12-16 (NIV), we read:

> *The apostles performed many signs and wonders among the people. And all the believers used to meet together in Solomon's Colonnade. No one else dared join them, even though they were highly regarded by the people. Nevertheless, more and more men and women believed in the Lord and were added to their number. As a result, people brought the sick into the streets and laid them on beds and mats so that at least Peter's shadow might fall on some of them as he passed by. Crowds gathered also from the towns around Jerusalem, bringing their sick and those tormented by impure spirits, and all of them were healed.*

As I saw here, people were healed, set free, and came to Christ. But they got the attention of our enemy. He knows about jealousy more than anyone else because it was his downfall. Satan was jealous of God. He wanted to be like God, and that pride led to his fall. But what do we read in the next verse in Acts 5:17 (NIV): "*Then the high priest and all his associates, who were members of the party of the Sadducees, were filled with jealousy.*"

They were "filled with jealousy." This is what happened here in B6, where I am now. God was moving, and then some people were filled with jealousy.

As I said before, a jealous person is more dangerous than a person with anger. Then, in the next verse, Acts 5:18 (NIV), they are jailed. *"They arrested the apostles and put them in the public jail."*

This is the pattern we see throughout the Bible, not only in Acts. We can look at Jesus with the religious people, Joseph with his brothers, David and Saul, the Apostles, and even you and me—if we have something people can be jealous about.

Suppose we're just living "normal Christianity," going to church on Sundays and going home without any spiritual growth, without any power, without any real change or evidence of God moving. In that case, there's nothing to be jealous about, and therefore there is no persecution. But as soon as we start to see God move, jealousy arises in people.

Another example was Stephen in Acts 6. Stephen was wise, and the religious leaders could not withstand Stephen's wisdom. In verse 11, we read how they caused people to lie. In another translation, it says they bribed people. So, they could not withstand Stephen's wisdom and were jealous of him, so they bribed people to lie about him. They stirred the people up and it ended with the stoning of Stephen. It was jealousy that caused people to do what they did.

In Acts 13, we read how Paul was in Antioch. He went to the synagogues and saw God was moving. We can read that in verse 44. God was doing great things. And what do we read in the next verse, verse 45? We read they were "filled with jealousy." It's the same thing that happened before. God was moving, some people were jealous, and the persecution started. It turned out that they needed to flee to Antioch, and they went to Iconium, which we read about in verses 44-52 (NIV):

> On the next Sabbath almost the whole city gathered to hear the word of the Lord. When the Jews saw the crowds, they were filled with jealousy. They began to contradict what Paul was saying and heaped abuse on him. Then Paul and Barnabas answered them boldly: "We had to speak the word of God to you

first. Since you reject it and do not consider yourselves worthy of eternal life, we now turn to the Gentiles. For this is what the Lord has commanded us:

"'I have made you a light for the Gentiles, that you may bring salvation to the ends of the earth.'"

When the Gentiles heard this, they were glad and honored the word of the Lord; and all who were appointed for eternal life believed. The word of the Lord spread through the whole region. But the Jewish leaders incited the God-fearing women of high standing and the leading men of the city. They stirred up persecution against Paul and Barnabas, and expelled them from their region. So they shook the dust off their feet as a warning to them and went to Iconium. And the disciples were filled with joy and with the Holy Spirit.

Like before, a few people stirred the crowd against the disciples. *"At Iconium Paul and Barnabas went as usual into the Jewish synagogue. There, they spoke so effectively that a great number of Jews and Greeks believed. But the Jews who refused to believe stirred up the other Gentiles and poisoned their minds against their brothers"* (Acts 14:1-2 NIV).

When I read these verses, it's like reading about my own life. When you know my story, you know that this is my life. Again and again, I've seen a few people become jealous, then they poison the minds of many, and then suddenly, I am the enemy. And as we read in the books of Acts, in Iconium, people wanted to stone Paul and Barnabas, so they needed to flee again—this time to Lystra. But then we read that the people, the Jews who were filled with jealousy and were against them in Iconium, now came to Lystra and caused the same problems there. *"Then some Jews came from Antioch and Iconium and won the crowd over. They stoned Paul and dragged him outside the city, thinking he was dead"* (Acts 14:19 NIV).

Again, it's so special to read this because I've now found out that the team behind my being jailed here in America are some of the same people who were behind the problems I had in Denmark. I know who they are, and I know this is because of jealousy. This is where it all started, first in Denmark and now here.

There's nothing new under the sun, as we have said. I've also experienced this here in B6. God was changing lives. People were delivered, baptized, and filled with the Holy Spirit. We also saw powerful healings.

One time, in my cell, a guy had been unable to bend his knee the whole way for many years. I asked one of my new disciples, who had never prayed for anyone before, to lay hands on this guy and pray for him, and God came through! The guy was healed, and he could bend his knee. From that day on, he told his story to many people in the jail!

There was another guy, two cells down from me, who had a wound on the front of his lower leg that was infected and bleeding. When he walked around, he pulled his trousers up over his knee so there wouldn't be blood on his pants and to get air to the wound. This wound kept bleeding for two or three weeks. It wasn't healing. Then, one day, I stopped and asked if I could pray for him, and I laid my hands on him and prayed. One hour later, he came back very excited and showed me that the wound had stopped bleeding. It was now dry, and the day after, he was completely healed!

Then jealousy arose. A few men started to get irritated with me, and one day I had a public meeting in which everyone joined us. Two people were talking to each other during my teaching, and they were talking loudly. They were there physically, but not with their hearts. When they were talking, I very quietly said to one of them, "Shhh," and I said, "Can you be a little quiet?"

But when I said, "Shhh," everything just exploded.

One of the men jumped up and yelled, "You should not say 'Shhh!' I'm not your dog!"

He went crazy.

He stood up and yelled in my face, and I wondered what was happening. It was so evil and demonic and everyone thought he would jump at me and hit me.

"Who do you think you are? I am not your dog! You should not come here and do what you are doing!" he screamed.

He went on and on and started to curse me. After he had done that for some time, he went into his cell very angry. One more person joined him in his cell, and then three more joined him. He ended up with six people in his cell, which was all chaos.

I knew something was about to happen. I thought, "Okay, let's continue teaching with the rest of the people and see what will happen."

I knew they were talking about me, which could go in any direction. I was expecting a big fight or something like that, but I tried to keep my focus and continue my teaching.

After a few minutes of teaching, they all came out of his cell as a group, took the television remote on the table in front of me, and stood in front of me with their arms across their chests, very firm and provoking. Then they turned on the television as loud as possible, stopping the meeting to the irritation of everyone else.

From that moment on, there was nothing I could do. I couldn't continue teaching in the Pod as we had done every Sunday.

That day, when we moved to one of the cells, a few more people stayed behind. People now had a choice—Who do you follow?

So now the group was down to thirteen, as five more people decided to stay outside with the group there. From that day on, the fight was on. I could feel it. The hate was not a secret anymore. It was out in the open. It was somehow them against us, or them against me, and I felt like Paul.

But I wanted to do what Paul did—and that was just to continue in another place with those few who really wanted it. But that was the difference here. There was no place to go. I could not do the meetings at any other site. So, I just kept doing it in my cell with those who wanted it. But the pressure was there. And I felt the mindset of others was being poisoned against me.

Jesus, in Luke 10:11, said that if people do not receive us, we should shake the dust off our feet and move on to the next town, just as Paul did. I could not do that because there was no place to go. I was just in the middle of it all. Some people hated me, some people loved me. Why? Because their lives had been transformed.

I've been in three "fights" here as of now—just not physical yet. People hold back because of the cameras here, and guards are always watching from the security room. But I've been in fights with shouting, yelling, and screaming, and it's hard.

It is hard to be in an atmosphere of so much hate and have people cursing you. Out there, I would leave right away and probably never come back, but inside here, I just need to stay in it.

Jesus was very radical when it came to what we shall do when we have enemies hating us. In Luke 6 he said this:

> *"But to you who are listening, I say: Love your enemies, do good to those who hate you, bless those who curse you, pray for those who mistreat you. If someone slaps you on one cheek, turn to them the other also. If someone takes your coat, do not withhold your shirt from them. Give to everyone who asks you, and if anyone takes what belongs to you, do not demand it back. Do to others as you would have them do to you."* (Luke 6:27-31 NIV)

All of this has allowed me to grow in my love for people—to love those who hate me. As I said, I've learned many things and felt like God was preparing me for war—to help me stand firm in Him even when it is storming around me. The prophecy I got said at one time that He would make me into a war leader to help me equip the church for the hard times that are coming in the future. And I really believe this.

In Paul's teaching, in Ephesians 6, we read this:

> *Finally, be strong in the Lord and in His mighty power. Put on the full armor of God so that you can take your stand against the devil's schemes. For our struggle is not against flesh and blood, but against the rulers, against the authorities, against the powers of this dark world and against the spiritual forces of evil in the heavenly realms.* (Ephesians 6:10-12 NIV)

Paul continues, talking about the whole armor of God, which we so much need. But I want to say that our war, as we read in Ephesians, is not against flesh and blood, even if it feels like that. It was flesh and blood shouting in my face and cursing me. It was flesh and blood who was filled with hate for me. But they are not my true enemies. It's Satan who is a liar, and he has poisoned the people against us with his lies. We are in this war, and I want to share more about that later.

Jail is genuinely the best Bible school one can get. Experiencing these things in here has really been hard because I don't like conflict. If you know me, you know I am a lovely person. People like me, and I like them. And when I often say to people that I don't like conflict, they often laugh at me and say, "Torben, then you need to find another job."

And that's correct. Not that this is a job. This is a calling. But I know with this calling of following Christ, we will have many conflicts, and many people will not like us, which we need to learn to handle.

I hate conflicts, but I love Jesus more. And I want to be a faithful servant. Therefore, I've learned to get used to it without taking it personally, without getting bitterness in my heart, and keep loving those people who are persecuting me and praying for them. It's all part of following our Lord Jesus Christ. When you obey His Word and see fruit in your life, you can be sure that when people around you begin to see it, the enemy will notice this, and then persecution will also come your way.

But like we saw with Joseph, he struggled when they threw him into the pit, but God was in control. God used Joseph's brothers to throw him into the pit so Joseph could come to Egypt and fulfill the call God had for him. It's the same way with us. Persecution is just part of helping us come to Christ—to go to the cross, to become more like our Lord Jesus Christ.

But what a life God has called us all to!

Chapter Fourteen
Life Outside

People who know me and have been walking with me know the phrase, "Look at the birds." Jesus tells us to do this in Matthew 6:26-30 (NIV) when He was teaching us not to worry:

> *"Look at the birds of the air; they do not sow or reap or store away in barns, and yet your heavenly Father feeds them. Are you not much more valuable than they? Can any one of you by worrying add a single hour to your life? And why do you worry about clothes? See how the flowers of the field grow. They do not labor or spin. Yet I tell you that not even Solomon in all his splendor was dressed like one of these. If that is how God clothes the grass of the field, which is here today and tomorrow is thrown into the fire, will he not much more clothe you—you of little faith?"*

Jesus says we should look at the birds and the flowers in the fields because God takes care of them, and if He takes care of them, is He not able to take care of us?

Jesus also says, in Matthew 6:31-34 (NIV):

"So do not worry, saying, 'What shall we eat?' or 'What shall we drink?' or 'What shall we wear?' For the pagans run after all these things, and your heavenly Father knows that you need them. But seek first his kingdom and his righteousness, and all these things will be given to you as well. Therefore do not worry about tomorrow, for tomorrow will worry about itself. Each day has enough trouble of its own."

I often use these phrases when there are problems and things we can worry about. I say, "Look at the birds or the flowers in the field." That is true out there, but it's also true inside here. There are so many things I could worry about because so many crazy things are happening all around me. When it comes to Jesus' words about looking at the birds, there is a problem in here: there are no birds here I can look at, as there are no windows!

One of the first times I went outside, I tried to find birds, but there were no birds. So, I tried to find flowers, but no flowers were to be found. But one day, while walking into my cell from outdoors, I found a tiny flower growing between some stones. It was only an inch tall, but I picked it up and took it with me into my cell, and then I said, "Jesus, now I can look at a flower. When you take care of this flower, You will also care for me."

Learning not to worry is essential for all of us. We need to learn to stand firm. We must learn to keep our eyes on God because He controls our lives.

I've gone through many times when I needed to keep my eyes focused on not worrying and not giving up. The last nine months have been like that. I want to take some time to talk about life outside, about my family, and about everything that's going on outside these walls where I'm now sitting. I hope this can show you how crazy this is and how much there truly is to worry about.

If I didn't have a family, or hadn't been accused of false things, or if I knew why I was in jail and when I was getting out, or if I didn't have crazy YouTube videos out there with people acting like experts on why I'm in prison and spreading all kind of lies, then it would not be as challenging to be in a place like this as it is in this case.

But this is not how it is in my case at all.

The truth is, the things outside have stressed me out the most, caused tremendous pain, made me worry and want to give up, and made me feel helpless in a way I've never felt before. When it comes to my family, the pain of being away and then seeing them suffer at the same time, has indeed been hard.

I've been married to Lene for twenty-six years. Last year was our 25th anniversary. It was our silver-wedding anniversary, a big thing people celebrate a lot in Denmark. We also celebrated it with a big party in the United States where we had amazing friends from all over America, which was so beautiful. In the twenty-six years we've been married, we've only been away from each other for two weeks. Even when I've traveled all over the world, to many different nations, we've only been away from each other for two weeks. Most of the time, we have been traveling together as a family.

We have our two girls with us here. Our youngest daughter, Simone, turned eighteen while I was here, and I could not be part of her eighteenth birthday. Then we have Stephanie, who is twenty-one. Back in Denmark, we have our son Sonni, who is married to Hannah, and they have three children, so I have three grandkids. I talk with them on the phone, but I've not seen my grandkids for the last nine months. They were supposed to have come a while ago to be with us here, but now they're all waiting for me to get out so they can finally be with us again.

But being away from my wife, my daughter's eighteenth birthday, and not being there for all of them as a husband, father, and grandfather has been hard for me. In the crying and pain, I've very often missed my family. And in some ways, what Lene has gone through outside has been more challenging than what I've gone through inside here. She's had to stand alone with all the pressure as I'm not there. She's used to having me around to take care of the house and be there for the kids.

But there are also many new things on her shoulders, things she's never taken care of before. She must talk to the lawyer, and she has to pay the bills. She needed to go through moving without me, as the house we rented in California was a one-year rental, and we were not able to rent the house any longer. I still remember calling her one day. She was crying on the phone, and then she told me that we needed to move. We had hoped the owner would let us stay longer, but they needed to move into the house themselves, so that was impossible.

So, there we stood with immense pressure, and it was tough. But we've always seen God come through and give us manna repeatedly.

When I heard we would not have the house, I asked, "What now?"

I felt the pressure, worries and anxiety trying to come. Then I thought, "Remember the verse Torben, remember the flowers of the field," and then I went in and prayed.

I was very sad, but suddenly God spoke to me. He came and said, "Move down to San Diego. Move down and be close to the church you had started working with."

And then He reminded me of something He'd been speaking to me a lot about before when I received the same vision to work with the church out there.

"Whoa!" I exclaimed, and suddenly, sadness was changed to excitement.

I immediately called Lene, but God had already spoken to her, putting the same idea in her heart. She was already excited about the move to San Diego to be close to the people there.

Then I called my friend Josiah, the pastor down there, and he felt the same thing: God confirmed things in a big way. God was moving beautifully.

But another thing needed to happen: Lene still needed to find a house, and she found one. When we saw that house, we were like, this is it, this is the house. She sent me some pictures—that was all I could get, so that was very special, but we both felt this was the house God wanted us to have.

There weren't many options because they were costly, but we found our house close to the church, only seven minutes from it. So Lene went to look at the home with the girls and had an excellent impression.

"This is it, this is the house," she said.

But three other couples were interested at the same time. The owner would then get back to us if we were the ones who got the house.

Three days passed, and we did not hear from them. Then, after four, five, and six days, with nothing new, I really felt the pressure again. I felt the stress coming over me. I felt worried.

"God, we don't have a lot of time." We needed to move in two or three weeks. "Look at the birds, Torben, look at the flowers in the field," I reminded myself.

If God can take care of them, He would also take care of us. But as I said, it was difficult because there were few options because the houses were so expensive in San Diego.

Then it suddenly came to me, "Relax. Don't worry."

And the words came to me; I felt God said, "I have the last word."

And it was really a special experience: "I have the last word."

This phrase exploded in my spirit. The day after we heard from the owner, the answer was no.

"The house is not yours; we've rented it out to somebody else," they said.

"What? No," I said.

God didn't give us the house; we didn't have a lot of time; it was a no.

But then the Spirit spoke to me again, "Relax, don't worry. Remember, I have the last word."

Peace came over me. Even if it was a no, I felt it was not the last word because God had it. But all this was just extra pressure on us and everything else. Then, one week later, ten days before we had to move, Hallelujah, God had the last word!

I don't know what happened. I can only imagine that something happened regarding the other couple who the owner rented the house to. I didn't find out; I just know we got the house. The owner spoke with Lene, saying we could get the house anyway.

Ten days before we were going to move, God had the last word! This testimony became powerful to us, and I will return to that later in this book.

We've seen this many times when it comes to moving, how God is there and is taking care of us. But this time was special because God used this to give us strength as far as my asylum case.

But then we came to the whole practical process of moving. I was not there. I was always in charge, but now Lene had to organize moving without me, even though we had some amazing friends who came to help. And thank you, guys, all of you, who came to help us! It was beautiful!

A lot of work was needed. Everything had to be taken down, organized, packed, and moved. Lene needed to take care of the water, the internet, the cleaning, and the organizing, and I was absent. I was here, just sitting. I wanted to help more than anything else. I wanted to move with my family. I wanted to move into the new house but couldn't do anything.

One prayer was answered—and another pressure rose up. The lawyer needed money: an insane amount of money. We needed financial miracles. As with moving, many times in our lives, God has taken care of us and helped us, but this was a new level we'd never been through before.

But until now, we have seen God provide every time. And thank you to the many of you out there who have been giving! We will never forget it; it really means a lot!

The pressure over the money often made me cry more than anything else. If I had known how much this would cost, I would never have started it. But now it has somehow begun, and we are here; we cannot just leave it, and the bills just keep coming. And then there was all the confidentiality required as part of my legal defense, those things Lene knew but could not tell me over the phone. We often tried to speak to each other with codes and find different ways to say things, and it was just weird.

Then there were all the YouTube videos against me. As I often say, I'm used to people coming against me; that is part of the job description following Jesus. But this time was very different because in some of the videos they said they had been involved in my case and been in contact with U.S. Immigration and Customs Enforcement and the Department of Homeland Security. My legal team was very interested in these videos, so Lene needed to watch many of the bad videos out there to tell them what was true and what was not.

I have always protected Lene from the poison that has come out of people like in some of these videos. But I could not defend her this time, as Lene needed to watch hours of bad videos spreading lies against me. Sometimes, it was not only against me, but they also talked about her and the girls. She knew some people who did this, which made it so much worse. When you know the people and how they live and the truth, it hurts so much more when they spread lies like that. Sadly, it is so easy today to become a voice people are listening to and yet hide behind the camera. You would never have listened if you had known about their lives and who they are.

Lene often cried because of all those things when I called her. And I was here, helpless, and couldn't do anything. I want to say that I truly have an amazing wife, and she's very strong. Yes, I don't know many as strong as her and all the things she had needed to endure the year we have served God together, but this time it has been so much for her.

In Matthew 5:11-12 NIV), Jesus says, *"Blessed are you when people insult you, persecute you and falsely say all kinds of evil against you because of Me. Rejoice and be glad, because great is your reward in heaven, for in the same way they persecuted the prophets who were before you."*

A man made a YouTube video falsely claiming I had raped a handicapped girl in Denmark. Even her mother appeared in the video, confirming it. It seemed so "real," and seemed so true when a mother is "confirming" it, but it was a lie from the pit of hell. First, she came out with accusations about spiritual rape by being delivered, even though none of us ever prayed for deliverance for her. Later, the accusation became physical rape. Then it became that I raped her at a demonic ritual at our Jesus Hotel in Denmark, while Lene and six others watched.

The truth was, she had been at a meeting when I was not there. I did not talk with her, but other people in Denmark have confirmed she's very mentally challenged.

The story just changed again and again. And we know the truth, but many don't. Lene had to bear all the lies being spread while I was sitting here, having never seen one of those videos because I don't have access here.

I am guilty until proven innocent—yes, it's the opposite in today's world.

The trouble with these stories is that they are poison—poison deceiving people, even people who know deep inside it's not true. Somehow, they still get influenced by what they hear one way or the other. Many people today think, "No, it can't all be true. Torben is not like that. He has not raped anyone; he has not been involved in weapons smuggling; he has not been involved in human trafficking, and he has not been involved in financial fraud. This cannot be true."

But somehow the poison still goes in and people start to doubt. "Yes, it is not true, but maybe some of it is. Maybe there is something with the money, or maybe there was something with the girl, not rape, but maybe some of it is true."

That is the poison working, and people start to think, "Torben cannot be in jail if he's innocent."

I've heard that phrase many times: "Nobody innocent would be in jail."

And when a phrase like that comes from a Christian, it just makes me so sad and reveals some of the big problems we have.

What about our Lord Jesus Christ, I will ask? Do you think He was guilty when He was arrested, whipped, had a crown of thorns put on His forehead, and was crucified? Do you think He was guilty of some of it since no one who is innocent would go to jail? No, we know with Jesus, He was without sin, but they still crucified Him. And He promised we would be unjustly persecuted too.

What then about Paul, Peter, or Silas, and all the other disciples who went to jail in the Bible? One of those was the brother of Jesus, James, who also was killed by a sword. Was he also somehow guilty? What about him?

And what about the hundreds of thousands of people around the world who, through the years, have suffered for Christ by being put in jail? We are not prepared if this has started in a country like America.

This has all been frustrating, and there is so much I want to teach the body of Christ when I am released. We all still need to learn so much, and I believe God will use this to teach us. But being here in jail and seeing the poison spreading to many people I knew, and that some had started to doubt, was hard for me.

It was mainly those a little further away who I was not close to because those close to me knew me and that I was innocent.

Some brothers and sisters in Christ took this position, and some helped spread the lies. But this is the world we live in. So, what is there to say, other than, "Look at the birds. Look at the flowers in the fields. If God takes care of them, will He not take care of us?"

I still don't have a clear picture of exactly what happened. More and more pieces are coming together, so hopefully soon, the truth will come out, and that has been my most significant prayer, that the truth would come out and the lies would be revealed.

But all the things we sometimes need to go through are just insane. So, we need to learn how to look at the birds from the beginning. We need to learn to throw our worries on Him, otherwise they will become too much and take us down. I just wanted to use this chapter to share this with you, to give you a clearer picture of what it is like to be here.

This is our battle, the war going on in our minds. We can decide to worry, to give up, to get depressed—I've felt it. I've wanted to do it, but I've needed to keep my eyes on Jesus and to remember His words about looking at the birds and the flowers.

They say what doesn't kill you makes you stronger, and this is what is happening here. We are learning through all of it. And very often, those prayers on our knees, crying from the depths of our hearts, are the most powerful. And this is where God is breaking us and weakening us, so there's nothing left—so we can be strong in Him.

I want to remind you to remember the wives, remember the families of those suffering and going through hard times. I've gotten many greetings and love from many people out there. But most people think of me and don't think of my wife, who is suffering with me and what she is going through. And this is true not only in my case but also with every ministry, any minister of the gospel who is experiencing hard times in their lives, because we all go through hard times. Remember the wives. Remember the families.

Paul says in I Corinthians 12:26 (NIV), *"If one part suffers, every part suffers with it."* This is true when it comes to the body of Christ, but it's even more true regarding a marriage, where we have become one flesh. But as you can hear, God was working in our lives. He was teaching us the truth and preparing us for something amazing that awaits us in the future.

Chapter Fifteen
My God, My God

We have now come to one of the most painful moments here, something that happened three months ago. But like so many other times, I saw how God came through amidst all of it.

Before I share what happened that day, I want to share a little about yesterday because I'm still shocked. I've been locked up for two hundred and ninety days, and it's just unbelievable the things that are happening here. As time passed, I started to understand more and more about my case and how crazy it is.

Yesterday was Thursday. It was time to cut our hair and nails in another room. I clearly remember when I first got detained. Thursday came and we could go in and cut our hair. I went into the room with twenty others in my Pod, and there in a room beside us were white plastic chairs all around, but not enough for everyone, so some people were sitting on the floor and others on the plastic chairs.

Then, there was one trimmer and one white bucket with a nail trimmer attached to a metal string so no one could take it with them.

There we were, in a room for two or three hours where we could cut each other's hair with one hair trimmer and cut our nails with the nail trimmer and the bucket. The hair trimmer was a cheap fifteen-dollar trimmer. It was awful: it is used every day by twenty people or more.

That's when it's not broken down. In my time here, we've had three or four trimmers break down. Sometimes, it happens in the middle of cutting someone's hair, and they've had to look funny until we get a new trimmer.

The room was dirty; the bucket had a lot of toenails and fingernails. It was just a different world. When it was my turn to cut my hair, the trimmer was burning hot. When I asked them to cut under my beard on my throat, it was the last time I asked that because it not only burned, but it cut me, and I bled across my throat. The warm, dull trimmer was very, very painful.

When it was all over, I went back to my cell, and it looked like somebody had been trying to cut into my throat or that I had tried to commit suicide. I went and took a shower, and the water streaming down my neck hurt. It was excruciating, and I had big wounds from the trimmer.

Another guy in my Pod saw how my neck was bleeding, so he gave me some cream to put on it. He told me that's why he doesn't cut his beard that way. I learned something important that day.

I was in the room again yesterday, but it was unique in so many other ways this time. First, because it had been several weeks since I'd last been there, my hair was long (where I still have hair), and my nails were very long because the nail clipper had broken three weeks ago, and they hadn't been able to get a new one. My nails were almost like women's nails. They frustrated me when I read my Bible and got food up under my nails. I just longed to cut my nails finally, but it has taken them over three weeks to get us a new nail clipper.

I asked them once if they could get new nail clippers sooner, as it had started to be a problem for me. I had already waited many weeks, and then when I finally went in to cut them the nail clipper was broken. I could always do a sick call and cut my nails there, but then I needed to have handcuffs on and be taken to another place in the jail to cut my nails, and I didn't want to do all that. I don't like to have handcuffs on, even though I got used to it.

But yesterday, after several weeks, I finally had the chance to cut my nails. What a relief! But that was not all. At the same time when I was in the room cutting my nails and waiting to cut my hair, I was on a radio program—or my lawyer was on a radio program talking about me and my case. I listened over the phone because I called my daughter, and she put the phone up to the computer so I could hear the radio show.

Finally, being able to cut my nails after many weeks, waiting to cut my hair with a worn and dull trimmer, sitting there on a plastic chair listening to people talk about me on the radio, was surreal. On the radio, I heard people talk about things about me and my case that I had not heard of before, things that were very new to me. I didn't get a lot of information about my case here, and when I finally got more information, it was on the radio like this.

At one point during the radio program, people could call in, and suddenly, a guy was saying that he was from Denmark. "I have known Torben for many years; I'm a pastor."

The interviewer got so excited, "Oh, you are from Denmark, and you're a pastor, and you know Torben?"

Then, the interviewer started to ask him questions. At one point, he asked him, "So, tell me about the persecution you, as Christians, are experiencing in Denmark."

He said something like, "No, I don't follow Torben there. I don't see persecution in Denmark."

I sat there thinking, "What is happening? What a crazy world we are living in."

Why? Because I knew this man. He was a young boy in my boarding school many years ago. I got to lead him to Christ, but he's not a pastor. He has never been a pastor.

He's a man with many personal problems, who left his wife several years ago, and I haven't had anything to do with him since. I know that he is not following Christ the way he should, and because I addressed that he could not just leave his wife like he did, he has been after me ever since. And here he was talking like an expert about me on the radio, telling many lies and even saying he is a pastor. Yes, I wanted to shout it is all a lie, don't listen to him, but I could not do anything.

We live in a world where it is so easy for people who have no life with God, no fruit, no good testimony, to suddenly become an expert everyone is listening to. And people believe it.

The truth is that everyone who knows this man would know that he's not a pastor and he's not the right person to talk about what it means to experience persecution as a disciple of Christ.

The radio host and my lawyer did not know that. I and my family were the only ones who knew about this man, but I couldn't say anything. Why? I was sitting on a white plastic chair, cutting my nails into a white bucket, waiting for a haircut with a trimmer that I hoped would not cut me again.

As the show continued, I heard for the first time my lawyer speaking clearly about me being a national threat. I've heard it before, but it is clearer now than ever that they see me like this. And that's the problem that I encountered repeatedly and why I could not get released on a bond. And this is now in my papers, even though there have been no trials, no proof, no investigation, and I've not been found guilty in a court.

Some people spread many rumors about me, and somehow, I was guilty without any proof. And it was extraordinary to sit there listening to all this on a phone. But I know God is in control, and that is what I have held onto. I know He will save me from this place and finally clear my name.

Why? Because at my lowest moment I cried out in the deepest, deepest pain, "My God, my God, why have you forsaken me?" There, God came and spoke to me.

The day was December 13th, 2022, two months ago, and I will never forget it. It was the day I had my court hearing when I could be set free, when I could get asylum, and it would all be over. When I was detained on June 30th, 2022, I came here. A few weeks later, I received a piece of paper with my first court date. But it was not an actual hearing; it was just a five-minute meeting where I got a new date, and the date was October 19th, 2022. That was an awful day because that was our wedding day, and I was thinking, "No, that can never happen. Not that day; that is the worst day ever."

Later it was changed again, from October 19th to December 13th, 2022.

So, the day has been changed a few times. But now, the day had come, and my legal team was ready. They were optimistic that it would go well and that I would get asylum because I had a strong case. They had even bought a ticket for me to fly home to California, and they would pick me up and take me the whole way back home to my family.

Everything was ready to go.

I was so ready to finally go home. I'd been here a half year and was missing my freedom and my family. I was so ready to celebrate Christmas with them. Our son, his wife, and grandkids would fly in from Denmark and be with us, and I could see my grandkids again and have a perfect family time.

Then the day came. In the morning, I was picked up in my orange jumpsuit, handcuffs on, and taken to a room with a white chair, a big TV screen in front of me, and a camera on me. To sit there in that room and look at the TV was so special. I looked so small because the camera was pointing down at me. On the screen, I could see the judge sitting in the court; one of his secretaries was there, and then there were several people joining online—some with me and some with U.S. Immigration and Customs Enforcement.

The court hearing lasted nearly four hours. They had asked for plenty of time, as we had a perfect and solid case, but there were many things to look at. During those four hours, I answered over two hundred questions from my lawyer. We covered a lot of things, from my time in Denmark and what happened with the television network there and the persecution to how I came to be here. It was genuinely harsh. I cried often, and it hurts to relive it all over again, especially in the way I was right then, locked up, filled with emotions and longing to see my family after a half year—just wanting to go home.

That day was like running a marathon, one of the hardest times in my life. After I answered all the questions from my lawyer, the lawyer from ICE turned to ask me some questions, and I answered. I thought everything went well. Then we came to the time for the judge to decide my case, but he said he would not make a decision that day because he needed time to write everything down. He said we would return on December 16th, 2022, three days later, and he would announce his decision.

When I got to my cell, I called my team, and they were encouraged, saying I did an excellent job. I answered everything well and they felt confident we would win. Three days later, it was December 16th. I went out again, with handcuffs on, and was taken to the same room, and I sat there waiting for the judge's decision. I could see who was there on the television screen, waiting to be invited into the court. We were all there, ready to start.

I was nervous but also felt good. I thought it would soon all be over. I will finally be free, we will get our asylum papers, and I could continue the work God has called me to do here in America.

But then a thought suddenly came to me, "It will be a no."

It will be a no to the asylum.

I thought, "Oh, no. Oh, no. Go away Satan." I went against these thoughts, as I thought it was an attack from the enemy.

But the thought came again that it would be a no.

And I thought, "No, it can't be. It can't be God. It must be the enemy. It's the enemy."

And I started to get nervous.

I hadn't been nervous until that moment, not like this, at least. The judge began to give his decision. He said a few words, and then I heard, "And therefore, we've decided to deny Torben Sondergaard."

And he continued, talking some more, and used the word "deny" again. I did not fully understand it the first time he said it, and he used many words I did not fully understand as it was very technical. But I knew enough to realize that it was a no.

But still, it did not sink in. So, then he said it a second time. And then he continued speaking and said it a third time, and suddenly, it started to sink in. I started slowly to understand what it meant and was just in shock.

And I was in shock while he continued explaining why he decided to deny me asylum.

There I was, listening to what he said, but it was so unreal for me. He just denied me. What? And according to his words, it almost sounded like I had no chance to win, like I had no case at all.

But I thought I had a good case. That is what I was told. At that point, it's tough to explain the feeling that came over me. I have never in my whole life experienced anything like it before.

I suddenly felt so lost, like it was all over. I lost, it's over. This is it. Like, I lost. I needed to leave America. Goodbye America, goodbye California. But what about my family? How do I get them out? What should we do? God, what is happening? Have you not spoken, God? What about the dream of us getting our papers? What about the things you talked to me about regarding the revival? What about our house? Yes, all those questions were running around in my head.

The judge continued talking, and I felt smaller and smaller and smaller. But what about my legal team? Everything they told me was, then, lies? I didn't understand. I thought we had a good case, but now, listening to the judge, we had nothing. I'd been lied to; I'd been deceived. God, where are you? God was truly far away, like God was not there. He had left me.

Something deep inside me broke, and continued to break, to a point where I just put my hand on my head. I cannot begin to find words to describe that moment and what I felt. All I believed in, everything I thought—it's over, it was wrong, all of it. God had left me here alone. God has left me to myself. And in that moment, I was crying inside from the deepest of my being, and the words just came out of me very quietly, "My God, my God, why have you forsaken me?"

After a half hour, it was all over. I stood up, and a guard took me back to my cell. And there I was alone. God had forsaken me. I was alone; yes, so many things were going through my head, and at the same time, I was so empty. I then called Lene, and we both cried over the phone. We both felt so lost.

I then called my legal team, and they told me they were disappointed because I had a good case, and that they disagreed with the judge's decision and said there were so many things the judge had left out and things he did not address. It was a wrong decision, but we needed to speak in a few days about our next move.

Then I stood there again, alone in my cell. I was like, "Okay. God, it's over. We have lost. I have lost. But God, what about everything You said to me? What about the prophecy? What about You calling us here to America? What about the revival? Your hand put me here, and You will get me out? And now it is suddenly over, and there's nothing more. It's all over."

In Psalm 22 (NIV), David starts by saying, *"My God, my God, why have You forsaken me?"* His words describe a painful separation from God during great trouble. These words are also the words in Matthew 27:46, which our Lord Jesus used when He hung on the cross, *"Eli, Eli, lema sabachthani?" (which means "My God, my God, why have You forsaken Me?")* during this most painful moment in His life. And now, these have been the words I've used, not that I thought about it when I said it, but I found myself in a place where I've never felt so alone.

I truly felt God had forsaken me, that my life had ended, and God had left me all alone. I felt a pain I'd never experienced before, and in that moment, from the depths of my innermost being, these words came to me, and I said it out loud.

It was so scary, and I felt it was the only thing I could say. It was the only thing that came to my mind: "My God, my God, why have You forsaken me?"

The words came, as I said, from the depths of my soul.

But then, at that moment, something happened to me. Suddenly, something rose up in me.

"No. No, it is not over. It cannot be over before you say it is over. You have the final word. You have spoken. And You, God, You are still in control. You brought me here, and You will get me out."

I was reminded of how our house, at first, was a no, but later a yes. And I knew that God would also turn this around, and He had a reason for it to be a no today.

Even though the judge said no, God is the one in control. It is His will that will be done, not the judge. You, God, know what You are doing because You are still in control, and I trust in You. Faith suddenly compellingly rose in me, like I've experienced only a few times. And I raised my voice and excitedly said, "Whoa! Hallelujah! God, You are faithful! You have not forsaken me. You are in control. And it is far from over. You are God, and You have not forsaken me."

I was jumping. Hallelujah! I started to praise God. I began to thank God. What a moment I had there with Him alone in my cell! Just a short time before, it was, "My God, my God, why have You forsaken me?"

Now, I was praising Him, thanking Him, because I knew He was in control like always, no matter what just happened. It was so powerful and beautiful, and I will never forget that moment.

Two hours later, I called Lene again, and she told me, "Torben, your court hearing is all over YouTube."

And I said, "What?"

"Yeah, I just heard it is all over YouTube. Someone recorded it and put it on YouTube. Some people are sitting there mocking you, laughing at you, making fun of you while they show you sitting there and the judge denying your asylum. Yes, some are even sitting eating popcorn while laughing at you."

And she said it in a way that you could truly hear how she felt sorry for me.

At that moment, it was like God said, "Now, Torben, you shall see what I can do. I'm going to turn it all around."

I called my legal team, and they also saw it. They said they'd never seen anything like this. It was a closed court hearing; it was only our team, two guys, the judge, and the secretary. And the judge needed to check everyone before he started; he was the one to let people into the hearing, and it was his responsibility. But somehow, he had let one of my accusers from YouTube come in and join, and they had illegally recorded it and then put it on YouTube, which is very illegal.

My legal team told me, "They have overdone it this time. This is going to change a lot."

And I knew it would because God had just told me. This is where we are now, three months later. We are now waiting for the decision about a retrial or what will happen, as everything about this is not normal. A criminal investigation was also started against the people who recorded it and put it on YouTube. This has gone big. It has been in newspapers in Denmark, and politicians in Denmark have discussed it. It has changed a lot.

What a ride. I have been seen as a national threat. Now, somebody illegally recorded my hearing and put it on YouTube, making fun of me. They even spliced it together, taking some things out and leaving others in, and sometimes playing certain scenes repeatedly, mocking me.

But isn't this precisely what Psalm 22 (NIV) is saying? *"My God, my God, why have you forsaken me?"* But if you read verses 6, 7, and 8, we read here, *"But I am a worm and not a man, scorned by everyone, despised by the people. All who see me, mock me; they hurl insults, shaking their heads. 'He trusts in the Lord,' they said, 'Let the Lord rescue him. Let Him deliver him, since he delights in Him.'"*

That was what I felt. That was what those people were doing. In the lowest moment in my life, they were eating popcorn, laughing, and making fun of me, saying, "Look, where is his God now."

But we know that in verses 22 and 24 of Psalm 22, God has not hidden His face from the afflicted one, and He listens to his cry for help. And this is also what I saw: God did not hide His face from me. He has not forsaken me. He heard my cry for help.

In the last line of Psalm 22, we read, "He has done it." I believe we will see this, this time also, that God will do it again. What a life!

When I was writing this chapter, I found out it's Good Friday today. I did not know that. I don't have internet here. I know very little of the things happening out there. I don't have a calendar. I can't watch television. But today, at this moment, I'm writing about my experiences, and in Psalm 22, people all over the world are reading these exact words in churches, "My God, my God, why have You forsaken me?"

Yes, these are the words Jesus used, but they came from David, and now they're words I've used.

You may be out there, and you will use them one day. But I learned something significant, and you need to receive this too: Even if we feel like God has forsaken us, even if we feel like He has hidden His face from us and things look hopeless, we must remember God is faithful. He is in control, and He has the last word. Maybe Psalm 22 starts with, "My God, My God, why have you forsaken me," but it doesn't end like that.

Chapter Sixteen
Revelation

My asylum case was denied, and I did not go home as I had hoped. What I had prayed for, and my family had put their hope in, did not happen. It was a great disappointment, but as we have seen many times before, God did not leave us; He came and spoke to us.

He showed us there were several ways I could leave this place. The first was to get asylum. This did not happen, so we are appealing, which can take several months.

At the same time, there is an investigation regarding all the lies, which is why I am detained. Therefore, there is also a chance the revelations from the investigation can open doors for me.

Additionally, there is still a chance I can get a bond. We filled out all the documents for a bond and gave it to them, but it was denied again without any reason. And then there is always God, who can surprise us and do things we did not expect. But, as I heard on the radio the other day, they see me as a national threat, which is why they did not let me out on a bond.

Honestly, I don't know what is up and down anymore. It could still be a long time before I get out.

After I'd been here a few months, one person from my legal team said I needed to be aware that this was not a one-hundred-meter race—it's really a marathon, and that I, therefore, needed to be ready to run a marathon.

He said that to give me the strength to keep running and help me understand that it can still take some time. But when he used the same example when I lost my case in December several months later, it did not help.

I could only tell him, "But you said the same thing a few months ago, and I have now been running that marathon. I feel like I've just finished a marathon, and then you tell me this is not a one-hundred-meter race but a marathon."

This was indeed what I felt back in December. It was like I'd just run a marathon and was exhausted and ready to go home, but then, as I came to the finish line, giving all that I had to give, only to be told that I needed to run another marathon because of all the lies. But as you heard, God was faithful and had more work that needed to be done in my life.

Now, when I look back, I see why, and I am thankful I was not released that time or a few weeks later as I had hoped because then I would have missed what would happen next. The book you are holding in your hands is truly the next page in this story. Last time, the next page was the revival I would have missed if I had gotten out. But this time in December when I lost, it was a particular revelation I would have missed, and also this book you are reading.

The longer I am here, the more I start to understand God's purpose with it all and see how the prophecy I got is being fulfilled. God has a plan with it, and He knows when and how I will get out. This is also what the prophecy said, but even when I read it, I often had doubts as it was so hard. But I started to believe it more and more, which gave me more and more peace. Read a prophecy I got back in B8 some weeks after I arrived here:

"God's purpose alone is what has brought you where you are. Embrace that truth and settle it in your heart—lay hold of the peace that comes from knowing that. Don't allow the situation to trouble and depress you in any way, nor let it steal any joy from your heart. Take full courage and assurance of faith. Let it all go into God's hands, my dear brother. You don't have to live anxiously or strive regarding the entire situation. You don't have to fight or lift a finger to get yourself out. In fact, you can't—only God can. To try and get yourself out before God's purpose is fulfilled would actually be working against Him, and it wouldn't work anyhow. Save yourself the heartache. Just trust Him with His plan and the big picture He is working to accomplish. Don't think about how or when you will get out. Trust Him that He will get you out. Remember, this is only for a season. Remember, your time will come. He that promised is faithful. And again, don't you forget to rejoice! He did promise you!"

The message was very clear but still hard to receive. But God also spoke other things. God spoke about breaking me for a purpose and was teaching me endurance. I truly experienced that in a big way. When we read more about that now in the prophecy, I want to say I'm sharing this because I believe it is not just about me. I believe the way God has worked here in me He works the same way in many of us. And the words He spoke to me are speaking to many now. Be encouraged when you read this:

"There is also the strategic objective of what God is working in your own heart and mind during this time. He is building your faith and increasing your endurance for the days ahead. You will have to lead many through some very difficult times in the future. You will have to be able to impart endurance into others for the hard things the body of Christ will have to experience in the future. God is preparing and purifying you for the coming seasons of warfare. He is making you into a more effective war leader. This season is a great crushing of your character. Like olives being crushed and pressed to create fine oil—God has you in this process to bring you to an even greater glory. He is transforming who you are so that you will be even more effective in the future. The outcome of this crushing will bring forth greater authority, greater power, and greater character. You will become an even sharper weapon in the hand of the Lord. You will come out of this a greater man than you have ever been. Embrace it joyfully, knowing the reward ahead of you! Who you were before you came into prison could not accomplish the work God has for you to do in the times ahead. He is having to crush you in this season in order for you to become who you need to be for the next season of war. Rejoice because of this!"

Those were some of the words I got and some I had been reading daily and praying for. With these, I started to understand it more and more. I saw that God was working through all of this in me deeply.

It was still hard not to be with my family in December. Christmas and New Year are special for me because many years ago, God spoke to me during a forty-day fast, which transformed my life. Since then, every New Year, I have had a particular time of seeking the Lord and fasting for the following year. But this year, I was here and not with my family.

We continued the Bible Discovery Groups here, in which we looked at what it is to be a disciple, repentance, faith in God, baptism in water, and the baptism of the Holy Spirit. We looked at fellowship with God, judgment, eternal life, as the foundations of our beliefs that we read about in Hebrews 6.

At one point, I was teaching three times a day. I had a few group leaders in the morning, teaching them and preparing them for the Bible Discovery Groups they did in the afternoon. Then I had an extensive teaching session at 5 p.m. with everyone, and then I met with some disciples in my cell at 9 p.m. So, I was busy.

I love teaching, especially new believers and people who have yet to hear me. I love our two-month school because two months is a good length for me. I've always wondered about those people who love to teach the same group of people Sunday after Sunday, year after year. That was not me. I love doing my thirty to forty lessons I often share, then doing small videos with teachings on YouTube. But I am different from those who teach day after day. I often don't know what to teach about, and I normally only share things I feel God has made very clear to me and put in my heart in a special way, so two months was a good time for me.

But now I was in a new place I had not been before. And I did not know what to do about it. I had already gone through the teaching I love to share and what I had in my heart. And I felt empty, like I have nothing more to share. This, for some, will sound weird, but I am just not a teacher as my main calling, even though I'm teaching and love to teach, and my teaching has blessed many.

Then, over the next one to two months, my life changed. I was blind, but now I see. I would have missed this if they had let me out that day I wanted to be released. If the judge had given me my asylum back in December, I would have been out. But then, I would have missed what God did next. And I am genuinely thankful for this.

I reached the point where I didn't know what to teach anymore. I could always find something, but I wanted to bring what God wanted me to teach. Then, one day, I got a thought, and I knew this was God—to go back to the beginning of the Bible and teach Jesus and the Kingdom of God out of the Old Testament and then continue with the focus on Jesus and the Kingdom of God all the way up to the book of Revelation. To start in the beginning and go to the end.

When we read the book of Acts and the letters to the church, we often see, again and again, how they quote Scripture. Every time when the writers of the New Testament quote Scripture, it always leads back to the Old Testament because it was their Bible then. That was the Scripture they had. They did not have the Gospels. They did not have the book of Acts. They did not have the letters. They did not have the book of Revelation because they still needed to be written.

It hit me: I cannot do what they are doing—teach out of the Old Testament. I knew some of the prophecies, but I could not preach and teach the way they do out of the Old Testament. So, if I only had the Old Testament, I would be lost, not knowing what to say. So, this was a good place to start. Let's go back to the beginning and see what the Bible says there.

I started in Genesis and woah! Something began to happen to me. Scriptures came together in a way I'd never experienced before. And over the next one to two months, I did around thirty new lessons. Beginning with the Garden of Eden in Genesis and ending with the Garden of Eden in Revelation, a lot of revelation I'd never had before flowed into my life. This is the first time I have experienced something like this, it was so clear and intense. It was truly unique.

For some of you out there, it may be that what I learned is not new to you. But for me, God opened Scripture in a new way as many of those things were new to me. It started slowly, but it built up more and more as I read through the Bible. It was like everything came together as one story by one author, as the Bible truly is, even though He used many different authors to write it. God is the primary Author of the whole book.

Before I was arrested, I also had special times with God and experienced revelations of His Word. In a way it changed me, so I would never be able to go back to the way it was before that experience. Those times have truly transformed my walk with God, even my life. But prior to this moment, those times only happened a few times a year.

But here, during the last few months, it just became more and more intense. I had a period of a few weeks when I received revelations every day, sometimes, even several times per day—something I have never experience in such an intense way before. Many things opened up to me from the Bible in a new way. Let me share some of it with you. For some this will go very fast and be very new to you, but just hang on, this will be good.

But it was also important for those out there who need it.

Starting with the Fall—the serpent, the curse, and enmity between the woman and the snake, and the seed of the snake and the seed of the woman—this is why people today hate us without a reason, just as Jesus said they would. It all leads back to what happened in Genesis with the Fall and curse. This is why, even though we are in this world, we are not to be a part of this world—because this world is cursed.

It's a cursed world, and the world is like God's field, as you can read in Matthew 13.

In Genesis, we read about the seed of the woman, and we know that is Christ, and we also know that Christ is the Word that became alive and dwelt among us. By the Word, Christ, God spoke, and by His Word, Christ, God created everything, and that is how Christ became the Creator of all things, the firstborn of God. We become a new creation when we receive that Word, Christ, into our hearts.

We receive the Spirit of Christ, the Holy Spirit, Christ in us, the seed of the woman, that falls into the good ground and bears much good fruit. The Holy Spirit guarantees our promise, the eternal life we have in Christ. Christ, the Word, the Spirit of truth, is what sets us free, but the serpent, Satan, tries to come up with lies to put his seed in people, which will also grow around us.

It's a peculiar walk between truth and lies—between the seed of the woman, Christ, and the seed of Satan. I saw how it was all working together. Things started to make sense, how people indeed are like grass in God's field: they stand here today, but tomorrow, are thrown into the oven like the Bible says, so today we should focus on bearing the good fruit of God and letting the seed grow in us so we produce life.

And somehow, it all came together. I saw how God started calling people with Abraham, Isaac and Jacob. He is a personal God, the God of Abraham, the God of Isaac, the God of Jacob.

I saw how God's people came, and from there, a nation through Jacob/Israel was formed, God's holy nation. From there, under King David, it became a kingdom—an everlasting kingdom, and the One who was seated on the throne was the son of David, which is Christ.

But before King David, we see what Moses was shown on the mountain in Exodus. These were all shadows and copies of the New Jerusalem that will soon come down. And now, when we are born again, we are circumcised like the covenant to Abraham, but not by a human hand, but by Christ Himself, as we are baptized into Christ. And we become the seed of Abraham and part of the promise God gave to Abraham and David. Yes, Jesus is indeed the prophet Moses spoke about, that God would raise, the One we should now follow.

Matthew 1 starts with the genealogy of Christ, the son of David and Abraham, and now we understand it. Woah! Jesus is the son of David, the son of Abraham, the firstborn of God, born from above, with an imperishable seed, the living Word of God, Christ in us. The Holy Spirit is part of our inheritance, the promise to Abraham, until redemption, as we can read throughout the Bible. Yes, there is so much more to say about this.

This all just exploded in me. When I read Ephesians 1:9, it says that until our redemption, we have the seed of God in us, the Holy Spirit. The redemption are our heavenly bodies that we will finally receive as we who are in Christ. We will rule with Him here, first in the one thousand years of His reign and then on the New Earth, as God called us to from the time in Genesis before the Fall came and the curse and God's perfect order He created was destroyed.

But one day, He will restore it all. One day, death will be done away with, the New Heaven and New Earth will come down from heaven, and Eden will be restored, where we finally can reach out our hands, eat of the Tree of Life, and live forever. And God's home will again be with man, and we will see Him face to face.

Yes, it is so beautiful to see the big picture. And there are also so many other things I could share, where everything just became one story, one Gospel, one Kingdom. Yes, I could continue like this. And so many things are now connected and make sense. I also now understand why suffering and faith are not enough. We also need hope. And the end goal of our hope is the return of our Lord Jesus Christ. The day we receive our inheritance and what the Bible has promised us in Christ.

I did not understand much of this before, so I lacked hope, which I have now. So, when things came together, it changed so many things in my life, and I will share about that in the next chapter because I believe that the same truth will also change you and set you free.

Chapter Seventeen
The Gospel

A prophecy I received half a year ago has been an enormous blessing in these challenging times.

In the beginning, it brought a lot of hope to me: God had a plan with everything I was going through.

Later, it confirmed what God wanted to do in me in this time and season I am in. Yes, in all of us.

I've already shared some words, but I want to delve more deeply into this prophecy. I share this because I genuinely believe this is a word from God, not only for me but for everyone reading this book. The prophecy said:

"God is preparing and purifying you for the coming seasons of warfare. He is making you a more effective war leader. God is raising up leaders who will take over and lead His children into their true destiny. He's building an army. He's raising generals that will take His army of disciples into battle against devils—leaders that will restore the true Gospel, bring reformation of the church, and revelation of Jesus Christ to the entire world—and you are one of those leaders. Because of what is happening to you now, churches all over this country will be transformed and reformed to save souls."

I truly believe God is doing this in this season: God is building an army that can help restore the true Gospel, reform the church, and bring revelation of Jesus Christ to the entire world; an army that can lead His church into her true destiny.

I don't share this to say, "Look at me—God has called me to be a leader in His church." I'm writing this book to help, teach, and prepare you for what is coming. I want this to be a blessing in your life, and this prophecy is a part of that.

God is building an army and raising up leaders. God is at work, and we need to be obedient and join what He is doing.

I truly believe the words I have written here. I could share many more things regarding the prophecy, but here, I will focus on the idea that God is restoring the Gospel back to the church. All who know me know the Gospel has been on my heart for years. I want to bring the true Gospel back to the church. I genuinely love the Gospel, and sadly, many people in the church do not fully understand it. They are still in their sins; they are not free.

But to see them fully understand what the Gospel is and turn away from their sins once and for all, and be baptized into Christ, saying goodbye to the old life, and then be filled with the Holy Spirit, is just so beautiful. When there is a true repentance and true baptism, knowing they have buried their old life and are filled with the Holy Spirit, speaking in tongues, it is just so beautiful. The transformation that comes out of that is lasting, and now they can give this to others. I have, again and again, seen the power in the Gospel like that.

I dream of seeing a reformation of the church, where we begin to make disciples and not churchgoers. It's not about how many people come into the church on Sundays but how they walk with Jesus as disciples on Mondays, how they grow up in Christ and obey the Lord.

I dream of seeing the churches transformed to become a disciple-making movement. I genuinely want to see that.

But the Gospel and seeing people truly born again has always been the main thing in my life. That is number one. We cannot see the church succeed without the proper foundation—without seeing the people truly born again and experiencing the freedom there is in Christ.

Here in jail, God has done a great work in me regarding the Gospel. Some things needed to happen within me so I could be more effective in the future. There were still things I did not fully understand; I still lacked something very important regarding the Gospel, and I want to share that with you in the chapters to follow.

The prophetic word also said this: "Who you were before you came into prison could not accomplish the work God has for you to do in the times ahead."

The person I was before could not do what God wanted me to do in the next season. I can say I am not the same as before: not only has my understanding of the Bible changed, as God has opened Scripture to me in new and profound ways, but God has also done a great work deep inside my heart in other areas.

For example, He has put His love for the whole church in me, a love I did not have before, at least not in the same way. Today, I see that I have been too critical because I've seen the mistakes in the church. But I also know I've kept too much to myself instead of trying to help more. I see that now. It is often easier to start something new from nothing than to go in to help a more traditional, older church.

The Bible says that love hides a multitude of sins (1 Peter 4:8). These words have indeed been working in me. We are not to conceal sin, but we don't see all their small mistakes if we love people. We don't find fault in their lives. True love means we don't focus on all the wrong things people do. We easily see mistakes in those we don't like, and we overlook things in those we love greatly.

I confess I did not have the love I needed regarding the church. I was too quick to judge, especially people I'm not close with and those who do things differently than I do. I saw what they believed and moved on because I became frustrated and did not have the patience to give people the time they needed to learn and grow. I did not have the love and patience to give them the time they needed to really see what the Bible was saying and to get it into their heart where it become a revelation to them.

We have seen thousands of lives changed all over the world. We've seen powerful disciples being raised from nothing to become spiritual giants in a very short time. We have seen fantastic fruit. We have seen a movement—a beautiful movement of God that has been spreading all over the world in a few years. In the last four years, we have had Training Schools in over thirty countries: Poland, Spain, Germany, and all over Europe, but also Russia, Ukraine, Kazakhstan, and many other countries. Even locked up here, it is still spreading, and God is doing beautiful things.

I am honored by what God has done in my life and in our friends' lives. Not many can share the same testimony I can and have seen the same fruit I've seen. I don't say that to be proud—not at all. I don't say that to say, "Look at me," but I'm just sharing it to make a point: we have seen fantastic fruit everywhere we go because the Gospel is working. It is powerful. Authentic disciples are bearing a lot of fruit, just as in the Bible. I've seen that we can see fruit in a very short time.

In some areas, though, I have been disappointed with the church. Much of the church did not want, see, or think they needed it. So, at the time, I just let the church be, and started new fellowships, doing most of the work outside the church because it was much easier and faster. If they didn't want it, then it was their choice.

I see now that I should not give up on the church. I should lay down my life for her in a new way: service with patience to see God do great things inside the church walls. This is for the whole church, not only for the part of the church that shares my theological foundations. The entire church needs this, and I need the church.

So, these are some things God's been teaching me in the last few months here. It's easier to keep doing what we know and what is working and do it outside a large part of the church. But things have changed in me, and many changes will happen in our ministry. It had already started before I got detained, but God has worked deeper in my heart. We are all part of the same body and can learn from each other. And we need each other, especially in the times ahead.

I'm not talking about us compromising the truth. But how can we learn if we never sit down with people who see things differently and talk with them? We are brothers, and there is only one body, and I saw that those who are in Christ, even if they are very different, are not my enemies. I need them as much as they need me, and God has humbled me in this way.

He did this through the people I've felt wrong about in my heart, who suddenly stood up for me. They used their platforms to help me while I was suffering here. When that happened, it truly humbled me. I needed to repent for my attitude toward them, and God used this to teach me many things.

We often spend too much time fighting each other while our true enemy is busy stealing and destroying lives all around us. I now say, "The enemy of my enemy is my friend." And when I get out, I know changes will happen.

There was also another big area God worked in my life, having to do with the word that God wants to restore the Gospel to the church. I thought I knew the Gospel, but I needed to learn some things. I did not fully understand it in the right way. And how can I help restore the Gospel to the church if I don't understand it myself? How can I bring something I don't have?

I know people will be surprised when they hear this coming from me. "Torben, you have always talked about the Gospel and have been preaching it for over twenty years, so how can you say you did not fully understand it?"

In the next chapter, I will share how God suddenly spoke about the Gospel and changed everything for me. But before that, I must tell you something important about the Gospel.

I hope you will be able to receive what I will now share. What I will share now will be a lot for some of you, primarily if this is the first time you have heard about this.

So, I hope you are ready as I now move on.

We know that the Gospel is all about Jesus and the cross; in the next chapter, we will look more into that. I want to discuss how it is being told, and how we expect people to respond to what they hear. We can listen to beautiful preaching about how we have all sinned, how Jesus died in our place on the cross, and how we in Him can find forgiveness for our sins and eternal life. All that can be so good and biblical. But then many end up, if you believe this, praying a prayer and asking Jesus into their hearts. And that is where the biggest problem is today: how we respond to what we hear regarding the Gospel.

I have in my heart for everyone out there, and you who are reading my book, to know that it's not just about praying a sinner's prayer and being told that you're born again. This is truly a big problem in the churches today, and people think they're born again, but they're not.

There's nothing wrong with praying a prayer with people. The problem is that many stop there. "Yes, I prayed the prayer; therefore, I'm now born again." And very often, it's just a prayer they repeat after another person without understanding repentance or sin.

How can you repent if you don't know what to repent for? And then, to make it even worse, after they pray a prayer repeating after someone, they are told, "Congratulations, you are now born again, and nothing can take it from you." Nobody in the Bible got born again by praying a sinner's prayer. The sinner's prayer, asking Jesus into your heart, is not found in the Bible.

Many will say, "Well, Romans 10:9 (NIV) says, 'If you declare with your mouth, "Jesus is Lord," and believe in your heart that God raised him from the dead, you will be saved,' is that not the sinner's prayer?"

These words are very well known, but what we need to understand is that these words are part of a letter—a letter written for a church. It was not written to a sinner; it was not written to someone who needed to be born again. It was part of a letter written to a church that had already repented, had been baptized, and so on.

In the same letter, Romans 6 discusses when they were baptized in water, and Romans 8 talks about how they had received the Holy Spirit and should walk by the Spirit. If you take Romans, the letter to the church in Rome, as a whole, then the first chapter talks about sin and repentance, then it talks about the baptism in water in Romans 6, and then about the Holy Spirit in Romans 8. Then, Paul reminds these Christians, those who follow Christ, that if they go on believing and confessing Jesus as Lord, they will be saved one day. This is the context of Romans 10:9—to go on believing and confessing. He's quoting Moses from Deuteronomy 30, as Jesus was the prophet Moses wrote about. Jesus was the one we should now obey. So, we need to read Romans 10 properly and not just take a few verses out of context and build a whole theology.

It becomes even more evident if we look at the book of Acts and how the people in the early church came to faith in Christ and what they did when they believed. We don't see anyone praying a sinner's prayer and leaving it there. There, we also see repentance toward God, baptism into Christ, and receiving the Holy Spirit.

Remember, all the letters in the New Testament were written to the church in this or that city or to the disciple named in this or that letter. It is all written to already born-again believers. The letters are not addressed to sinners about what they must do as they come to faith. No. For that, we have the book of Acts as the only historical book where they communicate with sinners who do not know Christ yet.

That's the only book in which we see how the disciples shared the Gospel with sinners and how sinners came to faith in Christ. So, what do we see there? Not in one place do we see that they prayed a sinner's prayer by getting people to repeat a prayer after them and ask Jesus into their hearts (as we sadly often see in the churches today).

Many churches today focus on getting people to say the sinner's prayer and it stops there. But in the Bible, we see the necessity of ongoing repentance toward a righteous God. We see baptism in Jesus' name. Yes, they always got baptized the same day or even the same night. They always got baptized immediately, and they did not see baptism as just a symbol or an outward sign of inner faith, as many sadly do today. Baptism was a big part of being born again and following Christ. We also see how they got filled with the Holy Spirit; sometimes, it happens before baptism in water, and other times, it happens right afterward.

Some examples are found in Acts 8 with the eunuch or in Acts 10 with the house of Cornelius, who also were baptized into Christ. In every place in the book of Acts, they got baptized in water immediately after repenting and received the Holy Spirit. After the cross, after the Holy Spirit came down, combined with faith in God, there was always repentance, baptisms, and receiving the Holy Spirit. And this is what Peter also said in Acts 2:38 (NIV) when the people there ask what they should do.

> *Peter replied, "Repent and be baptized, every one of you, in the name of Jesus Christ for the forgiveness of your sins. And you will receive the gift of the Holy Spirit."*

It always starts with repentance—to turn away from our sins. Repentance was the first word from John the Baptist's mouth. It was the first word that came out of Jesus' mouth. It was the first word that came out of Peter's mouth and should be the first word that comes out of our mouths when we share the good news.

In Acts 2:38, Peter said to repent and be baptized for the forgiveness of your sins. When Ananias baptized Paul in Acts 22:16 (NIV), we read, *"And now what are you waiting for? Get up, be baptized and wash your sins away, calling on his name."* So here in Acts, we see words like the "forgiveness of your sins" and to "wash your sins away." Who talks like this today?

In Galatians 3:26 (NIV), we read, *"So in Christ Jesus, you are all children of God through faith."* The question is, when does a person enter into that faith?

In the next verse, Paul says something interesting, "For all of you who were baptized into Christ have clothed yourselves with Christ." So, when you're baptized into Christ, you put on Christ and are now in Christ. It becomes more apparent if you see the big picture or if you keep reading, so always keep reading.

Some say, "Yeah, but the robber on the cross did not get baptized." But keep reading. When the robber on the cross was hanging there,

Jesus had not yet died. It was still the old covenant. Jesus had not yet died or been buried. He had not yet risen. He had not yet ascended to heaven. The Holy Spirit was still not given here as He is now. The robber on the cross did not get baptized into Christ in water and did not receive the Holy Spirit but keep reading! After the cross, it becomes so much more apparent, which is the time we live in now.

Some will say, "Yeah, but what about Acts 16, where Paul and Silas were in jail, and then the jailer asks them, 'What must I do to be saved?" In verse 31, it says, "Believe in the Lord Jesus, and you and your household will be saved?" Yes, you see, there was nothing about baptism and repentance here. It was just faith. But keep reading, and what happened then?

Verses 32-33 (NIV) tell us that after they believed in the Lord Jesus: "Then they spoke the word of the Lord to him and all the others in his house," and "immediately he and all his household were baptized."

We need to believe in Jesus, but how can you believe in Him if you have yet to hear, and how can you hear if no one is preaching? So, after they said, "Believe in Jesus," they spoke the word of the Lord to them, and when they believed, they were baptized.

If we keep reading, we will always get the whole truth, and I want to point out here that I don't believe in baptismal regeneration. Baptism in itself does not save. But baptism is a part of salvation, together with repentance and faith. Baptism is our circumcision, where we put off the flesh, that is a slave to sin.

We need to understand the true Gospel and how to respond to it. We need to see people truly born again and set free from sin in their own lives. For years, I have seen the power of the Gospel and how lives are being truly transformed from the inside out, but we have also seen so many people in the churches who were not fully born again. They were still in their sins and were struggling. But when they started to understand true repentance, baptism in water, and baptism in the Holy Spirit, and they experienced it all, freedom came to them like never before.

This is the cross: Jesus died for us. Now, we need to repent and die to sin. He was buried; now we need to be buried with Him in the water of baptism. And like Jesus was raised from the dead; we need the power of the Holy Spirit to make us, even though we were dead in our sins, alive in Him. This is the cross we can carry. The cross is a death, burial, and resurrection, and we now need to do this, not just pray a prayer or have faith in God and go to church somewhere.

My prayer has always been, "God, if I could just be used for one thing in this world, then let it be to bring this Gospel back to the church." That has been my main dream for years. I want to see people healed and demons cast out, but this is my heart regarding the Gospel and seeing people truly born again and following Christ. This Gospel needs to come back to the church.

But then I was put here in jail, and God spoke that He is bringing a reformation to the church, and that He wants to restore the Gospel.

I prayed daily for the first seven months, "God, let this happen as You said. Let us see how the Gospel will be restored to the whole church."

When I prayed this, I thought about how important it is for people to understand what true faith, repentance, baptism in water, and baptism with the Holy Spirit are.

After seven months, my mind was blown when God spoke and revealed what I've been thinking for years that the Gospel is not the full Gospel or all of it. I will share more about that in the next chapter.

This picture was taken at LAX Airport before Torben flew to Orlando, Florida, to attend the meeting with Homeland Security a few days later. However, he was unaware of what awaited him.

Pod B6, the pod where Torben stayed the longest, for almost a year. His cell was cell N on the second floor. That is the third door from the right at the top of the stairs. *Image courtesy of News4JAX The Local Station.*

Here you can see Torben's cell, or one exactly like the one he stayed in for the most time. He stayed in this one for around a year, with 90% of the time alone and often for up to 22 hours per day.

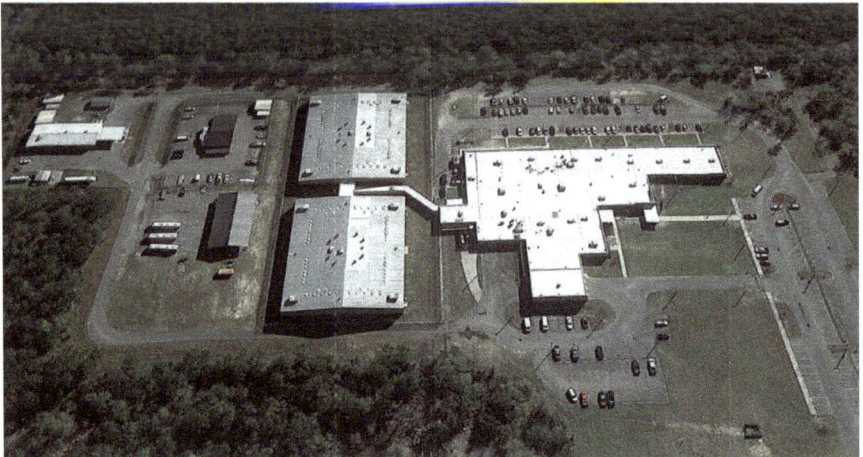

A picture of Baker County Detention Center, where Torben was held for over a year.

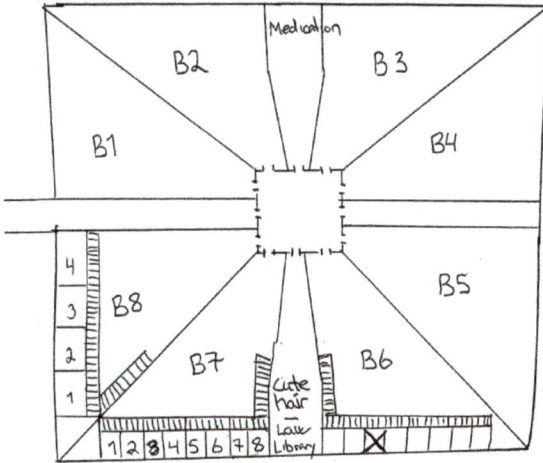

This is a picture that Torben created, showing the different pods B1, B2, ... B8, and how they are arranged around the square in the middle. The security room, located on the second floor of the square, is where they monitor the activities in the various pods.

Another image shows the computer in the pod where Torben was able to make video calls.

This picture is from December 16, 2022, when Torben lost the asylum case in the immigration court. This was the lowest moment for him, where he felt like saying, "My God, my God, why have you forsaken me?"

On July 26, 2023, member of Congress Clay Higgins made a statement about Torben saying:

"I also have a letter to enter into the record, regarding the case of Mr. Torben Sondergaard, who was a legal immigrant from Denmark, came to our country legally, applied for asylum properly, and no criminal charges. He was arrested for overstaying his visa. He has been incarcerated in solitary confinement for over one year. He has been persecuted by this administration and targeted, we believe, because he's an Evangelical Christian Minister. I'd like to enter this to the record without objection."

One of the many studies Torben did during his time in jail was called "Prison and troubles await me," and it was about the persecution that Paul was called to endure and how he managed to do so without losing his joy.

Here, you can see the papers that Torben wrote in his cell, which eventually became this book. After writing on the papers, he read the book chapter by chapter over the phone to his friends, who recorded it, as he was unsure if he could keep the papers with him.

This picture captures the moment when Torben saw Lene again for the first time at Hamburg Airport in Germany.

A warm hug between Torben and his son Sonni, the first time they see each other in a long time. It has also been a hard time for them back in Europe, not knowing what will happen.

First time Torben sees his new grandson Caleb, who was born while he was in jail. God used Caleb in a special way to remind Torben of Caleb and Joshua in the Bible and how he needed to be strong.

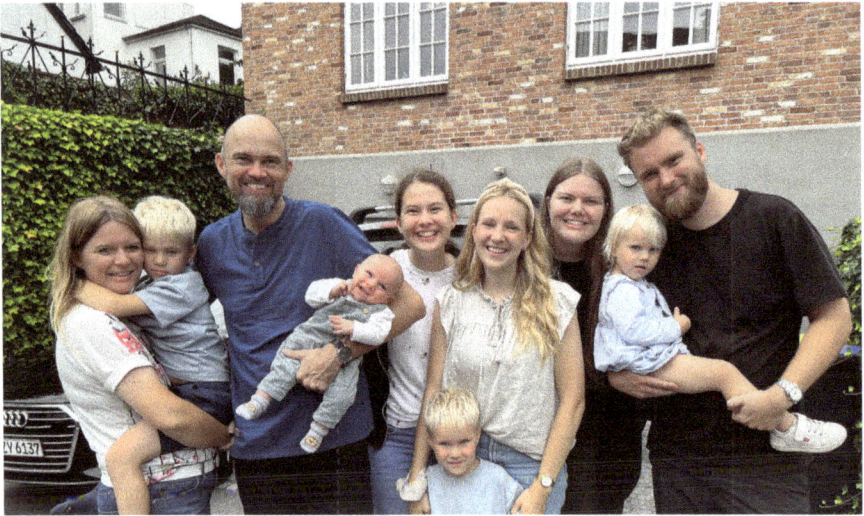

It also shows the first time the whole family gathered, with Torben, Lene, and the girls meeting their new grandson/nephew, Caleb.

One of the first pictures of Torben after he was released. Now with a beard and 35 pounds (16kg) lighter. But spiritually, he was also a different person than before he was detained.

One of several interviews Torben did after his release, sharing his story. This is from the ministry "Truth and Liberty," located in Colorado, USA.

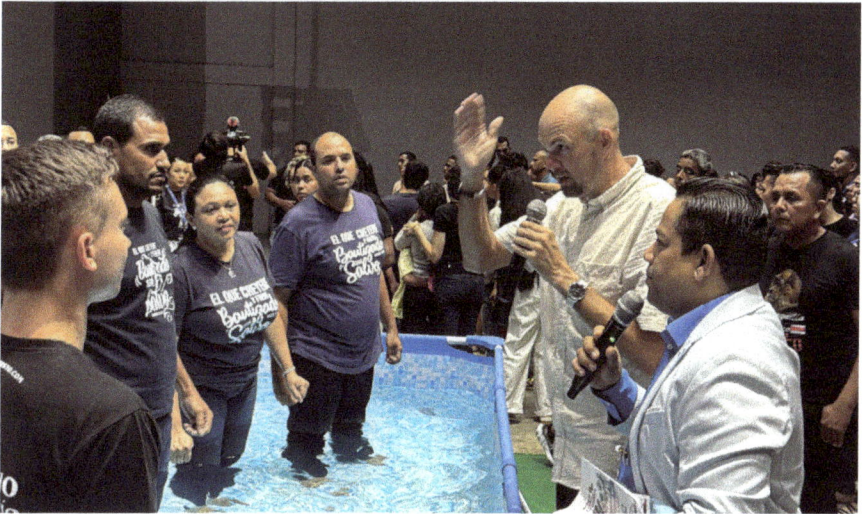

Torben is back doing ministry. This is from Colombia in June 2024 at a meeting with over 2000 people where hundreds were baptized. God has been doing beautiful things in many people's lives since his release, and he is witnessing the beginning of the fulfillment of the words God spoke to him in jail.

Chapter Eighteen
The Kingdom

Sitting here in my small cell, writing this book, I often think of how it must have been for the Apostle Paul to sit in chains, writing to the churches in the different cities. Or what it was like to write this to his dear friend Timothy:

> *"I thank God, whom I serve, as my ancestors did, with a clear conscience, as night and day I constantly remember you in my prayers. Recalling your tears, I long to see you, so that I may be filled with joy. I am reminded of your sincere faith, which first lived in your grandmother Lois and in your mother Eunice and, I am persuaded, now lives in you also."* (2 Timothy 1:3-5 NKJV)

I feel what Paul felt and the heart behind these words. I miss my friends out there. I love serving Jesus with you, and long to see you again.

Writing this book is like escaping to another place: it is like you are all here with me, sitting in my cell listening. But as soon as I am finished, I am suddenly back again alone in my cell.

It is the same when I'm reading the Bible. When I'm reading the Word of God, it lets me escape to another place, and I love it. It feels so good. I am away from this dreadful place, the noise, closed doors, and no windows. But sometimes it's hard to return or wake up in the cell again, returning to this reality.

Yesterday, I talked with an inmate in the cell beside me who's often sitting and drawing, and I asked him if he could draw my cell so all of you could see how it looked. So, he drew a picture so you could see my cell and see there's not much in it (you can see the picture at TorbenSondergaard.com/412days).

Yet, I am thankful because I know God is with me here. And I hope you have started to see the wisdom in me being here: God needed to put me in this place to show, teach, and do something with me so I could share it with you—and this book is all part of that.

I ended the last chapter by saying everything changed when God spoke to me concerning the Gospel. And I will now share what He showed me.

On Sunday, February 19, 2023, I felt like God spoke a few words and a veil was taken off my eyes and I suddenly understood so many things. It all fell into place in me in a very special way. God had been revealing many things to me from the beginning of Genesis to the end of Revelation. The Bible had become one long story about restoration—God restoring what was in the Garden of Eden that got corrupted and was destroyed. The fall of man changed everything dramatically, something we often don't understand or think about. But that is the world we live in now, a fallen world.

But God wanted to restore it, and He started doing that through a man called Abram (as his name was at that time), the father of our faith—God gave a promise to Abraham and to his seed, and then God came with the covenant of circumcision.

God became known as the God of Abraham, Isaac, and Jacob. Then, through Jacob, also called Israel, He made that family into a nation—God's holy nation. But as we who are in Christ, it is also our story. We who are in Christ are circumcised by Christ when we are baptized into Him. Christ is Abraham's seed, and Abraham's promise is now ours. Abraham is our father. The story moved on to Moses and David and then to Jesus.

I suddenly understood the big picture. Before, when I read Matthew 1:1, which starts with, *"This is the genealogy of Jesus the Messiah, the son of David, the son of Abraham"* (NKJV), I did not put much into it.

But now, when I read that our Lord is the son of Abraham and David, it just exploded in me. Jesus is the son. Jesus is the son of David who will sit on the throne forever and ever, and we will, therefore, reign with Him. Yes, He is the son of Abraham, the heir to the promise, and when we are in Jesus, we are, therefore, also heirs to that same promise.

Before, when I read those verses, I did not understand them, but now, they just make the Bible come alive in a new way.

As all of this came to me, and the truth set me free more and more. I was still praying daily for the church, that God would restore the Gospel to the church, as the prophecy said, and as I'd had on my heart for many years. "Do it, God! Let the church come back to true repentance, to a true baptism in water, and let them receive the true baptism in the Holy Spirit. This is not only for a few, but God, this is for the whole church!"

This was my prayer for years and is still my prayer today.

I cried to God, "God, we need it so much—we need it—we need it all. God, we need the Gospel to come back to the church. People need to be born again to be free from their sins. Many are deceived; they are still in their sins. They are not free. They need the Gospel."

And then, amid my prayer for the church and that the Gospel would come back to it, suddenly, like lightning, it came to me. God spoke to me: "Torben, this is the Gospel. I want you to help restore it back to the church, and THIS IS WHY I NEEDED TO BRING YOU HERE, TO REVEAL THIS GOSPEL TO YOU—THE GOSPEL OF THE KINGDOM."

I will never forget it when He said, "This is the Gospel," the "Gospel of the Kingdom." This is what I have been learning the last few weeks and months, this is what I've been sharing with the inmates—this is the Gospel that has been lost in the church.

Repentance, baptism in water, and receiving the Holy Spirit is the proper response and what we must do to enter His Kingdom. I saw that I often preach the Gospel (Good News) without preaching the Kingdom.

And I saw so clearly in that moment that God wanted me to help restore this Gospel of the Kingdom back to the church. The Gospel of His Kingdom, that one day will come down here on earth. This is what He promised to Abraham and David and throughout the whole Bible.

When this happened, everything changed for me. I understood so many things at that moment. I was so blind before, but now I see. And this is what the prophecy was saying:

"Your being where you are is critical and strategic for the purpose of the true Gospel breaking out across the entire state of California and spreading across this entire nation. Your situation is happening so that true salvation and freedom can come to so many who live in complete darkness—even the sleeping church."

I had been reading and praying over these words daily. But for the first time now, I understood it. God wants to break out the true Gospel of the Kingdom, the Gospel that God brought me here to teach me. And for that to happen, it was critical and strategic for this to happen. For Him to take me aside like this and teach it to me, so I am able to teach it to you.

Yes, we need repentance, yes, we need baptism in water, and yes, we need baptism with the Holy Spirit, but that's not all of it; there is so much more. That is the response we need to give to what we hear. But we need to understand why we need to be born again. Why? To be able to enter into the Kingdom of God. It's all about the Kingdom. We need to enter into it, but we also need to understand it so we are ready and will not be surprised on that day our Lord Jesus appears.

Four days before God spoke to me on February 19th, I had the worst day of being here. I was crying to God like I'd never cried before, and I was begging Him to let me out. The reason was that my amazing wife Lene had become very sick, and she ended up going to a hospital emergency room. It was incredibly hard for her and me to be in here unable to help. So, I was crying out like never before. I will share more about that later.

Despite my begging and crying like never before, God did not let me out at that time. But I understand why now. More needed to happen, which was a big part of why God brought me here.

When He said "this Gospel" I was also reminded of Matthew when Jesus talked about some signs of His return. One of the main signs of His return is that, *"This gospel of the kingdom will be preached in the whole world as a testimony to all nations, and then the end will come"* (Matthew 24:14 NIV).

This "gospel of the kingdom" God revealed to me and many others in these last days is why He brought me here and why He did not let me out before. And it all makes sense. I was blind, but now I see.

Last year, I had several friends in The Last Reformation, our ministry, talking about the Gospel of the Kingdom of God—that there were things we were missing, that we needed to preach more about the Kingdom of God, more about the day of the Lord, about the one thousand years of reign with Christ, about the New Heaven and New Earth, about the Kingdom. I heard what they and others were saying about it all, but to be honest, sometimes it just put me off.

At the time, some of it (not all, but some) was too much like it was only about the Kingdom and not about Christ (the King). But it was mainly because I did not understand it. They tried to get my eyes on the Kingdom, and that was why they tried so much. I did not fully understand what they were trying to tell me. I was not in a place at that time to receive it.

I heard what they said about it, and I also tried to listen to others preaching the Kingdom of God, but I didn't receive it.

At the same time, many had very different views, so who should listen to them? So, I wanted to make my own discovery and look into it myself, but did I do it? No, I did not have the time or take the time to do it. I was too busy with other things, and I've never been a big reader. I read, but not very fast, at least not then. I've grown a lot in that area since I came here.

I read the Bible, but besides the Bible, I read only one to two books a year or every two years. Reading the whole Bible from one end to the other takes some time. My family can read the Bible in three months. My son often does that. He reads the Bible two to three times a year, which is beautiful. I started with them to go through the Bible in three months. They read, and I did what I often do, which is to mostly listen on an audio Bible.

I love to listen to the Bible. I've always done that a lot, which has been my way to get the Word inside me. I started with them this time, but I dropped off quickly because I just didn't have the time. But now, I have no phone, no Facebook, no Signal, no internet, no YouTube, and no distractions. It was just me, the Bible, and the Holy Spirit teaching me. And I needed that.

After reading the Bible from one end to the other and studying the people in the Bible, I had the overview I needed to start putting the pieces together. With the details coming together, I became more and more free. And since God has spoken how this was the Gospel that He wanted me to bring, He said I should do a teaching series like the Online Pioneer School, a teaching I did back in 2011, which has transformed many people worldwide. God has used that teaching series in a mighty way to set many people free to live the life God has for us. (You can see a link to it at the back of this book.)

The Online Pioneer School also came at a time when God taught us a lot. God led us into the lives of the disciples in the book of Acts, who were led by the Holy Spirit, healing the sick, casting out demons, and seeing whole households come to faith. God transformed our lives then, and one day, God spoke. "Torben, we need pioneers. Start a Pioneer School."

It was an online school with twenty lessons in the beginning, which really helped to take off the religious glasses, as I called them, and bring people back to the book of Acts—a time of true discipleship when people truly followed Jesus and lived the Christian life, not only thinking about it, talking about it, and reading about it, but actually living it. These early disciples spread Christ in their everyday lives, and that life is also for us today. So, it was an extraordinary time with the Online Pioneer School.

And now, years later, I am here, and God called me to do a teaching in the same way with this. So, I got together some of the lessons I have already done here, and for the next month, I went through them all again, one by one. Some of them I took out, and a few I joined together, and then I added two new ones, and like that, I ended up with twenty-four lessons, twenty-four life-changing lessons about the Gospel of the Kingdom.

Some weeks ago, I went through the lessons one more time, and to be honest, it was the most fantastic experience I'd ever had regarding the Bible. During the week, God gave me so much more revelation; it all became more apparent to me as I went through the lessons again.

My head was always in the Word, from the morning when I woke up to when I closed my eyes at night. When I started teaching about the Kingdom of God about one and a half months ago, the more I talked about it to the others, the more I came into it, to the point where my last update here from jail on YouTube was, "Freedom Behind Bars." This teaching about the Kingdom of God had set me free and made me strong in a way I hadn't been before. I knew now what was coming, and it was good. I knew that God was in control of world history all my life, and I was becoming ready for it all.

But it was not only me who felt like that. I started to see it in the disciples around me. One of my newer disciples, Baka, had a powerful new birth, and God has truly transformed his life; he was hungry as I taught him about the Kingdom of God. But after a month, he had an incident where he was taken out of my Pod and put in the "box."

It was unfair how it happened. He was complaining about the food to a U.S. Immigration and Customs Enforcement officer, and because he spoke English, everyone was complaining to him. He then said it to the ICE officer, but the officer did not receive it, and instead, he became angry at Baka.

I was there when it happened, and yes, what Baka said was not good. Like the rest of us, he was frustrated, but I have learned to keep quiet because I have seen repeatedly that you don't win anything when complaining like that.

And instead of listening to Baka, a few days later, they announced: "Baka, pack your things; you are going home." When I heard that, I was like, wow, you are going home. Baka is finally going home, and we were excited for him, even though I will miss him a lot here.

But no. That was all just a dirty trick to get him to pack his things together fast. Instead, they put him in the "box." That is an isolation cell in a part of the prison where inmates go when they have been in a fight or have stolen things from other inmates. So, there is a lot of yelling and screaming there, as most are angry and frustrated. It is not a good place to be.

When I heard that he was put there, my heart broke for him. How evil was that to make him think he was going home, then to do this. I was so worried for him, and I often prayed that he would not lose his faith. He was still new in his faith, and it was not an easy place to be. Later, I heard he was moved to another Pod beside me, but even though there was only a wall between us, we could not contact each other. I just heard from others who saw him there.

A few weeks later, I met him outside during recreation time. As soon as he saw me, he was so excited that he came to me right away. He was on fire like I'd never seen before.

He said, "Torben, I'm like you now. I just spent time in my cell with God, and He has been teaching me, now, I don't see TV anymore; it's just me and God, and the others are coming to hear about God; it's been so amazing!"

And he continued: "Yes, I have just started a new Bible Discovery Group with eight others from my Pod." I was just amazed as he talked about what God was doing.

At that moment, I saw how this teaching had made him strong in a very short time. And then I began to think of the church, and not to criticize, but sadly, in many places we have a Gospel that is so focused on blessing "me"—a blessing "me" Gospel, give "me" a good life here and now, and make "me" rich here and now. The focus is on us in this world, not the Kingdom and the world to come.

This has been a big mistake in so many ways. If I think about what Jesus is saying in Mark 4, that there are those in shallow ground who receive the seed/Word with joy, but then when persecution sets in because of the Word, they immediately fall away. And that is what I think will happen in America and Western churches the day when persecution sets in.

The day persecution truly sets in, we'll see a falling away like never before, maybe even as high as 80 to 95 percent of Christians. Why? Because people are not ready and don't have deep roots in their life with God. We have focused too much on this world rather than the Kingdom to come. We have been looking backward to the cross instead of looking forward to Jesus's return. To look backward to the cross and what happened then doesn't help us in the same way as looking forward to the return of Christ. Jesus endured the cross by the reward set before Him. Yes, the cross is our beginning. But now we are on the road, we must fix our eyes on Jesus, and He is not hanging on the cross anymore. He is sitting in heaven at God's right hand and will soon return to bring us our salvation.

> *"And let us run with perseverance the race marked out for us, our eyes on Jesus, the pioneer and perfecter of faith. For the joy set before him he endured the cross, scorning its shame, and sat down at the right hand of the throne of God."* (Hebrews 12:1-2 NIV)

We read in Acts 2:38 that people must repent, get baptized in water, and receive the Holy Spirit. But in Acts 2:37, we read that they were all cut to the heart. Why were they cut to the heart? Because Peter had just quoted Psalm 110:1 (ESV) to them: *"The Lord says to my lord: 'Sit at my right hand until I make your enemies a footstool for your feet.'"* The first "Lord" is YHWH. The second "lord" is the Master—which points to Jesus. And this was written by David.

When they heard these words, they were cut to the heart. I've read these verses many times, and they've never cut me to my heart.

But now, I understand it. Jesus is the One God said, "Sit at My right hand." He is the son of David; He is the One in Psalm 110, and God proves that by raising Him from the dead as David prophesied.

You can read the whole context in Acts 2 in Peter's sermon. It's mighty. They understood that Jesus was the One because He was the son of David—He was raised from the dead as proof of that. He is the one now sitting at the right hand of God and He will return to judge the nations. So, therefore, they were cut to the heart. Then they asked, "What do we need to do?"

Peter replied, *"Repent and be baptized, every one of you, in the name of Jesus Christ for the forgiveness of your sins. And you will receive the gift of the Holy Spirit."* (Acts 2:38 NIV)

They truly understood that one day, Jesus would return and set up His Kingdom here. He would restore the Kingdom to Israel as it is spoken of.

And if you have that foundation and focus, you will come into agreement with the Lord's Prayer Matthew 6:9-13 NIV):

"This, then, is how you should pray:
Our Father in heaven,
hallowed be your name,
your kingdom come,
your will be done,
on earth as it is in heaven.
Give us today our daily bread.
And forgive us our debts,
as we also have forgiven our debtors.
And lead us not into temptation,
but deliver us from the evil one."

Our Father, Your Kingdom come, and Your will be done here on earth as it is in heaven. That is our prayer, that's our longing, that is our hope, and that is what we put our faith in. That is why we are strangers here on earth and don't fit in—we are in this world but not part of it, as we long for a new country, our real home, where we belong. A heavenly one, as the Bible talks about.

This is the Gospel of the Kingdom. If this is our focus, we will not fall away when persecution comes our way or we are treated unjustly. We know that when we keep running the race, we will one day be given our eternal inheritance. On that day, if we remain faithful to our Lord and King Jesus, we will rejoice in our heavenly bodies and we will reign with Christ here on earth for one thousand years. After that, God will make a New Heaven and a New Earth. We will see God face to face and walk with Him like Adam and Eve did before the fall. No more death, no more pain, because the old things are finished, and everything has become new.

God needed to bring me here to reveal this so I could help prepare others for what is coming over the earth in these last days. He made it so strong, and I saw the first fruit of that in jail, and it was beautiful.

Chapter Nineteen
The Cross and Salvation

One of the most significant changes in my life over the last month was my understanding of the Gospel of the Kingdom. God will soon set up a Kingdom here on earth. It is not so much us who will die one day and go up to heaven to be with God, but God will come down here on earth to be with us.

Yes, God will make His dwelling place down here—He will create a New Heaven and New Earth, which you can read about in the last chapters of the book of Revelation. I started to see and understand many new things about this Kingdom, especially the cross and the return of Jesus, which I will share now.

Because we in this chapter will look at the cross, I will share a testimony about something that happened last year on Resurrection Sunday.

It is important to share testimonies of God's work. But teaching can do something testimonies cannot. Testimonies can strengthen us, but the Word of God is what sets us free.

What I share here is what the early church taught, but today, we have gone so far away from what they taught in so many areas. What I will share here will help you remove those religious glasses, as I call them, and see more clearly. We often read the Bible through glasses we've gotten through our traditions and church denominations, which clouds our reading and understanding.

None of us have been so blessed that we, from the beginning, knew the whole truth.

None of us have been so blessed that we grew up in a church or denomination that had the whole truth.

Yet, we often believe we have the absolute truth because we grew up in what sounds like the truth. We think it's the truth because everyone else around us also feels the same as us, but then later, we discover, hopefully, that we are missing things. We may have been living in a bubble, and many others are out there seeing it differently and teaching it differently than we have thought, and they are right and not us.

At one time, I thought that our church and denomination were the ones. But then, years ago, I decided that if the Bible teaches it, I will believe it, no matter what people around me think. Since then, I've changed my views and learned many new things. I found that God revealed something entirely new to me from the Bible, and later discovered that it was only new for me, as many others have been teaching the same things for years because there's nothing new under the sun in that way.

Some people are strong in one truth and others in another. It would be beautiful if we would just learn from each other and bring it all together. So even though I'm very excited about what I will share—this new truth I'm seeing—some of you may be sitting back, thinking, "This is what we have been believing for many years." So, for you, there is nothing new here.

Others might be more skeptical, as this is different. My advice is always to check things with the Bible, not only what I am teaching here but also what you have been taught your whole life, what you grew up in, and what you thought was true—always check if everything is in the Word of God, no matter who is teaching it.

I will start to look at the resurrection of Christ. I did not plan on this when I decided to do this teaching, but as I write this, it is Resurrection Sunday. Today is an extraordinary day, the most prominent church day of the year. The churches are filled. People go to church and then have a good family time. I will celebrate the resurrection of Jesus here, just Him and me in my cell, while I'm writing these chapters to you.

But recently, I've found I celebrate this with Him daily. It has been Him and me here for a long time now. I love Him like I never did before, and I'm so thankful for the cross. Paul says in Philippians 3:10-11 (NIV), *"I want to know Christ—yes, to know the power of His resurrection and participation in His sufferings, becoming like Him in His death, and so, somehow, attaining to the resurrection from the dead."* No one talks like this today.

This is so beautiful, true, and valid for all of us. May this be the heart of all of us so that we may know Jesus personally and the power of His Resurrection and continue to take part in His suffering and His death to experience His Resurrection later! These words have been working especially for me while I have been here.

Most of us need help understanding what Paul is saying here. Last year, on Resurrection Sunday, I visited a church near our home in California. It was my first time trying to go to a bigger church on Resurrection Sunday. When I arrived there, there were many people, and I looked around me. A few rows further down, I saw a woman and her husband. The woman walked with crutches. And when I saw her, I immediately felt God wanted me to go and pray for her afterward.

So, while the sermon was going on, the preacher spoke about the resurrection and the power of God. I imagined going and praying for her, lifting the crutches over my head and shouting, "He is risen! He is risen!"

As soon as the pastor finished preaching, he said, "Go in the power of His resurrection."

Those were the last words in the sermon. Everyone stood up and went on their way out, but I stood up and walked over to that woman.

I talked briefly with her, and there in the church, I was allowed to pray for her, and God came. She got healed. She could walk without crutches. It was amazing! And there I did it as I had imagined; I lifted the crutches over my head and shouted to everyone in the church, "He is risen!"

Everyone who saw it was amazed; she was healed. Then I prayed again, and there she was filled with the Holy Spirit. It was so beautiful and powerful. We went out to the cafe and had a long talk with her and her husband. I even recorded it on video. (You can find a link in the back of this book.)

But then I thought afterward that everyone in the church could have done what I did, but none of them did it. Many saw the woman with the crutches; all had the power of the Holy Spirit in them, but none did it.

Why?

Maybe because they did not understand the power of His resurrection?

They did not understand what Jesus did for us and what we have in Him. There is so much more to the resurrection than we often think.

If I asked, "What is the cross to you? And what happened when Jesus died on the cross? And what will happen when He returns?" What would you say?

Most people think that Jesus died on the cross. Therefore, we can experience forgiveness for our sins and get a new life because when He died, the veil in the temple that keeps us from the presence of God was torn in two, and now we can enter into Holy of Holies through a new and living veil, which is His body.

Yes, that is beautiful. And Jesus dying on that cross is an extraordinary moment in our history. But as unique as it is, you must understand that Jesus' death on the cross was not enough. Paul, in I Corinthians 15:14, said it so clearly. He said that if Christ had not risen, our preaching would be useless, and so would our faith. And if Christ has not risen, we are still in our sins, and those who had died in Christ will then be lost. And that is the truth and something we need to remember. If Christ had not risen from the dead, then His death on the cross was not enough. Then, we would all still be in our sins, according to what Paul says.

All through the book of Acts, we see something exciting: when they preached, it was about Christ's resurrection, not the death of Christ. When Governor Festus explained to King Agrippa why Paul was in jail, he said that it was a matter of a person who was dead, but who Paul says was alive (see Acts 25:19). It was always about the risen Jesus and not the death of Jesus or Jesus on the cross. Jesus is truly alive; therefore, we can fellowship with Him.

The early church preached the resurrection of Christ, but it was not a Resurrection Sunday message but an everyday, year-round message. We also need to know that Jesus could not have risen if He had not first been buried. When we are baptized, we are baptized into His death so that we may rise up to a new life just as Christ is risen.

In Romans 6, we see it all; we understand Christ's death, burial, and resurrection in the Gospel. When we read that chapter, the death, burial and resurrection of Christ, along with new life, comes to mind.

> *"What shall we say, then? Shall we go on sinning so that grace may increase? By no means! We are those who have died of sin; how can we live in it any longer? Or don't you know that all of us baptized into Christ Jesus were baptized into his death? We were, therefore, buried with him through baptism into death so that, just as Christ was raised from the dead through the glory of the Father, we too may live a new life. If we have been united with him in a death like his, we will also be combined with him in a resurrection like his. For if we have been united with him in a death like his, we will certainly also be united with him in a resurrection like his. For we know that our old self was crucified with him so that the body ruled by sin might be done away with, that we should no longer be slaves to sin."* (Romans 6:1-6 NIV)

But it also does not stop with Christ's resurrection, which has been eye-opening. It's much clearer now that it doesn't end with the resurrection but with the second coming. It is with His second coming that all begins in a new and fantastic way. After Jesus was raised, He went to heaven, from where He will come back a second time to bring salvation. Then and only then is it all complete. And this is the part I have seen that many people are missing or have misunderstood; it's a part of the Gospel that I have been missing or misunderstood.

That Jesus rose from the dead was for everyone the proof that He is the one God has called to judge the world. And that will happen when He comes back the second time. Let's read Acts 17:30-32. Here, we read that it was not about the cross and that Jesus died, but the resurrection, that He lived—that was the truth for all of them. It convinced the early disciples, and the people at that time, that He was the one.

> "'In the past God overlooked such ignorance, but now he commands all people everywhere to repent. For he has set a day when he will judge the world with justice by the man he has appointed. He has given proof of this to everyone by raising him from the dead.' When they heard about the resurrection of the dead, some of them sneered, but others said, 'We want to hear you again on this subject.'" (Act 17:30-32 NIV)

In the book of Hebrews, it says that Jesus came the first time to bear our sins, but when He appears again a second time, it is not for sin, but to bring salvation to us that awaits Him and to judge the world.

> "Just as people are destined to die once, and after that to face judgment, so Christ was sacrificed once to take away the sins of many; and he will appear a second time, not to bear sin, but to bring salvation to those who are waiting for Him." (Hebrews 9:27-28 NIV)

To bring salvation to who? Those who are waiting for Him.

Are you waiting for Him? Are you waiting for that day He will bring salvation to us?

When you see this and get this into focus, you will see that this is all over Scripture.

I have missed this for a long time. I knew that Jesus would return once again, but it was not really part of my life, decisions, longing, preaching, and what I was waiting for. But now I see it; it is my life, my longing, what I preach, and what I live for and wait for. Yes, it is what I am preparing for—for that day when He returns.

Let me move on to teaching about His second coming, which includes some examples from the Bible we often misunderstand. We start with John the Baptist talking about the baptism of the Holy Spirit and fire.

"'I baptize you with water for repentance. But after me comes one who is more powerful than I, whose sandals I am not worthy to carry. He will baptize you with the Holy Spirit and fire."' (Matthew 3:11 NIV)

Sadly, many people in the church have misunderstood these important verses and what John was saying. In the gospels, the authors talk about this baptism in Matthew 3, Mark 1, Luke 3, and John 3. But if you look at all the gospels together and compare, you'll find something interesting: there are two times John the Baptist said that Jesus would baptize with water and fire, and then there are two times where he said that Jesus would baptize in the Holy Spirit, but where there is no talk about fire.

Why is that? Why does he leave out the fire in two of the gospels? He also talks about judgment in those two places where he said fire. But he does not talk about the judgment in those two places where he leaves out the fire. So, in Matthew and Luke, where he talks about the baptism with the Holy Spirit and fire, he's talking about the judgment fire. If you read the verse before and after what we just read, it becomes clear what the fire is:

"'The ax is already at the root of the trees, and every tree that does not produce good fruit will be cut down and thrown into the fire. I baptize you with water for repentance. But after me comes one who is more powerful than I, whose sandals I am not worthy to carry. He will baptize you with the Holy Spirit and fire. His winnowing fork is in his hand, and he will clear his

threshing floor, gathering his wheat into the barn and burning up the chaff with unquenchable fire.'" (Matthew 3:10-12 NIV)

The Bible is talking about two different baptisms and two different times. The first time Jesus came, He came to baptize with the Holy Spirit, but the second time, He will come to baptize with fire. And that will happen to those who did not receive the first baptism.

Many have misunderstood the fire here because, in Acts 2:3 (NIV), the Holy Spirit appears like "tongues of fire." But this is not the fire John the Baptist talked about in the gospels. In Acts 2, we also read it was not real fire. But it was like "tongues of fire." It was like fire, but it was not real fire.

But John said Jesus would baptize with unquenching fire and that fire is a real fire that would burn everything up on that day. So, Acts 2 is not the same as the baptism in fire John talks about at the beginning of the gospels. Acts 2 says it was like fire. It is similar to the language in the gospels where it says the Holy Spirit came down as a dove, but it doesn't mean that the Holy Spirit is a dove. No, it was just as a dove the Spirit came down, like in Acts 2, where it was fire. So, the tongues were not fire and that is not what John is talking about in the four gospels.

So, at Jesus' first coming, He came as a savior to die on the cross and to give us who believe in Him the Holy Spirit. But the next time is to bring salvation to those that await Him and to judge the rest in an unquenching fire.

Another thing that has opened my eyes to understanding many things in the Bible is the timeline. Let's consider the word "and" in "the Holy Spirit and fire" (Matthew 3:11 NIV). When we read the word "and" here, there is a gap of two thousand years between the words before the "and" and after it. Even if it is in the same line, it doesn't mean it is at the same time, and this is important to understand.

This is not the only place in the Bible where we see that. Several times in one verse or line, there is a big gap in time. In Luke 4, after Jesus received the Holy Spirit and went to the desert, where He was tempted, He came out of the desert in the power of the Holy Spirit.

He went to the synagogue in His hometown, and there He stood up, and started to read from Isaiah 61.

> "He went to Nazareth, where he had been brought up, and on the Sabbath day he went into the synagogue, as was his custom. He stood up to read, and the scroll of the prophet Isaiah was handed to him. Unrolling it, he found the place where it is written:
> 'The Spirit of the Lord is on me,
> because he has anointed me
> to proclaim good news to the poor.
> He has sent me to proclaim freedom for the prisoners
> and recovery of sight for the blind,
> to set the oppressed free,
> to proclaim the year of the Lord's favor.'
> "Then he rolled up the scroll, gave it back to the attendant and sat down. The eyes of everyone in the synagogue were fastened on him. He began by saying to them, 'Today this scripture is fulfilled in your hearing.'
> "All spoke well of him and were amazed at the gracious words that came from his lips. 'Isn't this Joseph's son?' they asked." (Luke 4:16-22 NIV)

Now when Jesus said, "Today, this scripture is fulfilled," and sat down, everyone was amazed because He stopped in the middle of the verse. He did not complete the sentence; He just stopped in the middle and sat down. Why? Because only this part was fulfilled. Going to Isaiah 61, we can read what He left out:

> "...to proclaim the year of the Lord's favor and the day of vengeance of our God." (Isaiah 61:2 NIV)

In this verse, we see that there is not only a year of the Lord but also a day of vengeance of our God. He left the last part out. Why? Again, we are also here seeing a gap of two thousand years. So, the first part

Jesus read is fulfilled as He said, "Today this scripture is fulfilled," but the vengeance of our God will be fulfilled at His second coming—a day of our God when Jesus will come back and judge the nations, this time with fire.

A third example is found in Acts 2. The apostles had just received the baptism of the Holy Spirit, and Peter stood up and quoted a segment from the book of the prophet Joel. But what is interesting here is that there is also a gap between the verses Peter quotes—a gap of until now two thousand years. The first verses happened at Christ's first coming when He was baptized with the Holy Spirit and has since baptized us with the same Holy Spirit, but verses 19 and 20 still need to be fulfilled; that will happen at the second coming.

> *"In the last days, God says,*
> *I will pour out my Spirit on all people.*
> *Your sons and daughters will prophesy,*
> *your young men will see visions,*
> *your old men will dream dreams.*
> *Even on my servants, both men and women,*
> *I will pour out my Spirit in those days,*
> *and they will prophesy."* (Acts 2:17-18 NIV)

Pentecost began to fulfill these verses when God poured out His Spirit—and it is still being fulfilled today. But the next verse is something we have not seen yet. This has to do with the end of this age and the second coming of Jesus.

> *"I will show wonders in the heavens above and signs on the*
> *earth below, blood and fire and billows of smoke. The sun will*
> *be turned to darkness and the moon to blood before the coming*
> *of the great and glorious day of the Lord."* (Acts 2:19-20 NIV)

Many go wrong here because we don't understand how there is often a big gap in the middle of a text. What is also interesting here is that he quoted Joel wrong, or he, by purpose, quoted it differently from what Joel said.

When Peter was preaching this, he said it would be a "great and glorious day of the Lord," but Joel did not say that. He did not say it was going to be a "great and glorious day" but that it was going to be a "great and dreadful day" of the Lord.

"The sun will be turned to darkness and the moon to blood before the coming of the great and dreadful day of the Lord." (Joel 2:31 NIV)

But what is it? Will it be a glorious day, or will it be a dreadful one? That depends on who you are—if you have received the Holy Spirit as the guarantee of your salvation, or not, if you are waiting and have been preparing for His coming, or not. This is what we see all over Scripture. In the Bible, they did not run the race ahead of them, looking backward to the cross, but they were running their race looking forward to the day of salvation, the day of the Lord.

They did not endure suffering looking backward to the cross, but they endured suffering looking forward to the reward when Jesus returned. Salvation in the Bible is not just a one-time thing that happened many years ago; it's throughout the Bible.

No, salvation in the Bible is something we are working out. We are not working for our salvation, which is essential to understand. No one can earn their salvation. That is all because of Christ and what He did. But now we have received the justification in Him, we are working out our salvation, and we are looking forward to that day so we will be ready and not ashamed, as the Bible says.

"Therefore, my beloved, as you have always obeyed, not as in my presence only, but now much more in my absence, work out your own salvation with fear and trembling." (Philippians 2:12 NKJV)

We are born again with a seed of God, the Holy Spirit, the Word of God, and Christ in us. When we receive that seed in our hearts, we need to let it grow by putting off the old life and putting on the new life. That is also called sanctification, and it is almost as big a part of salvation as the first step, justification. But sadly, most only focus on the first step, justification.

As justified children of God, we let the Holy Spirit work in us as we are being sanctified so we can be glorified one day. That is when we will receive our new heavenly bodies, as we read here in 1 John:

"Beloved, now are we the sons of God, and it doth not yet appear what we shall be: but we know that, when he shall appear, we shall be like him; for we shall see him as he is." (1 John 3:2 KJV)

But then John continues in the following verse:

"And every man that hath this hope in him purifieth himself, even as he is pure." (1 John 3:2-3 KJV)

Everyone has hope for the future, and they have purified themselves. They work out their salvation, letting God transform them.

Salvation in the Bible has always been written in past, present, and future tense.

Keep this in mind when you read the following passage from 1 Peter:

"Blessed be the God and Father of our Lord Jesus Christ, which according to his abundant mercy hath begotten us again unto a lively hope by the Resurrection of Jesus Christ from the dead, to an inheritance incorruptible, and undefiled, and that fadeth not away, reserved in heaven for you, who are kept by the power of God through faith unto salvation ready to be revealed in the last time. Wherein ye greatly rejoice, though now for a season, if need be, ye are in heaviness through manifold temptations: That the trial of your faith, being much more precious than of gold that perisheth, though it be tried with fire, might be found unto

praise and honour and glory at the appearing of Jesus Christ."
(1 Peter 1:3-7 KJV)

We are born into a living hope. We are born again into an inheritance kept in heaven until the coming of our salvation (in the future). So, we see it's into a living hope, that's Christ, into an inheritance that God gave to our father Abraham until our salvation comes. Here, we see the past, present, and future tense all over the Bible.

But right now, in this present age, our faith is being tested and tried so that when Christ is revealed, it will result in praise, glory, and honor.

The Bible teaches this, and the more I understood this, the more freedom came to me.

I understand my suffering here is nothing compared to the glory that will later be revealed when Jesus appears.

My hope and freedom increased as I understood this and started looking forward to all of this.

How can we rejoice when we experience hard times and testing? We can rejoice because we know it's all part of working out our salvation, and we know that it's a part of God blessing us because through all of it we will receive a great reward in heaven.

When I share a few verses with you here, notice the word "know." It is because we "know" it is like this. But if we don't "know," we will not be victorious in it all like we read here, but we will give up on the way.

> *"Not only so, but we also glory in our sufferings, because we know that suffering produces perseverance; perseverance, character; and character, hope." (Romans 5:3-4 NIV)*

> *"Consider it pure joy, my brothers and sisters, whenever you face trials of many kinds, because you know that the testing of your faith produces perseverance. Let perseverance finish its work so that you may be mature and complete, not lacking anything."*
> (James 1:2-4 NIV)

"Whatever you do, work at it with all your heart, as working for the Lord, not for human masters, since you know that you will receive an inheritance from the Lord as a reward. It is the Lord Christ you are serving." (Colossians 3:23-24 NIV)

It is by knowing this that there is freedom. Knowing all these things, you can rejoice amid suffering and testing.

If you want to know more about what is waiting for us one day, you need to read the last chapters of the Bible. Here's a sample:

"And God shall wipe away all tears from their eyes; and there shall be no more death, neither sorrow, nor crying, neither shall there be any more pain: for the former things are passed away." (Revelation 21:4 KJV)

One day, this pain I am in will be gone. One day, it will all be good. Even now, I suffer so that my life may result in praise, glory, and honor when Jesus Christ is revealed.

It is truly unique. I suddenly understood it in a way I had never done before, which brought a longing in me as I'd never had before. And I could rejoice even though I'm now sitting here in my cell, and it's tough. Why? Because something very good is waiting, and I know it will all be over one day. No more suffering, no more pain. Yes, no more jail, curse, death, and I will be free like never before.

The cross of Jesus is not only about His death, burial and resurrection, and somehow disappearing afterward. No, after He rose again, He went to heaven to prepare a place for us, and soon, He will come back the second time to bring salvation to those waiting for Him.

This is so beautiful when you see it all. Let's not stop with the death on the cross or even the resurrection; let's be ready when He appears a second time to bring us salvation, the glorification of our bodies.

In the next chapter, I will share more about this freedom—a freedom I did not expect to experience, not in here.

Chapter Twenty
Freedom Behind Bars

What God was showing me in His Word burns in me. The Word has deeply impacted my life and how in all this I have experienced freedom—the same freedom I believe will come to everyone as this is the truth for all of us.

When I got detained, I tried to update all of you out there and keep you informed about what was happening. It was a challenge; I had a hard time with it all. Looking back at the early updates, I realized they were a desperate cry for help. I was desperate for someone out there to listen to me and do something to get me out of this place.

I hoped every time I did a new update that it would reach someone who would hear my cry for help and could do something about it. I also hoped my lawyers would be able to do something. But as I learned more, and as the truth set me free, I saw that only God could get me out. I needed to put my hope in Him, even though He could use people. But God was in control of it all.

After a few weeks, a prophetic word came to me and I wrote it down and often read it: "No judge can keep me in, and no lawyer can get me out unless God allows it." I wrote that down in big letters on paper. God is truly in control, and it is all about His will being done and what is happening with me is part of God's plan and His Kingdom.

It took time, but the truth of it came all the way down into my heart. It became truth for me, and it set me free. So, the last update I did, which I actually called "Freedom Behind Bars," was not about a cool title, but how I felt.

I even wanted to call this book "Freedom Behind Bars," but then I found out that there are other books by that title. So, I asked God what title I should give the book. I soon realized that I should give it the title of my days here. If that will be 330 Days or 365 Days, I still don't know. God knows.

As this word brought freedom to me, I had moments when I just started praising God and thanking Him from the depths of my heart for sending me here. It was special to experience that. It was so very different from the beginning. I would never have imagined that I would come to that point. I remember how terrifying it all was in the beginning and how depressing it all felt to me.

Months later, I experienced that freedom; how unimagined it was that I would experience this. One day, I was sitting on my bed praying and thinking over all this, and suddenly, I just burst out in praise and began to worship God for doing this. Thank You for letting me come to this place and for what You've shown me. After this moment, I knew I would never read Acts 16 with Paul and Silas worshipping God in chains the same way again. It was like I had just been there with them— not in the same jail but in the same place of freedom and knowing God is in control no matter what happens.

> *"About midnight, Paul and Silas were praying and singing hymns to God, and the other prisoners were listening to them."* (Acts 16:25 NIV)

I was set free even though I was still locked up. And I saw that had I gotten out much earlier, I would have been full of fear and anxiety; I would have come out and spread that fear and anxiety to every one of you out there.

"Be careful! Be careful! Everyone, this is terrifying; don't do anything that could make you go to a place like this. You have to be careful what you're doing! God will leave you there for yourself. What we have heard of testimonies from jail, how God was with people is all a lie, or He was not with me."

I would have said that; I would have spread fear to everyone out there. I would have been a tool in the hands of the enemy to frighten people rather than a tool in the hands of God, setting people free. I would have done so much damage in the kingdom and given people the idea that God leaves us behind bars and that we cannot trust Him.

It was the place I was in at that time. I wanted nothing more than to come out; I was desperate; I did not understand why God allowed this to happen; I did not understand why there were thousands of people praying for my release, and still, it seemed like God did not answer. Why did God not answer and set me free?

Now I see why the author of The Heavenly Man, Brother Yun, said what he said about suffering:

> "When a child of God suffers, you must understand it is only because the Lord has allowed it. He has not forgotten you! I don't advise people to pray for their release unless the Lord reveals we should pray this way. Before a chicken is hatched, it must be kept in the warm protection of the shell for twenty-one days. If you take the chick out of that environment one day too early, it will die. Similarly, ducks must remain confined in their shell for twenty-eight days before being hatched. It will die if you take a duck out on the twenty-seventh day."

I fully agree with this statement. In the book of Acts, Herod had James, the brother of John, put to death with the sword, and he had Peter arrested—all while the church prayed.

> *"He (Herod) had James, the brother of John, put to death with the sword. When he saw that this met with approval among the*

Jews, he proceeded to seize Peter also. This happened during the Festival of Unleavened Bread. After arresting him, he put him in prison, handing him over to be guarded by four squads of four soldiers each. Herod intended to bring him out for public trial after the Passover. So Peter was kept in prison, but the church was earnestly praying to God for him." (Acts 12:2-5 NIV)

Just before Peter was put in jail, James was killed, and it pleased the Jews as we read here. So, King Herod had Peter arrested too. He attempted to do the same with Peter as with James.

Peter was put in jail, and the *"church was earnestly praying to God for him"* (Acts 12:5 NIV). If you read on, you can see how God answered their prayers and set Peter free. And we love stories like that.

"Suddenly an angel of the Lord appeared and a light shone in the cell. He struck Peter on the side and woke him up. 'Quick, get up!' he said, and the chains fell off Peter's wrists. Then the angel said to him, 'Put on your clothes and sandals.' And Peter did so. 'Wrap your cloak around you and follow me,' the angel told him. Peter followed him out of the prison, but he had no idea that what the angel was doing was really happening; he thought he was seeing a vision. They passed the first and second guards and came to the iron gate leading to the city. It opened for them by itself, and they went through it. When they had walked the length of one street, suddenly the angel left him." (Acts 12:7-10 NIV)

If not for God's intervention, Peter would probably have died the same way as James did. But it was not time for Peter to die—not yet at least. Therefore, God set Peter free. It was all part of God's plan.

But in Acts 24, you can read about how Paul was in jail, and God did not set him free there. No angel came to rescue Paul, as we saw with Peter. Paul was left there for over two years. We can then ask why God set Peter free and not Paul?

The answer to that excellent question is that God knows what He is doing. God always has a reason, even if we often don't see it. God had a plan for it.

But the story is different with Paul. God had a plan with Paul: to get him to Rome and keep him in prison. Like Joseph in Genesis, he needed to be thrown into the pit first by his brothers and then later ended up in the Egyptian jail. No matter how unfair it seemed then, we know it was all part of God fulfilling His plan with Joseph.

In Rome, Paul was also under house arrest for two years. No angel came to rescue him there. But I want to truly thank God for that. If God had rescued Paul from jail, we would not have the letters Ephesians, Philippians, Colossians, and Philemon, also called the Prison Epistles. It was better for us and God's Kingdom that Paul remained in jail and wrote those letters. It was better for all of us and God's Kingdom that He set Peter free. So, what happens is sometimes different, but it is all for the Kingdom.

We must understand why God doesn't always answer the same way. But remember this: if God had left Peter in jail, he probably would have died, and God was not finished with him yet. And if God had taken Paul out the same way as He did with Peter, Paul would not have come to Rome, and we would not have the letters he later wrote there under house arrest. God was not finished with Paul yet, and therefore, He did what He did.

We see God's hand in all the stories, even if they look different. And if God has not set me free yet it's because God has a plan in mind. Therefore, it is important that we are led by the Spirit in how we pray. We should ask God: "Shall we pray for his release now or for You to guide and help him in this season?"

There is a lot we all can learn from this.

I want to use this opportunity to talk about the importance of forgiveness and not becoming bitter against God. I have no unforgiveness against those who have spread lies about me, even those that had a big hand in me being locked up here. And I am in no way bitter against God for allowing this. I never have been.

Why should I have anything against those people when they're helping fulfill God's will for my life? God used Joseph's brothers to throw Joseph into the pit. They wanted to destroy him, but God did not allow that because it was not Joseph's time yet. God had another plan for him. Think about this: Joseph's brothers threw him into the pit to make sure God did not fulfill the "silly" dreams Joseph had. But God allowed them to do it so those dreams would be fulfilled. God understands how to turn things around for our good. If we look at Jesus' life, we can learn a lot about this. There, we see how Judas was necessary in Jesus' life to fulfill God's plan for Jesus to go to the cross.

I believe Jesus could have done without John, James, and Peter, but he had to have Judas. Judas was the only one of Jesus' disciples who was necessary for Him to fulfill the call God had for Him. It's the same for us. We all need a Judas in our lives to fulfill God's call. And why become bitter against God when He does it for our best? The current suffering we experience is nothing compared to the glory that one day we will receive.

If you can understand these truths, you will never have anything against anyone again and decide not to become bitter against God, no matter what.

You can forgive everyone from your heart, knowing everything works for good for those God has called, and He knows what He is doing. So, there is a great lesson here, and it's essential to see things through God's eyes to understand the bigger picture and His plans. This was also what He communicated to me in the prophecy I received. And over time, I saw it being fulfilled.

As time went on, I saw that God was in control and that this current suffering is something God has allowed as a tool to bless us and help us become more like Jesus. This, together with focusing on eternity, His kingdom, and the inheritance that was waiting for me, brought so much freedom and peace to my life.

Yes, I still long to leave, but at the same time, I feel peace knowing that God's in control. Initially, I often thought about when and how He would do it.

"God, now is a good time for me to come out; I hope you can see that."

Like when it was my birthday, I thought this was a good time for God to get me out. I prayed a lot for it and tried to convince God how important it was for me to be out for my birthday, but it did not happen. "God, don't you like birthdays?" I asked. Then it was our wedding anniversary! "Yes, God, it will soon be our anniversary! That is the right time for me to come out. Why? The Bible says that God has joined my wife and I together and let no one separate us (Matthew 19:6 NIV)."

Yes, these words may have been taken out of context to be used like this, but I was looking for everything I could, and why not?

I thought He'd get me out by our wedding anniversary, October 19th, but no. "God, don't you like our anniversary?" I asked.

Then, maybe it would be my daughter's 18th birthday, Christmas, or New Year.

But God didn't see things the way I saw them. Though it seemed like He did not care or listen to me every time I put a date on it, He was there, in control, and knew what was best because He had a plan.

God said that it would be in His timing and way in the beginning, but it took time for me to really receive it, as it hurt so much.

"To try and get yourself out before God's purpose is fulfilled would actually be working against Him, and it wouldn't work anyhow," the prophetic word said. "Save yourself the heartache. Just trust Him with His plan and the big picture He is working to accomplish. Don't take thought for how or when you will get out. TRUST HIM THAT HE WILL GET YOU OUT."

It is written here in black and white, but it's still difficult. But as time went on, it all became the truth for me. The prophetic word and the dream I received have been an enormous blessing for us. They have helped me a lot, and they will always be a part of my life, as I know they are from God.

But I also want to add that I got many other "prophetic" words and dreams from people while I was here. Sadly, so many people got it wrong. They think they heard from God but did not. It was their flesh and their own thoughts.

Sometimes, it was directly from the enemy, and there were times I needed to say like Jesus said to Peter: "Get behind me, Satan! You are a stumbling block to me; you do not have in mind the concerns of God, but merely human concerns" (Mathew 16:23 NIV).

Initially, I often got words like, "You will come out in two weeks," or "I got a dream that you would be out at the end of this month," or "I see you being home for Christmas," or something like that.

It created a lot of hope for us, but a hope that wasn't real and didn't last because when it did not happen, it hurt a great deal, but I'm not saying that to you out there to stop hearing from God and giving prophetic words, as the Bible says we should not despise prophecy (see 1Thessalonians 5:20), but eagerly desire to prophesy (see 1 Corinthians 14:1).

But the Bible also talks about the importance of discerning when it is from God or not and to test every spirit (see 1 John 4:1).

We need to hear from God; prophecy is a beautiful gift to the church. But we need to be better listeners as to when it is God's actual words to us and test what is said. Does the prophetic word align with the Word of God? I see how this can be very dangerous because it is so easy to be led astray when people are desperate for an encouraging word, and like Jesus needed to rebuke Peter, we all must be alert to the enemy's schemes.

For instance, a woman who has been to our training school has been an enormous blessing. She has sent me letters in jail, which has been a huge blessing. I was encouraged whenever I read her letters and got something out of them.

Every time I got a letter from her, I got excited because there was so much wisdom and hope in them. But one day, I was down, hoping for a word from God or help because it was hard, and then I saw a letter from her. Yes! Please, God, I need a word from you. I was excited, but the word was the opposite of what I needed this time. She wrote something against everything God had been showing me, which hit me hard.

After reading it, I spent quite a bit of time trying not to get discouraged and give up. It's not that it was all wrong. But some words were just not from God, or how she interpreted them was wrong.

God has given us the Holy Spirit to help guide us, and I knew by the Spirit right away that this was an attack to discourage me and tempt me to give up. I also felt this way because the other words God had spoken to me said the opposite. Those words I knew were from God. So, like Jesus, I needed to say, *"Get behind me, Satan! You are a stumbling block to me"* (Matthew 16:23 NIV).

Our enemy wants to hit us in every area and persuade us to give up. Yes, we should not despise prophecies, as the Apostle Paul says. But we should be alert and test them. Then, hold on to what is good.

> *"Do not quench the Spirit. Do not treat prophecies with contempt but test them all; hold on to what is good, reject every kind of evil."* (1 Thessalonians 5:19-20 NIV)

I still appreciate the women who gave me the word of the Lord. God used her, and I will still listen to her another time, even if this one time I needed to rebuke her.

We all need to be alert, not just those who receive prophetic words but also those who give them. Know that your words can bring comfort and help from the Lord, but the enemy can also use them to do the opposite. So don't be too fast to give words until you know it is from God, and ask for wisdom on how and when to say what needs to be said.

I want to say that I came to that point, as I said, that I experienced freedom, and that is a freedom God has for all of us, no matter if you are out there without bars or inside here behind bars. You can be out there and still be bound, or you can be in here and be free. I pray that God will use this book to set you free no matter where you read it.

But now it is time to end this chapter. It is also time for me to take an afternoon nap. We only get a few hours of sleep at night, as the lights first turn off at 12.30 a.m. or sometimes even at 1 a.m. and wake us up at 4.30 a.m. Therefore, we are often tired, and many try to sleep during the day.

I try to get thirty to forty minutes of sleep here and there during the day. Now I have a tablet on which I can listen to worship, and I love it. I lie down on my back and listen to and worship Jesus in my heart until I fall asleep. This is one of the highlights of my life here right now.

Chapter Twenty-One
Well Done

I have found I love being able to write from my small cell, now my home. Yes, it feels like my home. When I need to go to another place, for example, like the doctor for a checkup, it feels so nice to come back "home" again to my cell.

I don't have a lot of fellowship these days. Most of the men I became friends with are gone, sent away, and I'm spending most of my time alone writing this book.

I still have to get my food, change my clothes, and be ready when the guards come four times per day and count us.

I also still sleep every afternoon as I otherwise have difficulty keeping awake until they count us for the last time and lock us down overnight at 12:30 a.m. to 1 a.m.

But outside of this, I am alone with God, reading my Bible, and now having fellowship with you, the reader. I know this is still just me writing on paper and you are not here. But I know one day you out there will sit with this in your hand and read it. And because I know that, in some ways, it feels almost like you are here with me and I don't feel so alone. So, thank you for reading this. I pray that this will be a blessing to you, as it has been for me.

This chapter is an exciting one to write. I have some very special and personal details to share, and I believe one day, I will stand on a platform, or in churches, sharing this message with many people. This is unique, and God will use this to teach us something very important.

I hope you are ready; here we go.

A lot of Christians talk about the second coming of Jesus and long for His appearance. I was one of them. But being here has not only helped me understand the theology behind the second coming, but it has also given me so much more. I now not only understand it with my mind, but I feel it; I long for it.

I dream about it in a way that I had not before I came here. I'm not sure I could experience it the same out there. At least, not the way it was for me here. There is something that suffering and hardship can do: it helps us see things in a different light and get the right focus.

It's difficult to understand things when life is good, and the days just move on. When life is good, we almost feel immortal. We don't stop and really think about life. But when crises happen, suddenly, everything has a unique value, our whole focus changes, and we tend to understand truth in a much deeper and more profound way.

Let me explain with an example I know I will share again. A song, which I really love, used to play often on Christian radio stations before I was detained. I ended up downloading it on my phone so I could listen to it again and again. The name of the song is "Well Done" from the group The Afters. Part of the lyrics go like this:

"What will it be like when my pain is gone.
And all the worries of this world just fade away?
What will it be like when You call my name.
And that moment when I see You face to face?
I'm waiting my whole life to hear You say:
Well done, well done. My good and faithful one
Welcome to the place where you belong.
Well done, well done. My beloved child.
You have run the race and now you're home.

Welcome to the place where you belong"

What a beautiful song. I truly live to hear Jesus say to me: "Well done, well done. My good and faithful one."

Try to imagine that day, when we see Jesus, face to face.

Try to imagine that day when He calls our name, and we are finally home.

As this song says, we should all live for that day, to hear Him to say, "Well done."

Being here has made everything they sing more real to me. I believe, see, and feel it now even more. The words here are real to me. I can say it from my heart in a new way, and I can see it in front of me like I have never been able to do before. Being locked up here has brought me to a place I have never been before. I've lost my freedom, and I still don't know what will happen to me. I know something is off: I have not done what they have accused me of, and because of the lies, I have no idea how this will end.

From a human perspective, they took me away from my family and everything I love. The uncertainty and loss have changed me. It has been harder than anything I have ever experienced, and I have needed to die to myself again and again in a deep way. But in all of that, it has also created a longing in me, a longing I never felt before. A longing for this to be over, a longing to be with my wife, to be with my girls, to go home where I belong.

When I could finally get a tablet in which I could hear some music instead of all the noise all the time, I bought different songs I know very well, including the song, "Well Done." When I found it and was ready to listen, I was so excited. I remembered how I loved this song, but when I listened to it, it brought a lot of emotions up in me that were not there before. I could not listen to it in the beginning because of all the emotions and thoughts that were going through my head. It brought up deep pain in me because a lot of memories were of being free, driving in my car, listening to this and other songs.

Then, when I heard the words in the song, like: "What will it be like, when You call my name?" I did not think of Jesus calling my name, but I imagined that day when I heard the officer in here call my name and say, "Torben, pack your things, you are going home."

And when I heard the words in the song, "When I see you face to face," it was not Jesus' face I was thinking of anymore; it was my wife, Lene—to see my wife face to face. I so longed for that. And it was all those thoughts that rose up in me instead.

And then the words: "My pain is gone and I'm finally home." When I heard those words, I was not thinking of the New Heaven and the New Earth, but I was thinking of my home in California. I imagined how I would step through that front door to our home, the home we have rented, but I have not been in yet, to step inside the house and know I'm home, I'm home, and my pain is gone.

I so long to be free and to be with Lene again. Those thoughts, that longing, is always there. During the day when we wait for the food at the door in the Pod, there is sometimes a small crack at the window that is not covered by the curtain on the other side, so I can see people walking on the other side. One day I will not be here, looking through the crack and dreaming. Or when I was outside in the recreation area looking through the fourteen-foot-high fence around us with spiky barbed wire, or when I was alone in bed here in my cell, I was longing for my wife, longing for this to finally be over.

I have thought about that day when I will finally see my wife, Lene, and I can go to her and give her a big hug, and be with her and the girls, or my son, daughter in law and grandkids. To stand there and cry together with them, knowing that we are finally together again as a family and it's over. I am smiling and crying at the same time, just writing this to you.

All these emotions were in me, and still are, and when I heard that song for the first time, all of this came to me. And it broke me. So, I couldn't listen to it, because it brought all of this up in me instead of what the words were truly saying. I longed so much to see my wife and to be home. Not that I did not long to see my Lord Jesus's face and be home in heaven. I really want that. That is truly what I live for.

But you need to understand, somehow, to see my wife, Lene, was so much closer to me. I knew it was just in front of me, and I believed it could happen any moment.

Because this song made me think of her and all this instead of Jesus, it felt wrong, as I know it was not about Lene and being home in California. So, I didn't listen to the song for a long time. It was just too painful. I started a few times, but I couldn't finish the whole song. I took it off my playlist again.

Then I started to see what the Scripture was saying about the day of our Lord. The more I saw it in Scripture, the more I longed for that day, when our Lord will appear. As the longing to see my Lord Jesus face to face grew, my emotions started to shift.

When I read the words of Paul, Peter, James, and John, I saw the longing they had for that day. And I felt their words. I did not just understand it with my mind anymore, but I felt it deep within me. Woah! This is how they felt, lived, and showed us all how to live for that day, long for that day, in the same way, that I long to be free from here.

How I feel about leaving this place, seeing Lene, and finally being home, is how we all should feel about going home to be with Jesus. We will one day leave this world and finally be home, home where we belong and then, finally we will see our Lord face to face. God used this place to teach me how it should be in our lives as disciples of Christ. Yes, this understanding grew, the longing grew, and the more it grew, the less I saw Lene, and the more I saw Jesus.

I can now hear the song again, and have a deep longing finally to be home, where I truly belong, with my Father in heaven, and experience that day when I'm home and there is no more pain, as you read at the end of the book of Revelation. A longing to see Him face to face as the song was saying.

In Paul's letter to the Philippians, he mentioned that he was waiting for the verdict of the Imperial Court. He said that he rejoiced over the Gospel being preached, even though some were doing it with the wrong motives. And then he said this:

"Yes, and I will continue to rejoice, for I know that through your prayers and God's provision of the Spirit of Jesus Christ what has happened to me will turn out for my deliverance." (Philippians 1:19 NIV)

So here we read that Paul believed their prayers would deliver him. But when I read those words, it suddenly hit me. How would he be delivered? What was Paul thinking of here? Because Paul had two possible ways of being delivered. First, someone could release him from jail, and he could leave, thus gaining his freedom. But he could also be set free from the jail through a verdict and be killed, and that way finally leaving that place and being home where he belonged.

So, this verse doesn't make it clear what Paul was thinking. When we read on, you see that he had a deep longing to leave this place to be with God. In referring to leaving this place, he was talking about this life.

"I eagerly expect and hope that I will in no way be ashamed, but will have sufficient courage so that now as always Christ will be exalted in my body, whether by life or by death. For to me, to live is Christ and to die is gain. If I am to go on living in the body, this will mean fruitful labor for me. Yet what shall I choose? I do not know!" (Philippians 1:20-22 NIV)

Paul was not just talking about being delivered or set free from jail, but from this life. Why? Because he truly longed to be with Christ. Christ was his life, and he wanted to be here so others could experience Christ, but he also wanted to leave and be with Him.

"I am torn between the two: I desire to depart and be with Christ, which is better by far; but it is more necessary for you that I remain in the body." (Philippians 1:23-24 NIV)

As you read this verse, understand the person behind the verse. Paul's focus was on the longing he had, and the hard choice before him: to stay here or to die and go home where he wanted to be. Paul was torn between those two. But he ends up saying that he will remain here, for their progress and joy in the faith (see Philippians 1:25).

Paul was really living for the day he would finally be home, with Jesus, because he knew that was by far the best thing for him. But there was one thing that kept him here: that others would progress in their faith through Paul's works for the Kingdom.

Paul was not the only apostle that felt that way. The other apostles in the early church were all living for that day. And they were all torn.

Let me then ask you: Where do we see that in the churches today? I've heard people saying that they hope Jesus doesn't come back soon so they can get married, have kids or travel the world. Some have just bought a new house and therefore they are not interested in Christ coming soon.

How many people think like that? How many can say, like Paul, that they are torn between this life and the next, that they long to leave this place and be with Christ, but what keeps them here is that they could help bear fruit in other people's lives?

Paul didn't want to stay here because he longed for anything this world had to offer. It was not the house, money, or even family and friends that were drawing him to stay on earth. He wanted to stay here because other people would find Christ like he did.

Why are we in the state we are in? I think one answer is that our lives are too easy. Most of us who live in the Western world live very comfortable lives. We don't experience suffering or persecution and hardships like in other places, as Paul did. And therefore, somehow, we have fallen asleep.

Some years ago, I saw the movie Sheep Among Wolves, a story about an Iranian woman who had come to America to get away from the persecution in Iran. But after a short time living the American dream, she wanted to go back home to Iran, to her home where the persecution was happening. Why? Because she said it was easier to live close to Jesus there. She said, in America, there is a demonic lullaby playing, and it's so easy to fall asleep here.

I have seen this demonic lullaby, causing people to slowly fall asleep. What a powerful picture. But it's not limited to America—all the rich Western countries are under its spell. Sadly, we see most of the people have fallen asleep spiritually.

In many places around the world today where they are experiencing persecution, we see a dependence on Christ there that we don't see in other places the same way. They have a deep dependence on Jesus and an understanding that life cannot be lived without Him.

But in the good times, we all tend to become lukewarm. We sit in front of the television for hours; we spend time enjoying trivial things in life; the focus shifts to how we can get the best out of this life. We forget that this life is just *"a vapour, that appeareth for a little time, and then vanisheth away"* (James 4:14 KJV). And that *"the world and its desires pass away, but whoever does the will of God lives forever"* (1 John 2:17 NIV).

So, we should all have the same attitude as the Iranian woman. Not fearing persecution but fearing falling asleep.

This is the attitude Peter said we should have as far as suffering and trails:

> *"In all this you greatly rejoice, though now for a little while you may have had to suffer grief in all kinds of trials. These have come so that the proven genuineness of your faith—of greater worth than gold, which perishes even though refined by fire—may result in praise, glory and honor when Jesus Christ is revealed. Though you have not seen him, you love him; and even though you do not see him now, you believe in him and are filled with an inexpressible and glorious joy, for you are receiving the end result of your faith, the salvation of your souls."* (1 Peter 1:6-9 NIV)

If we look at the early church, persecution, suffering, and hardships were a regular part of their lives. For that reason, the early church loved the book of Revelation. Why? Because it brought them hope for relief, for change, that one day, this suffering and the pain would be over, and everything would change.

But the Western church, or those that lived a good life, often don't like that book the same way. They are living the good life now and don't want things to change. If people are enjoying life, they rarely want Jesus to come back, the same way others are longing for it. Not right now, at least, because they are too busy enjoying this life and there is so much they still need to do before Jesus comes back.

If we look at the Western church, we are often the one that is like the Laodicean church. We think we are rich and on fire for Jesus, and the ones truly trying to help the persecuted church with our riches. But we are the ones who are lukewarm, wretched, pitiful, poor, blind, and naked.

As we read about Jesus talking to the church in Laodicea in Revelation 3, remember that we might have all the enormous churches and we have a lot of money, something the persecuted church rarely has. But they have something we don't have. They understand something we cannot understand before we experience it through true persecution.

"To the angel of the church in Laodicea write: These are the words of the Amen, the faithful and true witness, the ruler of God's creation. I know your deeds, that you are neither cold nor hot. I wish you were either one or the other! So, because you are lukewarm—neither hot nor cold—I am about to spit you out of my mouth. You say, 'I am rich; I have acquired wealth and do not need a thing.' But you do not realize that you are wretched, pitiful, poor, blind and naked. I counsel you to buy from me gold refined in the fire, so you can become rich; and white clothes to wear, so you can cover your shameful nakedness; and salve to put on your eyes, so you can see." (Revelation 3:14-18 NIV)

There is good news for the Western church. Persecution is coming! I am the living proof of that. As God has shown me, it starts with a few and then it will come to the many. In the end, it will be all of us who confess Jesus as Lord.

But I am here to prepare you and give you hope. The last month has truly opened my eyes in so many ways. And it has brought me to God's Word to find hope. The more I understand about the Kingdom that will come, the more I have died to myself, and the freer I become.

There are many things that have been growing in me. Together with my suffering, I have come to a place where I can surrender to God, die to myself, so I can truly live by Him. And that is the goal for all of us.

But I also know that there is still work God needs to do in me before I am done here. I know when the time comes, I will be with the church, to strengthen the church for the difficult times we are all heading into. I believe we are heading into very difficult times, but it will also be a time when the Gospel of the Kingdom is going to be spread. We are going to see a reformation of the churches and freedom is going to come to many.

Let's not be afraid. Let's live for that day when we hear, "*Well done, good and faithful servant!*" (Matthew 24:23 NIV).

When we are finally home, where we belong, when our pain is gone, all the worries of this world will just fade away.

Yes, that day we will see Him face to face.

Amen!

Chapter Twenty-Two
Lene in Jail

While I have been here, what has happened around my wife Lene is very touching. She is a big part of my story, yet people forget about wives when they hear testimonies like mine. But Lene has suffered like I have and has been on a journey with God, who has also been dealing with her in so many things. We are one flesh and God's plan with this is not only God's plan for me, but God's plan for us.

As I write this chapter, today is a very special day, a day when she takes a big step in faith. Yes, at this moment writing this, she is truly stepping out on the water, and I therefore have my wife and my girls in my mind, especially right now.

Today is April 11th, 2023, but let's go back a few months. In September 2022, after being here for three months, we were informed that we could not renew the lease on our rented house, so Lene needed to find another house for us as a family. She found a new house forty minutes away. However, when they moved into the new house after Thanksgiving at the end of November 2022, I was still here. Therefore, Lene and the girls had to pack everything and move without me, which was very difficult for all of us. During their move from our house in Vista to Spring Valley in San Diego County many things happened

First, Lene was tired. It had already been a few long months, and then suddenly she needed to move and oversee all the things around that. Crazy attacks came her way. The toilet in the basement of the new house suddenly ran over. No one was using it. It just ran over, and sewage water flooded the basement. It destroyed the floor and the walls in the restroom. They needed a whole new restroom.

The next week, the plumber made a big hole in the garage to clean the pipes, but every time they thought they had fixed the plumbing, it went wrong again.

After they finally got the toilet to work, it was time to rebuild the bathroom. Over the next three weeks, workers came and went every day, putting extra stress on the family. On top of this, we had a problem with our car, and then the washing machine suddenly did not work.

Then our daughter Stephanie's computer overheated. The keyboard on the computer rose up in the middle and become very warm. It happened so fast they were afraid and threw the computer out of the house in case it exploded.

As this was going on, Lene had to go to the bank and pay some bills to the lawyer, and there was a problem with that. The bank had a problem with paying the bills and she needed to go to the bank several times before she found one that knew how to get it done. Something so easy suddenly became a big problem that stressed her deeply.

Moving, the restroom, car, washing machine, computer, bank and me being in jail—everything was on her. Suddenly, she just shut down. Her body could not take any more. It became too much. She had problems breathing; fear and anxiety arose because everything changed at once. She ended up going to a hospital emergency room.

And for Lene to go to the ER things must be very bad. I have known Lene for twenty-eight years, and she has never had to go to the ER like this before. She's not a person who goes to the hospital for a problem. She never went to the ER or hospital except to give birth to our children.

She was now in a place she had never been before.

She received a check-up at the ER, where the doctors examined her, and everything looked fine. But when she arrived home, things just grew worse and worse. She had problems with breathing, problems with air in the stomach, and improving it by burping, which led to problems sleeping because laying down was too painful.

Fear grabbed her, and in the end, she couldn't do anything about it. It was a very hard time. Some good friends helped by staying outside our house in their camper and helping as they could.

In my diary on the day she went to the ER, I wrote, "Today was the worst and hardest day since I got detained."

Out of those three hundred days I have been here, I can honestly write that this day was the worst of them all.

There were so many days when Lene cried. It's been hard for her not having me around. The pressure was all on her out there and she continues to need to hold it all together. She was strong until she couldn't be anymore, and everything shut down.

Until the ER trip, Lene and I had spoken a lot on the phone. We encouraged each other to stand firm in the faith. We shared about God's faithfulness and the testimonies we have seen through the years serving Him. Sometimes we spoke for hours a day if we could.

I realize now we spoke more while I was in here than we did when I was out there. In many ways, we have gotten much closer to each other than we have ever been before. When I was out there, I often needed to deal with so many things. But in here there was not so much other than this.

Out there, I rarely sat down and just spent time talking about life with her. Not the way I've been doing here, at least. Many things will truly change when I get out. I am in love. I was always in love with Lene, but it has become deeper this time. We have become closer than we have ever been before. We also did video calls for thirty minutes per day where we could see each other. I loved it. It gave me so much to see her, even if it was hard not to be with her.

Suddenly, it all stopped. No more video calls and no more long phone calls. It was just too much for her. We went from an hour or more per day to a few minutes. We might talk for five minutes here and there, if she was doing well that day. But she could not handle more. It was too much for her just to talk to me. Just thinking of it and writing this to you has stirred deep emotions. I missed her and it was so hard to see her like that. She was crying in a way I've never seen her cry before.

Suddenly, the weight of being in jail was on top of me once again. I felt so locked up and bound, and the amazing freedom in Christ I had experienced was all gone. I wanted to go and be there with her, but I could not. The longing to be there was like nothing I have ever experienced before. I am her husband. I am the father of our girls. It is my responsibility to be there for them. My family needed me more than ever before and here I was, locked up.

The day Lene went to the hospital, I did not know what was happening. I heard that she had gone, and I tried to call. When I got hold of them, I only had a few minutes. The access to our phones was about to be closed at 10:30 p.m. in Florida and that was 7:30 p.m. in California. Lene was still in the hospital, waiting to hear from the doctor. So, I had to say goodbye to my family, not knowing what would happen to her. Would she go home? Would they keep her in the hospital? What was going to happen? I had no choice but to wait until the next morning to call to hear what happened. It was truly one of the hardest nights since I've been here.

It was much easier when it was "just" me suffering in here than to see my family suffering out there. She is my wife; I'm her husband. These are my girls; I'm their father. It is my responsibility to be there for them. It's my job as a husband and father to be there for them all, but I was not. I really felt like a bad husband and a terrible father. I have disappointed them so much and it hurt me. I know they are proud of me, and God was in control, but the thought was still there.

I continued to pray; I truly did. I cried out to God from the deepest part of my soul, but I wanted to do more. So many thoughts went through my head.

Lene came home that same evening, but over the next few weeks, everything was about survival. We were truly in a desert again, but God gave us manna every day. He gave us manna, like He did with the Israelites in the desert, in the form of a word from Him of encouragement, a visit from somebody, or something that just kept us going that day.

Lene, however, felt like she was in a fight for her life, not in physical danger, but emotionally. I was concerned that she might lose hope or be permanently disappointed and never truly recover from this. We both were in a fight like never before. The pressure was so enormous. I even reached a point where I was ready to give up. It was the hardest battle we both had faced.

At one point, I put the number of our legal team into the phone, ready to call them to tell them to stop it all. I would do anything for it to end; no more fighting for my rights and for the truth. I was ready to abandon my asylum claim, agree to leave, and never return. I was willing to accept whatever they wanted, even if it was all lies. I was prepared to comply no matter what it meant if I could escape this place and be with my wife. They could send me to Mexico, to any other country. I didn't care where; I just wanted to be with my family. But I didn't make the call, knowing I couldn't simply give up and leave this place, even if I wanted to. That wasn't an option, and I understood that no matter what I tried, I was stuck there. I was genuinely desperate in a way I had never experienced before, and it was frightening to see myself in that state.

Then God began to reveal things to us about this fight we were in. We saw that God was using it all to transform and change Lene, like he has done with me. I saw major changes begin to happen in Lene.

There was also more God needed to do in me. God started to teach me about the importance of really trusting Him and letting go of it all—also Lene and the girls. That God was enough not only for me but also for them.

Jesus wanted me to love Him more than them. He wanted me to give them over to God and let go, trusting Him. Jesus said we cannot be worthy of Him if we love others more than Him. *"Anyone who loves their father or mother more than me is not worthy of me; anyone who loves their son or daughter more than me is not worthy of me"* (Matthew 10:37 NIV).

I saw that I had to lay Lene and the girls on the altar, and let His will be done, not mine. It was difficult to let go and trust that God was also enough for them. It's easier for me to go through suffering and know that He is enough for me, but it's much more difficult when it involves my family and wife.

When I finally let go and gave them over, the freedom came back to me again. I was free again. It's difficult to understand, but if you one day are in a place like this, you will know what I am talking about. Let go. Give it over. Surrender to God's will. Let go of all control and you will be free.

But Lene was still not doing well even though I saw God was working with her. She didn't have any energy, was full of stress and fear, pain in her body, and trouble breathing. She only went out driving two times in an entire month. One time with another person and the other time she drove alone. Both times involved driving just a few minutes away from our house in San Diego.

The time she drove alone was very special. She wanted to drive to a church that we work with, and even though it was only seven minutes from our house, this was incredibly hard for her. She wanted to drive there and just take a little time to pray at the church. But as she sat in the car ready to drive, she felt all the fear and anxiety coming over her.

A massive panic attack hit her! Her mouth dried up, and she felt almost paralyzed in her body. She could not drive. Ten minutes later, she was still there in the car.

I called her and we prayed together over the phone while she was under attack in her body and mind. I tried to speak the truth to her and help her through it as she took the big step to drive to the church.

She finally made it, and it was a significant victory for her—for both of us. She was so happy afterward, but also extremely tired. It exhausted her for the next few days.

Then one day a few days later, in the middle of all of this, God spoke to Lene. "Drive to Florida," He told her. "Drive to Florida to be close to Torben."

The message was powerful. Yet, it was also unthinkable, as she had only been out in the car two times in the last month and only for a few minutes each time. But now she felt she should drive the entire way from California to Florida. Across America. It is over two thousand miles and thirty-five hours' driving if you try to do it nonstop. It is not a seven-minute trip down the road, but a three-day trip.

When she told me the plan, I didn't like the idea. The idea of her and the girls taking a trip like that without me was nerve-racking. She could also not just call me when she wanted, so I did not like it at all. But she was so desperate to be free, for things to change, and she felt God had spoken to her.

Despite not liking it, I know my wife: if God speaks to her, no one, not I or anyone else, can stop her. We joined in prayer about it and sought God. We also knew she would feel more at home in Florida as we lived there before and knew more people that would be there for Lene and to help her. Lene prayed, "God, confirm to us if I should go back to Florida. I feel more at home there, and we know more people there. But I cannot do it if You are not with me. I need You to speak clearly also to Torben."

Very shortly afterwards, we received our answer. A good friend in Florida who knew nothing about what we felt God was speaking to us sent a prophetic word to us. For most people, this word will mean nothing, and for the woman that received the word, it was also strange. She struggled over the idea of sharing it as it made no sense to her. For us and in our situation, it was an explicit confirmation. As she prayed, she heard the following verse:

"Therefore this is what the LORD Almighty, the God of Israel, says: 'I will punish the king of Babylon and his land as I punished the king of Assyria. But I will bring Israel back to their own pasture, and they will graze on Carmel and Bashan; their

appetite will be satisfied on the hills of Ephraim and Gilead. In those days, at that time,' declares the LORD, 'search will be made for Israel's guilt, but there will be none, and for the sins of Judah, but none will be found, for I will forgive the remnant I spare.'" (Jeremiah 50:18-20 NIV)

What a word from God at the right time. God desired to bring my family back to Florida and clear my name, as they would witness my innocence amid the outrageous accusations. Lene's appetite will be satisfied, as she surrounds herself with friends and familiar places.

For us, this was the ultimate confirmation. It convinced me that God was in this and I did not need to fear for them to take this trip, because it was not our idea only, but God's.

Today as I write this here from my cell, my family and two good friends are on the way to Florida from our home in San Diego. Our friends, Dewayne and Tabitha, have been such a big blessing to us in this time, helping Lene. They agreed to drive my family to Florida and then fly back to California.

They will all soon be in New Mexico and it has been a good trip until now. If you knew what happened last month, the fight that has been going on, and see how Lene in faith is doing this, it is so very special.

God is working in her life. I will come back to Lene later in this book as many more things are happening in her heart and soul, and I'm convinced that when I am free, you will not only see a new version of me, but you will see a new version of my wife.

Every desert time has led to something new, like the time fifteen years ago that lead to the online Pioneer Training Schools (PTS) and out of that The Last Reformation was born and is still growing all over the world today. In the last three years while I have been in America, there have been Pioneer Training Schools in thirty nations all over the world. Holland, Spain, Germany, and all over Europe, Russia, Ukraine, Kazakhstan, and the countries there, as well as Canada, America and many other countries. And now the first schools are starting in Chile and Argentina.

This is a move of God, by God's hand. It's not dependent on me, but God has done something beautiful. Countless lives have been transformed worldwide, also through the movies. Much of this started in the hardest season of our lives. It was also in that season that Lene recorded her songs and we started to travel around the world.

But now we are here again. It is painful. It is hard to go through a desert period. But we believe that this time, there will also be a lot of fruit coming out of it. We've already seen growth in our lives. Lene is saying and doing things I have never seen her say or do before. When you are broken and desperate, your surrender is deeper compared to when everything is fine or going well. True and deep surrendering often comes because of true suffering and pain. And that is where God is doing the greatest work in our lives.

I want to share a quote from a book by Steve Addison, Pioneering Movements: Leadership That Multiplies Disciples and Churches. It was a quote I read in here that really spoke to me as he said it so perfectly.

"Like the children of Israel in the wilderness, the leader can't go back, and they don't know how to go forward. They're lost. We may think of the wilderness as a place to avoid, a place of testing. Yet the wilderness is also a place where we encounter God. It is a place of profound change. We are given the opportunity to surrender and trust God before there are any answers. Pass that test and clarity will come as a byproduct of surrender. Most movement pioneers have faced God in the wilderness and allowed him to remake them. Breakthroughs in pioneering movements often occur as the byproduct of crisis encounters with God."

These words, when I read them, hit me. This is exactly what we see is happening in our lives. Wilderness is a place we try to avoid, but we need to understand it is not only a place of testing, it's also a place where we encounter God. It is a place of profound change because we

251

get the "opportunity to surrender and trust God." This is exactly what I feel, again and again is happening.

I asked myself: "Am I ready to surrender and trust God with my life? With my family?" I am ready to lay all of my life down and say it is only Your will, God, no matter what that is?

The text Addison wrote here is so true. I saw it was true last time and we also believe it will be true this time. And we are already seeing it happening with both of us. Changes are happening. And it also lines up with the prophecy we got that, "The one I was before could not do what God wanted me to be in the next season." And therefore, I needed to be here.

When you are in a desert period and suffer, remember it is a time to encounter God in a new way. It gives you the opportunity to surrender everything. And when you do, you will be free. Let God remake you to be the one He wants you to be.

I will end here with the words of our Lord, Jesus, who truly suffered many things. He was rejected by His own people and then killed in the cruelest way you could imagine. But God was in it all the way and He raised Him to life afterward. Have this in mind when you read these words of Jesus:

> "Whoever wants to be my disciple must deny themselves and take up their cross daily and follow me. For whoever wants to save their life will lose it, but whoever loses their life for me will save it. What good is it for someone to gain the whole world, and yet lose or forfeit their very self?" (Luke 9:23-25 NIV)

We need to follow Him as His disciples, picking up our cross and following in His footsteps. Yes, we are called to walk like Him and that is a life with much suffering. We will be rejected like Him. Many will even be killed for His name's sake. If we try to avoid it all by holding onto our lives, we will lose what God has for us.

But if we lay down everything willingly, and give up our lives to His will, we will truly win, see God's blessings, and see His restorative power in our lives. We will come out of it even stronger than we were when it all started. Don't be afraid when you go through a desert period but surrender all and let God remake you. He will bless you. If not in this life, then in the life to come.

Chapter Twenty-Three
Faith and Hope

When I received my first Bible here in prison, it stands out as one of the most beautiful moments of my life. It was so special, filled with many emotions. As I dove into the Word, I had many special encounters in which God highlighted specific places in the Bible.

One of the first places God spoke to me was through Romans 4. This chapter is about Abraham and God used it to carry me throughout this journey. Since then, I've read those verses again and again, and it has become a foundation of my life. It is the word I stand on in this season in my life. Specifically, Romans 4:18-22 (NIV) has become the lifeline I depend on daily:

> *"Against all hope, Abraham in hope believed and so became the father of many nations, just as it had been said to him, 'So shall your offspring be.' Without weakening in his faith, he faced the fact that his body was as good as dead—since he was about a hundred years old—and that Sarah's womb was also dead. Yet he did not waver through unbelief regarding the promise of God, but was strengthened in his faith and gave glory to God, being fully persuaded that God had power to do what he had promised. This is why 'it was credited to him as righteousness.'"*

God used these verses to instill a level of new hope in my heart. I must be honest; I did not fully understand the importance of hope before I came in here. When I read these passages now, I fully understand that I needed what Abraham had. There was something special about the hope we read in these verses. How could Abraham face the facts surrounding him and still grow in his faith while holding on to the hope at the same time?

The Bible says that it is by faith that we overcome in this world (see 1 John 5:4), but what is faith? Hebrews 11:1 (NIV) says: *"Now faith is confidence in what we hope for and assurance about what we do not see."*

I have, like many others, read this verse so many times. This is one verse most people can quote. But I see today that I never really understood it before. We read that faith is the confidence of what we hope for; that means that if there is no hope, how can there be faith? Abraham had hope—a hope that did not get smaller even though he faced many trials and tribulations. Amid his travails, many might think it would take away his hope, but Abraham faced it all and was strengthened.

Despite not being blind to the facts—that his wife Sarah was beyond childbearing age and that they had tried for years and had no children—we read in Genesis that he did not waver in unbelief because he had faith, not in himself, not in Sarah, but faith in God who gave the promise. He knew that God has the power to fulfill every promise, regardless of the circumstances, and he believed that God would indeed do it. Therefore, we read that righteousness was credited to him.

These words became powerful in my life. God had promised him and therefore He would do it. In this case, what was the promise? The promise was that he would have a son and that he would be a father of many people; that he would inherit the land. He believed in faith and was strengthened, so he received a son according to the promise. But it did not stop there.

As soon as he got the promised son God tested him and again it was by faith that Abraham overcame that test. We read this in

Hebrews 11:17-19. This is truly beautiful and these verses also began working in a unique way.

> *"By faith Abraham, when God tested him, offered Isaac as a sacrifice. He who had embraced the promises was about to sacrifice his one and only son, even though God had said to him, 'It is through Isaac that your offspring will be reckoned.' Abraham reasoned that God could even raise the dead, and so in a manner of speaking he did receive Isaac back from death."* (Hebrews 11:17-19 NIV)

We so often give up if we don't see things happen right away, but Abraham is an example for all of us to keep going, keep hoping, keep believing in God's promises.

Faith and hope in what God promised needs to go hand in hand with perseverance and endurance. I realized that I needed to have faith and hope in what God has promised during this time of testing. We so often give up if we don't see things happen right away, but Abraham is an example for all of us to keep going, keep hoping, keep believing in God's promises.

Faith is an assurance of what we hope for, meaning what God has promised He will do. We have hope in what He has said. Hope is impossible without a promise to hold on to. We need to have something to put our hope in. Faith is nothing if we don't have something to hope in, and that is in God and what He has promised us. But to see this happen, we also need endurance and perseverance. And that often comes or grows with a lot of testing and trials.

In Hebrews 10:36, we read something very important that allows us to understand chapter eleven. We need to remember that the authors of every letter or book in the Bible wrote them without chapters and verses. And we need to be aware of this or we often miss the context like we see with Hebrews 11. If we start in Hebrews 10:36 (NIV), we find:

"You need to persevere so that when you have done the will of God, you will receive what he has promised."

It starts with a promise, and when we have a promise, we can put our hope in it. And faith comes from our hope in the promise.

Being put in isolation, and then at the outset of being in B8, I was in a bad spot. It was hard and as things moved forward, it looked like I was truly stuck. I heard people say, "Torben's situation is impossible; time to give up. Recognize that you have lost, give up, go back to Denmark, your time in America is over for good. You will never come back here. Just face the facts."

These voices were all over the place, and it really looked like it was over for me with America forever. But I could not just let it all go. There was always one thing that stopped me from giving up on that hope. I believe because I have hope. I have hope in what God has promised, no matter how it looks right now.

God had spoken to me. He is righteousness and is truthful. All of this is not my ideas and thoughts. He talked to me about His plans to move to America, particularly California, and His goal of sending revival and reformation to the country, and many other things He has promised.

All of this grew in me more and more. I prayed and meditated on it, and hope stirred in me, a hope that it would be exactly how God had spoken, even if the facts right now suggest something completely different. By His words to me directly, and by the words I got through the prophecies, hope was growing.

God does not leave His servants to be destroyed by the enemy. He is a righteous judge and hates lies. It's throughout the Bible. This is who He is. God is faithful, He is righteous, He is just. Especially in Psalms, it is so clear.

"I trust in you; do not let me be put to shame, nor let my enemies triumph over me. No one who hopes in you will ever be put to shame, but shame will come on those who are treacherous

without cause. Show me your ways, Lord, teach me your paths. Guide me in your truth and teach me, for you are God my Savior, and my hope is in you all day long." (Psalm 25:2-5 NIV)

God is my savior; my hope is in Him all day. As hope grew in me, I could look at my circumstances, see that it wasn't good, but still be strengthened in my faith because I did not put my faith in the circumstances but faith in Him who spoke, Him who gave the promise, because He is faithful.

I saw that this was how the early disciples and the early apostles had it. When they went through persecution, they could rejoice and stand firm. Why? Because of their faith, faith in the hope they had that God is faithful.

If we look at the American or the Western church today, I see a church that in so many areas has become weak. We may have big church buildings, lots of members, programs and money. But because we have not experienced real persecution, many Christians are weak because their faith is not tested and tried like in other parts of the world, and because of the lack of persecution, it's so easy to fall asleep. Life is too easy and we slowly lose our focus and hope in God's promises, and when we lose our hope, we die spiritually.

People die when they lose their hope of living. This is true in the natural and it is also true in the spiritual. My father died six years ago. It was very hard when it happened because it happened so fast. He was 80 years old, but he was still doing good. He actually died that day he was supposed to move to another home with a sizeable garden he could care for. He got a cold, was sick for a week, and then he died. When that happened, we saw right away how my mom lost hope. She lost hope to live and because of that, a few months later, she also died.

This is what we are seeing now in our culture. People are losing hope and for many, Jesus is no longer the anchor of their souls. Hebrews says:

"We do not want you to become lazy, but to imitate those who through faith and patience inherit what has been promised."

When God made his promise to Abraham, since there was no one greater for him to swear by, he swore by himself, saying, 'I will surely bless you and give you many descendants.' And so after waiting patiently, Abraham received what was promised. People swear by someone greater than themselves, and the oath confirms what is said and puts an end to all argument. Because God wanted to make the unchanging nature of his purpose very clear to the heirs of what was promised, he confirmed it with an oath. God did this so that, by two unchangeable things in which it is impossible for God to lie, we who have fled to take hold of the hope set before us may be greatly encouraged.

We have this hope as an anchor for the soul, firm and secure. It enters the inner sanctuary behind the curtain, where our forerunner, Jesus, has entered on our behalf. He has become a high priest forever, in the order of Melchizedek. (Hebrews 6:12-20 NIV)

There is so much in this text we just read. Hope is an anchor for our soul and Jesus is our forerunner. In the second century, the word forerunner was used to refer to small boats that could enter the harbor where large boats could not enter because of the waters.

The small boats carried the large boat's anchor, went into the harbor, and dropped the anchor, ensuring the large boat would not drift out to sea. That is where the word forerunner comes from. Jesus is our forerunner, the anchor of our soul.

In the same chapter we can read how Abraham waited patiently and therefore he received God's blessings, and we can say he really did. Twenty-five years of waiting was rewarded when he received what God promised to him.

We as Christians are not ready for what is coming, not that I believe that we can ever be fully ready, but we need to be much better prepared—prepared by the truth, prepared by the things I'm sharing in this book. As it is right now, when persecution really sets into the church, I believe we will see a great falling away. In some areas, I think we will see whole churches disappear where there will only be a few left standing strong in their faith. Why? Because the American dream, the bless me here and now gospel, has created a weak church; a church that has their hope in the wrong things, the wrong place.

Jesus lays this out for us in Mark 4. In the "Parable of the Sower," the four types of ground show us the condition of the church. The soil may look good, but only one type is the good ground that bears a lot of fruit. If we look at the second type of ground, rocky places, then we see how the seed that is sown there springs up fast. The plant looks good, but as soon as persecution sets in, it withers and dies. People fall way. This represents those people who receive the Word with gladness but they've never really put down roots in Christ in their lives.

The third type of ground, the thorns, is where the deceitfulness of riches prevents people from bearing fruit. Or they get lost in their pursuit of the American dream and the worries of this world. And then we have the good ground that bears a lot of fruit. The good ground is what we all should strive to become.

I thought I had what it took. I thought I knew what I needed and I've often taught Mark 4, but I didn't fully understand it. I was not ready, so God needed to teach me a lot here to prepare me so I'm able to help the church and to prepare believers.

What God has been teaching me here, He has been showing Lene out there. I know He's showing it to a lot of people all over the world. He's preparing us by teaching us so we can be ready for what is coming. We don't need to fear the future if our hope is in Christ. This hope is the anchor for the soul. It takes us the whole way to the goal, no matter what waves are hitting us.

The world is changing rapidly. We all see and feel it. When God called me to America, He said, "Make my people ready; they are not ready for what is coming."

Then God put me in here. He needed to put me here to teach me faith, hope and endurance so I could impact the church out there with a teaching series and a new book.

Faith is the confidence of what's hoped for. It's not enough to just have faith. We need to have both, especially hope in God's promises.

Has God spoken to you? Then hold on to that promise no matter what circumstances you're seeing, no matter what you face to the contrary.

Abraham received what God had promised in the end. He was given a son and became a father of nations just as God said he would. Why? Because God is faithful.

As I read these words, I felt God said that my name would be cleared, I would be released, and that I would leave this place a different person, that God would use this for His Kingdom's sake. I don't know what God has spoken to you, but hold onto it.

We all have different callings and assignments God has spoken for us to do. But in the end, it is the same for all of us: the salvation of our soul, a new heavenly body, a New Heaven and New Earth where righteousness will live, where God will make His home with us, and we will finally see Him face to face. Then, He will wipe every tear from our eyes, and all will be as what God created it to be before the fall of man.

We are putting our hope on that day when our Lord returns and makes everything new again. Until that day, we stand firm in our trials and look forward to what the Bible calls our "blessed hope"—our Lord Jesus Christ's return:

> "For the grace of God has appeared that offers salvation to all people. It teaches us to say 'No' to ungodliness and worldly passions, and to live self-controlled, upright and godly lives in this present age, while we wait for the blessed hope—the appearing of the glory of our great God and Savior, Jesus Christ." (Titus 2:11-13 NIV)

It is also in this hope that we stand when we say no to ungodliness and want to live upright and godly lives, ready for His appearance.

The main promise for all of us is the day of our Lord Jesus, the day He returns when we will receive our blessings, our rewards. That is our hope and where we should place our faith. Even if in this life, for a short time, we suffer and go through all kinds of trials, we can endure knowing that there is hope in the future.

The hope that one day everything will be good, and when we endure, we will receive the crown of righteousness that is waiting for us. Yes, it is not so much the American dream and God's blessings here and now, even though He can provide that, it is an eternal blessing to live in Him when that day arrives. That is the true dream we all should seek, no matter where we are in our lives.

Chapter Twenty-Four
Love Each Other

Even though God is truly working in all of this, it is difficult to explain the pressures my family and I are under. But I'd like to share a little from the prophecy I received when I first was incarcerated:

> "This season is a great crushing of your character. Like olives are being crushed and pressed to create oil, God has you in the process of bringing you to even greater glory. He is transforming who you are so you will be more effective in the future."

I feel crushed in so many ways. But also, as I shared in this book, God is moving. He has truly transformed us in so many ways. We have faith, hope, and love like never before. Love is the key to it all, and we will look at love in this chapter and what God has been showing us.

This is one area in which I have needed to repent. Or, more precisely, my lack of love for the church as a corporate body. God has showed us a place where we did not love the way we should. We love Him. We love His Word. And we also love our brothers and sisters, our close family out there. But we lacked love toward the rest of the church.

People have been praying for and supporting me all over the world, and they still do. It feels good, and I am thankful for it. All that love toward us from friends around the world is meaningful. Yes, we are truly blessed by having so many amazing friends and family members in Christ out there all over the world. People we know personally and people we don't know personally love us and help us in amazing ways.

There have also been some ministries who stood up for me on their YouTube channels, which I did not expect. I did not expect help from them.

When that happened, it did something very deep inside of us. It profoundly humbled Lene and me. It is difficult to describe being here in the lowest moment of our lives and having someone we are not close to stand up and help in this way. It is humbling because the people who stood up for us were people I had been speaking against or not speaking well about.

It was not like public slander, but in my heart or to some of my friends when they asked me what I thought about so and so, I found the negative and focused on what we did differently instead of the positive there was to say about them. And now, in this darkest moment of my life, they reached out a hand to help me. Woah! It hit so very hard when that happened. It hit deep in my heart. God used it to break me. He used it to show me something fundamental about my heart and teach me something we all need to learn.

But first, I had to check my heart. I asked myself some very deep questions about what was inside me.

I suddenly saw how they were not my enemies, but they were my family, and they were there for me.

At the same time, there was total silence from so many other ministries and other faith leaders whom I had expected or hoped for some help from. Yes, in many ways, I got really hurt. I felt left behind and forgotten by a significant part of my body. It hurt me deeply, and I needed to bring it to God in prayer so as not to let it cause me to become bitter. It is so vital we constantly guard our hearts from bitterness and unforgiveness. But it was not easy.

God has used this to teach me many things, not only about those ministries and faith leaders but about me. I see things today in a new way regarding the body as a whole.

First, I saw that many of those churches and ministries did not help me because they didn't know me, and perhaps they thought I had done something wrong, and that is why they were silent. Many lies have been spread about why I am here, and maybe they believed that I had overstayed my visa or broken the law and done something wrong and I, therefore, was just getting justice for what I had done.

We sadly often see that when a church leader is accused of something terrible; we think there must be some truth to the allegations. And sadly, there are a lot of testimonies of sin and abuse in the body that it's almost difficult to believe someone is innocent when we hear of things they have supposedly done.

I see now that I can help with this by being an even more significant part of the body and by better connecting with them. People who truly know me know that I did not do those things, but those who don't know me—how can they know what is right and wrong in all of this?

I need to be connected with the church in a way I hadn't been before. I know I need to be closer to other ministries and church leaders. I have been isolated for too long, not that I don't have many friends, but as far as the rest of the body, I have not done enough. I have been busy doing my own thing. I didn't take the time to meet and make friends outside of our network. And now that I need the body, I don't have many faith leaders to reach out to.

It has also hit me that I should stop believing everything I hear about other faith leaders. I have often drawn away from ministries I have heard bad things about without really knowing the truth about it all. Satan is our enemy, and he is busy spreading lies to create division between brothers.

God showed me how my enemy has worked to create mistrust toward others, often because of small things we see or do differently. He has managed to get us to believe we are each other's enemies, so we don't know who our true enemy is and how he is behind much of the lies and division we see in the body of Christ.

God has made it clear to me that people who love Jesus, even if they do things differently and believe differently in some areas theologically, are not my enemies. Even if they were my enemy, which they are not, I am still called to love them; I am called to pray for them and not find anything wrong with them or think or even speak evil about them. We often treat our brothers and sisters in Christ worse than we treat our enemies. I am not talking about false prophets and those who directly preach another gospel—I am talking about our brothers and sisters in Christ, those who sincerely love and serve the same Lord and Savior as we do.

I was reminded that we all have the same Shepherd. They also follow His voice even though they differ from me in some areas. They are still sheep, and they have the same Shepherd.

The true enemy we must watch out for is the wolf out there. The problem is that today we are starting to see each other as the enemy. And we spend so much time fighting each other that we don't know when the wolf is standing right amongst us.

But when you go through hard times, you truly discover who the wolves are. It is clear they are there to kill and destroy. But you also see who's not your enemy and who is there to help. And this has opened my eyes to the fact that I, in some areas, have been fighting the wrong people. Listen to our Lord Jesus' words here:

> *"But to you who are listening I say: Love your enemies, do good to those who hate you, bless those who curse you, pray for those who mistreat you. If someone slaps you on one cheek, turn to them the other also. If someone takes your coat, do not withhold your shirt from them. Give to everyone who asks you, and if anyone takes what belongs to you, do not demand it back. Do to others as you would have them do to you.*

"If you love those who love you, what credit is that to you? Even sinners love those who love them. And if you do good to those who are good to you, what credit is that to you? Even sinners do that." (Luke 6:27-33 NIV)

Jesus is truly radical here, but we need to obey Him. This is how we should live our lives. We should all love each other, but we should also love our enemies and pray for those who persecute us. Jesus is very radical when it comes to love. When, for example, I got my asylum denied in an immigration court, someone illegally came into the closed court hearing and recorded it. They recorded the most challenging moment of my life.

They then put it on YouTube, where they spliced it together. They left some things out, and they showed other things again and again. And there on YouTube, they were laughing and making fun of me. I have heard some were eating popcorn like they were watching a funny movie, having a blast.

And those who did it were Christians, or they say they are Christians. They laughed and mocked me in a way not even our enemies deserve. It doesn't matter if I was right or wrong; we should only treat people as we'd like to be treated ourselves. Many people saw this video, and they laughed, rejoicing over my downfall. I'm not saying this because I am bitter against them. After all, I love and pray for them, and I have forgiven them right as it happened.

All of this revealed something not only about them but also the time we live in, where the love of most is growing cold, as Jesus said when He talked about the signs of His coming. *"Because of the increase of wickedness, the love of most will grow cold"* (Matthew 24:12 NIV).

Jesus said in the prior verses:

"Then you will be handed over to be persecuted and put to death, and you will be hated by all nations because of me. At that time many will turn away from the faith and will betray and hate each other." (Matthew 24:9-10 NIV)

Jesus said this will happen. How can we, therefore, say that there must be a reason when someone who follows Jesus is in jail? They must be guilty in breaking the law one way or another.

Jesus said that people will hate us because of Him and Him alone. I see this is also an area in which the church is asleep. We need to understand how persecution can happen. And as time goes, we will see this more and more.

I know it is difficult for the body in the Western world to understand that this is the time we are living in. It has begun to happen in a way we haven't seen before. But we need to wake up here and not to be too fast to accuse and think the worse of each other. Let's instead start with loving one another and being there for each other.

We should be known for our love for one another, for how we treat other believers and our families in Christ. Yes, we sometimes treat our families in Christ worse than we are called to treat our enemies. Yes, we can disagree. Yes, we can see things differently. But it doesn't change what Jesus has commanded us. And that is still to love one another, even our enemies. All throughout the Bible, love is the most vital and significant thing we have.

> "Therefore, as God's chosen people, holy and dearly loved, clothe yourselves with compassion, kindness, humility, gentleness and patience. Bear with each other and forgive one another if any of you has a grievance against someone. Forgive as the Lord forgave you. And over all these virtues put on love, which binds them all together in perfect unity. Let the peace of Christ rule in your hearts, since as members of one body you were called to peace. And be thankful." (Colossians 3:12-15 NIV)

In 1 Corinthians 13, we read that without love, we are nothing. Love binds everything together; without that, nothing matters. Let's read a longer text about what love is, and then let's see if we have that love in us:

"If I speak in the tongues of men or of angels, but do not have love, I am only a resounding gong or a clanging cymbal. If I have the gift of prophecy and can fathom all mysteries and all knowledge, and if I have a faith that can move mountains, but do not have love, I am nothing. If I give all I possess to the poor and give over my body to hardship that I may boast but do not have love, I gain nothing.

"Love is patient, love is kind. It does not envy, it does not boast, it is not proud. It does not dishonor others, it is not self-seeking, it is not easily angered, it keeps no record of wrongs. Love does not delight in evil but rejoices with the truth. It always protects, always trusts, always hopes, always perseveres. Love never fails. But where there are prophecies, they will cease; where there are tongues, they will be stilled; where there is knowledge, it will pass away.

"For we know in part and we prophesy in part, but when completeness comes, what is in part disappears. When I was a child, I talked like a child, I thought like a child, I reasoned like a child. When I became a man, I put the ways of childhood behind me. For now we see only a reflection as in a mirror; then we shall see face to face. Now I know in part; then I shall know fully, even as I am fully known. And now these three remain: faith, hope and love. But the greatest of these is love." (1 Corinthians 13:1-13 NIV)

Love is the greatest of all traits. Without love, we are nothing. Everything we do doesn't matter if there is no love. Love is greater than faith and hope and this is what binds us all together. I have just talked about faith and hope. And as you see, we need that. But we need to add love together with it, as love is the reason for all of it.

Here are some of the last words Paul wrote to the church: *"Be on your guard; stand firm in the faith; be courageous; be strong. Do everything in love."* (1 Corinthians 16:13-14 NIV). We need to work for God, but it must all be done in love like everything else. But the question is, do we truly have that love? Do we truly have the love we read about in the Bible?

How often do we, as brothers and sisters in Christ, as a family in Christ, use the word of God to fight and hurt each other instead of bringing healing to each other? Hear Jesus's words to: *"Put your sword back in its place for all who draw the sword will die by the sword"* (Matthew 26:51 NIV).

He said that to Peter just after he cut off the ear of one of the guards who came to arrest Jesus. Jesus healed the guard's ear. Even though he was there to arrest him, Jesus healed him.

But what Peter did with his physical sword is what we often do with our spiritual sword, the Word of God. When we use it without love, it doesn't bring healing. Instead, we cut off each other's ears—our spiritual ears—and we bleed spiritually all over. We are unable to hear what we are supposed to. Love does not delight in evil, as we read, but rejoices in the truth.

The truth is essential. We need truth, and I'm not saying we should compromise for the sake of unity. I don't believe in that. Truth is very important. But love hides a multitude of sins, as we read in 1 Peter 4:8. And if we don't have that love, we only see mistakes people are making and the areas we disagree with when it comes to doctrine. Let us not be like them and be ready to cast the first stone, but instead love them and help them see the truth.

Maybe it's not them who have a wrong doctrine. We could learn from each other by sitting down and getting to know one another. We will never really find people with whom we agree 100 percent anyway. There are, of course, areas where we need to be firmer and things we cannot overlook—very important things that have to do with salvation. But often, we fight with people over things that do not have to do with salvation. Going back to 1 Corinthians 13:

"Love is patient, love is kind. It does not envy, it does not boast, it is not proud. It does not dishonor others, it is not self-seeking,

it is not easily angered, it keeps no record of wrongs. Love does not delight in evil but rejoices with the truth. It always protects, always trusts, always hopes, always perseveres." (1 Corinthians 13:4-7 NIV)

We know that God is love, and therefore, God embodies all these attributes. God is patient and kind. God is all the things we read here. As God's children, we are to be like Him.

"For this is the message you heard from the beginning: We should love one another. Do not be like Cain, who belonged to the evil one and murdered his brother. And why did he murder him? Because his own actions were evil and his brother's were righteous. Do not be surprised, my brothers and sisters, if the world hates you. We know that we have passed from death to life, because we love each other. Anyone who does not love remains in death. Anyone who hates a brother or sister is a murderer, and you know that no murderer has eternal life residing in him." (1 John 3:11-15 NIV)

We should not be surprised when the world hates us. But if we hate our brothers and sisters, how can eternal life be in us? If you say you love God but hate your brother or sister, you are deceived. How can you say you love God, who you have not seen if you don't love the brother or sister you have seen? We are called to love God and love each other.

Love is patient and kind, does not envy, does not boast, is not proud, does not dishonor others, it is not self-seeking. Just to name a few. Can I say the same about me? Can you tell me the same about you? Do I have patience the way I need? I see now that there are areas in which I need to improve.

God has broken me in here and is still doing it. I see that I need so much more love in my life. I did not have the patience with other people that I needed. I saw that I have said and done things out of envy toward some people or their ministries. And therefore, it was not done out of love as it should have been. In those cases, I should have kept my mouth shut and dealt with my heart first before saying anything. I don't say that there is not a place to correct and rebuke. We are still fighting for the truth here because it is the only thing that can free people. But even correction and rebuke need to be done in love with the right motives.

We must check ourselves before we say and do anything. Is what we are doing motivated by the right motives? If not, repent, ask God to forgive you, and fill you with His love. We need each other, and we all need to be more like Jesus. There shouldn't be any room for sin, envy, pride, or any other thing in our lives. We all need to deal with our hearts. I needed to deal with my heart, when it came to the lack of support from pastors and other ministries. It was not easy. It's not easy to be in here and know that if the churches out there just came together as one voice, they could get me out right away. But one reason many are saying nothing is what I heard again and again: "Yes, we know Torben is not a weapon smuggler or human trafficker. That is insane. But no one is in jail if they are innocent, so he must have done something wrong."

I understand people can think like that because they don't know me. And therefore, they are saying that I must have done something wrong because no one goes to jail if you are innocent. As I said before, we are not used to this kind of persecution, especially not in our Western world. But when people say that no one goes to jail unless they have done something wrong, they have forgotten one very significant person, Jesus! He is a perfect example of an innocent person going to jail.

"Yeah, Torben, but you are not Jesus."

No, I am not. But let's continue because Jesus said again and again that what they did to Him they would do to us. When He sent out His disciples, He sent them out with these words:

"I am sending you out like sheep among wolves. Therefore be as shrewd as snakes and as innocent as doves. Be on your guard; you will be handed over to the local councils and be flogged in the

synagogues. On my account you will be brought before governors and kings as witnesses to them and to the Gentiles. But when they arrest you do not worry about what to say or how to say it. At that time you will be given what to say. The student is not above the teacher, nor a servant above his master. It is enough for students to be like their teachers and servants like their masters. If the head of the house has been called Beelzebul, how much more the members of his household!" (Matthew 10:16-19, 24-25 NIV)

I know I'm here because of you, because of the church. But I also know I need you as much as you need me.

We need each other.

I know for myself that I need to stop listening to rumors and evil talk about different ministries and brothers and sisters in Christ. Our enemy has been busy creating divisions through lies and slander. And we know that God looks very seriously at these things. I feel very strongly about this because I've experienced the fear of God when it comes to this.

We should not close our eyes to bad people—people who are willfully sinning, teaching heretical things, and bearing evil fruit. No, we should never close our eyes to this type of conduct. We have a responsibility to deal with it. But it must be the right way and with the right people. It must involve the elders, and it must be done in love. Only some people are called to play policeman and find mistakes. One of the signs in the end times is that the love of most people will grow cold. And we see that all over the place.

In Revelation 2, Jesus spoke to the church in Ephesus, and said, *"I have this charge against you, that you have left your first love. Repent and do the deeds you first did"* (Revelation 2: 4, 5 NIV).

This shows me that I can stay in my first love. I have loved Jesus for twenty-eight years. I met Him, and He transformed my life. But it has exploded while I am in here. In fact, I'm almost afraid to leave and reenter a busy world full of online pressures or my constantly buzzing phone. I'm preparing my mind for it as I don't want to lose what I have been given here.

Have you lost your first love? Then repent! Let's go back to what we did in the beginning: love Jesus, worship Him, read His word, and spend a lot of time with Him. I'll end this chapter by showing where our love starts. As I said, it starts with God, but it doesn't end with God.

When discussing love, we must understand that it all starts with God. We love Him because He first loved us. We need to know that He loves us and then let His love grow in us so we can love like He loves. *"This is love: not that we loved God, but that he loved us and sent his Son as an atoning sacrifice for our sins. We love because he first loved us"* (1 John 4:10, 19 NIV).

But the greatest commandment does not stop with our love for God or God's love for us. We are also called to love others as we love ourselves. Jesus replied: *"'Love the Lord your God with all your heart and with all your soul and with all your mind.' This is the first and greatest commandment. And the second is like it: 'Love your neighbor as yourself'"* (Matthew 22:37-39 NIV).

"But who are our neighbors?" the Pharisees asked. The neighbor is someone you meet. But it also starts with our wives, husbands, and families. "In this same way, husbands ought to love their wives as their own bodies. He who loves his wife loves himself." (Ephesians 5:28 NIV)

We are called to love our friends. Jesus said, *"Greater love has no one than this: to lay down one's life for one's friends"* (John 15:13 NIV). But we are also called to love our brothers and sisters in Christ, the church. *"We know that we have passed from death to life because we love each other. Anyone who does not love remains in death"* (1 John 3:14 NIV).

But it does not even stop here. He also talks about the brothers and sisters we don't see eye to eye with. We are even called to love our enemies.

"You have heard that it was said, 'Love your neighbor and hate your enemy.' But I tell you, love your enemies and pray for those who persecute you, that you may be children of your Father in heaven. He causes his sun to rise on the evil and the good, and sends rain on the righteous and the unrighteous. If you love those who love you, what reward will you get? Are not even the tax collectors doing that? And if you greet only your own people, what are you doing more than others? Do not even pagans do that? Be perfect, therefore, as your heavenly Father is perfect" (Matthew 5:43-48 NIV).

Let's all strive to be perfect as our Father is perfect, and do as Jesus has commanded us: love others. I know I have changed when it comes to this. I've always loved God since that day He saved me. Since that day, I have wanted to serve Him. But there were areas in my life where I needed more love. And that is especially true with my brothers and sisters, those I do not see eye to eye with.

God is changing me, and I love it.

Ask God if there are areas in which you need to love more—God, your husband or wife, your kids, your family, your friends, the church, or even your enemies. Or maybe all of them.

It starts with you!

Chapter Twenty-Five
National Security Threat

As I am writing this to you, I'm currently sitting outside in recreation. Today, it is mandatory for the whole Pod to be outside, as every Tuesday morning they clean our showers with bleach and chemicals. The cells often become very nasty in here.

The air conditioner sometimes makes it very cold. Other times, it doesn't work—which has been a lot lately—and the entire building becomes very humid. Sometimes I see water running down the walls. Then when we shower in the cell at the same time, with no air conditioning, it gets nasty in there. Often our towels are dripping wet the day after as nothing can dry in the humidity. Because of that, mold appears a lot, so they have begun cleaning with bleach once a week. After a few hours, when we are allowed back into our cells, it is like entering a swimming pool facility with the smell of bleach everywhere.

But right now, it's 7:30 a.m. I've slept about four and a half hours, and now we are outside. We sleep so little because they don't turn off the lights until 1 a.m. and then wake us up around 5 a.m. for breakfast. After breakfast we try to sleep a little more, but because they count us again after breakfast, it's often difficult to sleep.

Where I am outside, there is a basketball court, sixty-five by thirty-five feet (twenty meters by eight meters), with a sixteen-foot-high (six meter) fence around us with spiky barbed wire. There is a half basketball court with one basket. Next to that are two stationary exercise bicycles that people can use for training, and some equipment to do pull-ups. There are also some benches where we can sit. There is almost always somebody playing football in the middle of all of it.

I often run around the area, and do exercises. But not today: the yard is jammed with fifty-five people from two Pods, waiting to get their Pods cleaned so we can come back. Therefore, there is no space to run around or do anything like that.

Besides this, there are six smaller places with fences all around—I call them dog houses—that are eight feet (2.44 meters) by fourteen feet (4.3 meters) where the more dangerous inmates are kept. Right now, there is one from our Pod in the doghouse. He was in a fight last weekend and they put him in the box (isolation). This was his time to get out and see the sun.

There is grass outside the fence and trees in the distance. This is the closest I come to nature. Everything is concrete and cold. I truly miss hiking in the mountains, and riding my bike, or just being able to run out in nature and feel the grass under my feet. But I can see the green grass and trees, and remember there is life outside of here.

I'm here as a national threat. I'm detained without any option for bond, because I am considered a national threat and therefore very dangerous. When I heard that for the first time, I was truly shocked and I did not know what to think of it all.

If you think of who's behind all of this, knowing that it is our enemy, according to his kingdom, I truly am a national threat. So, what an honor it is to get that label when you think about it. We should all be a national threat toward Satan and his kingdom. But here I am, and I have put my hope in God's promise that it will be as He has said. I will use this chapter and the next few to talk more about the battle we are in to help you understand what is going on, and also to help you to be ready for what is coming.

There are still many things I don't know when it comes to my case and why I am still here. It is truly hard not to know what is really going on. One reason is that the things I hear are changing all the time. I am being told one thing, and as time goes on and we get more information, it seems like what I was first told wasn't correct.

Looking at all the inmates around me right now, every case is unique. But everyone here has a chance to get out on a bond. Everyone beside me. Everyone here is illegally in the country, or has broken the law one way or another, except for me.

Most people have been here for three or four months at most, but I have been here over ten months. I am the only one here labeled as a national security threat, mandatorily detained even though I have not broken the law in any way.

Weapons smuggling from Mexico to America was the first thing I heard as the reason they detained me. But since I've been here for ten months, I have not one time heard anything about that again. There are currently no charges against me for weapons smuggling from Mexico, or any other charges for that matter. But it was all over the news in the beginning: "Torben is a weapon smuggler; Torben loves weapons. Just see his pictures."

Then they showed a picture with a long rifle over my shoulder, looking cool. "Here is the proof that Torben loves weapons."

In one of the biggest newspapers in Denmark, they showed that picture of me taken from my Facebook account. But the truth about that picture is very different than what they said in the article. I know very little about weapons. That picture was taken in Canada and not in the United States as they said. And that was not my weapon I stood with. We were in Canada some years ago, and during a meeting there was a guy who had some rifles and guns, and he asked if we wanted to try them. We went to his house and tried his weapons. A picture was taken and I put it on Facebook.

Later, in Florida, I bought a gun and a rifle because I thought it could be fun to use them for target practice, but I only used them three times and then I sold the weapons, as it was not something for me. I know it can seem strange for somebody from Europe to buy a gun and rifle, but in this part of America many people own rifles and guns and there is nothing strange about it. It's like buying a bicycle. Perhaps more people own guns than bicycles in this part of the country.

I know very little about weapons, but suddenly I was in the newspapers and on YouTube with the picture of me with a rifle as proof that I love weapons. I am now in many eyes here as a weapon smuggler. This shows how crazy it all is and how little we can take anything we see on the news or on YouTube as truth. I have learned I should not have posted a picture like that, as it is so easy to be used against us.

Another thing I heard in the beginning, a thing that they still hold on to as an excuse for keeping me here is that I overstayed my visa and therefore I was illegally in the country.

I arrived in America on January 26, 2019, on a three-month visitor visa from Europe. That meant that I could stay for ninety days legally. In those three months, I met with my lawyer to find out what options I had.

My lawyer informed me that I needed to send in my asylum papers before the three months were over or they would label me as an overstay, and I had as good as lost my case already. So, we gathered the evidence and managed to get it done in time.

We sent in the application within the three months, and I got a receipt that they received my application on April 22 and sent me an I-797 form, allowing me to stay while my case was pending. So that was three days before April 25 when my visa expired. Everything was wonderful—at least we thought so. But everything has been upside down in this case because we have an enemy that will do anything to stop me and destroy me.

What I and my lawyers did not know in the beginning was that this system had written that I overstayed. Why? The answer is because they had secretly canceled my visa one and a half months after I arrived in the United States. So, while I was still preparing and sending in my papers, they had already canceled my visa and from that moment I was illegally in the country. Someone contacted U.S. Immigration and Customs Enforcement and falsely accused me of money fraud, exploiting sick and elderly individuals, and mistreating children. That's why we hadn't heard about it.

Yes, my enemies from Europe were in contact with immigration in the United States shortly after I arrived in America, and they got them to cancel my visa. We now know who some of the people are behind the lies. It's the same people from Denmark, and the main reason I fled Denmark. As in Denmark, they influenced the media, the government, and came after me. I fled Denmark to come to America to find out that the same people were very active here.

But even though I overstayed according to their system, it is not the main reason; it cannot be. Why? Because why did they not arrest me before now. If I had truly overstayed, why did they wait three years and why did they bring up weapons smuggling when I was at the meeting? And why did they put me in mandatory detention as a dangerous person and a national security threat without any chance of getting out on a bond if the reason that I was here was because I just "overstayed"? Nothing makes sense in all of this.

It is all built on lies and leads back to the same people in Europe. But I know I have a clean conscience because I know I've done nothing wrong. I know God will reveal the truth one day. But the lies did not stop here, the lies did not stop with weapons smuggling, taking money from sick or elderly people, or even abusing children. The people behind this have been very active for years. One of them is from Denmark, and he was actually a man who worked with me back in 2016, and I saw him as a friend.

At one point, I saw that something was off with him, and someone warned me about him, but it was much worse than I thought. Even though I knew something was off, I did not see how bad it really was until much later. Many of us did not see what he was up to. But when we finally discovered what he had been doing behind our backs—lying, manipulating, putting people up against each other and getting rid of people he did not like by spreading lies—I fired him right away. Since that day he has had as his primary goal to destroy me.

There is a documentary out called "Revealed" that you'll find on our YouTube channel where we talk more about these people behind it all, how they are working, and as documents keep coming out with new information, you'll find so much more information there than I am able to share here in my book.

When I came to America, I got an email from one guy in France, someone that is working close with the guy from Denmark. Both of them are really smart and have a lot of money and influence, also with the American government. They are ready to do anything. He wrote that he was happy I came to America so he could finally destroy me and put me in jail through his contacts in Washington, D.C.

I've never met people like this before: deceiving, narcissistic and evil.

But the man in France and the man in Denmark weren't the only ones working against me. An American man who has a YouTube channel who at one time was in one of our training schools has made videos of my case, and his videos got the attention of our legal team. What he revealed in them was very serious: he knew how I got arrested and many others things, which meant he was in personal contact with people from U.S. Immigration and Customs Enforcement, as well as people from Europe.

So our legal team did a deposition with him under oath. They had him for two days and fourteen hours, and he sat in front of two lawyers who asked a lot of questions.

This deposition revealed many things we did not know, like where the human trafficking accusation came from and why I was labeled a national security threat. He explained how the officer who detained me called him months later and told him to contact the U.S. Department of Homeland Security and falsely report me for human trafficking. It then appeared in my files that I was under investigation for human trafficking, and the officer who initially lied used that to label me as a national security threat. It is truly scary and feels like a movie, but this is real, and that is why I'm sitting here in my cell.

There is even more to the story, and when I'm finally out and it is all over, we will create a new website where we will provide you with even more details about this crazy story as things unfold. Even though I know some details, there are still many things I don't know myself.

My legal team has information they will not disclose to me over the phone, as they do not trust the people in here. I am not entirely certain as to the reasons for this. I can only speculate, and it is unsettling to dwell too much on this and speculate. Therefore, I try not to delve too deeply into it.

But I don't want to focus too much on this here. Instead, I want to focus on what we can learn from this, and what I have learned. In the book of Acts, the early church faced persecution, and I have experienced so many things similar to what they went through.

In Acts 14, Paul and Barnabas went to Iconium, and like any other place they went, they saw people coming to faith and miracles. But like every other place and like so often, a few people became jealous and stood up and spoke against them. They spread lies and poisoned the minds of the many.

> "At Iconium Paul and Barnabas went as usual into the Jewish synagogue. There they spoke so effectively that a great number of Jews and Greeks believed. But the Jews who refused to believe stirred up the other Gentiles and poisoned their minds against the brothers." (Acts 14:1-2 NIV)

But they just continued doing the work of the Kingdom until the people there plotted to mistreat them and even stone them, and they fled to another place and there continued to share the good news of the Kingdom.

> "There was a plot afoot among both Gentiles and Jews, together with their leaders, to mistreat them and stone them. But they found out about it and fled to the Lycaonian cities of Lystra and Derbe and to the surrounding country, where they continued to preach the gospel." (Act 14:5-7 NIV)

But it didn't stop there: the same people in Iconium came to the new place, spread the same poison, and the people ended up getting Paul stoned.

> "Then some Jews came from Antioch and Iconium and won the crowd over. They stoned Paul and dragged him outside the city, thinking he was dead." (Act 14:19 NIV)

But the story doesn't stop here. Paul came back to life and he just got up and went back to the city.

> "But after the disciples had gathered around him, he got up and went back into the city." (Acts 14:20 NIV)

Back in Denmark, we saw amazing things, and the ministry exploded. We had a big Jesus Center where people came from all over the world to get trained. Sometimes we had students from over thirty nations at one time. Many people met God, received training, and were sent out to share the gospel, seeing more lives transformed.

But a few were against it and they plotted to stop me. They started to spread their poison, and through the media, poison the minds of many people, even within the Danish government. This resulted in me leaving for the United States. However, there, the same people from Europe began to influence individuals in America, including those within ICE and the American government. The poison influenced people with authority to detain me and place me in jail. The plot was not to stone me like Paul, but to destroy me and put me in prison, as one of them from Europe wrote in the email: "I want to destroy you, and I will put you in jail." They managed to get me put into jail, but they did not destroy me. God is still in control, and it is not over yet.

It reminds me of when I was new in the faith. I really wanted to live the life I read about in the book of Acts, and I can say I have gotten to live that life.

I can add one more thing to my testimony that reveals Jesus is just like we read about Him in the Bible. But when it comes to persecution, I want to say that it's much nicer to read about it than to live it. It really hurts. It is hard. But I can see that God uses it. And I've learned so much through it, and I understand Paul and his boldness even more. Paul, after he got stoned, just stood up and went back to the same city. There is a place of no fear, knowing God is in control and if He says go, we go.

We also need to understand that all of this is truly what Jesus has promised us. When he sent out His disciples, he sent them out with these words:

> "I am sending you out like sheep among wolves. Therefore be as shrewd as snakes and as innocent as doves. Be on your guard; you will be handed over to the local councils and be flogged in the synagogues. On my account you will be brought before governors and kings as witnesses to them and to the Gentiles." (Matthew 10:16-18 NIV)

And:

> "When you are persecuted in one place, flee to another. Truly I tell you, you will not finish going through the towns of Israel before the Son of Man comes." (Matthew 10:23 NIV)

He said so much more in Matthew 10. I encourage you to read the entire chapter for yourself. But this is what Jesus said, and this is what those who follow Christ can expect, also today. I am not bitter toward the people who have caused so much pain for me and my family.

Joseph wasn't bitter toward his brothers who threw him into the pit and sold him as a slave to Egypt, or toward Potiphar's wife who lied about him and got him thrown into jail. It was part of God's plan.

Jesus wasn't bitter toward Judas who betrayed him. Of course it hurt to be betrayed by a friend. But the truth is Jesus could have completed

His mission without John, James and Peter, but He could not have done it without Judas. Judas was the only apostle necessary in Jesus' life to get Him to the cross and fulfill what God had for His life.

In the same way, we all need a Judas in our lives to help us get to our cross so we can die to ourselves and fulfill God's plan for our lives.

The people who hurt us most are the biggest blessing because it brings us closer to God, and causes us to die to ourselves so we can become more like Christ and live for all that God has for us. There is no reason for me or anyone else to become bitter.

We're also called to love our enemies and pray for those who persecute us. It's not as easy to do as it is to say, but I've grown in this last year. God has really been teaching me the importance of this, of loving our enemies, of praying for those who persecute us, and to not become bitter when people hurt us.

So, remember, it all helps us to become more like Jesus. When people speak evil against us and lie like Jesus said they would, it can turn to a blessing.

> "Blessed are you when people insult you, persecute you and falsely say all kinds of evil against you because of me. Rejoice and be glad, because great is your reward in heaven, for in the same way they persecuted the prophets who were before you." (Matthew 5:11-12 NIV)

These lies have been in my life for years—just Google my name and you'll find a lot of lies out there. The more fruit we see in our lives, the more God does through us, the greater the persecution will become. It all helps humble and keep us closer to God.

But while we are in it, it can be overwhelming. I've never experienced anything on this level before. I know that this is truly new for all of us, especially in the Western world. But it is what we see in the Bible, and it is something we will see more of in the future as we come closer to the appearance of our Lord Jesus Christ.

The lies I've heard in the last month include accusations of my involvement in human trafficking, money fraud, money laundering, tax abuse, child abuse, and more. Shockingly, someone on YouTube even claimed that I raped a handicapped girl in Denmark. Yes, the story claims that I supposedly raped her while my wife Lene and three other couples from our leadership team watched, as part of a demonic ritual we supposedly conducted at one of our training centers. Yes, there seems to be no limit to how crazy these lies are and how quickly they spread. This girl is someone I have never personally met, but that doesn't hinder someone from believing the lie and boldly sharing it on YouTube.

I expect there are many more lies out there that I've not heard yet. I'll use the next chapters to share more about how it is important that we watch out for these things and understand what the battle is all about. I believe that the things that have happened to me are for all of us to learn and grow.

Chapter Twenty-Six
Watch Out!

Jesus has called us to love our enemies and pray for those who persecute us, also for those who hurt us, as we have already looked at. But He has also called us to watch out, to be alert.

I've learned this the hard way the last few years, especially in this season I am in now. In Matthew 10, when Jesus sent out His disciples, He said they would be arrested, but He also said, *"I am sending you out like sheep among wolves. Therefore be as shrewd as snakes and as innocent as doves"* (Matthew 10:16 NIV).

And after this He continues in the next verse with "be on your guard" or "be aware of man" or "watch out"—depending on which translation you read.

> *"Be on your guard; you will be handed over to the local councils and be flogged in the synagogues. On my account you will be brought before governors and kings as witnesses to them and to the Gentiles."* (Matthew 10:17-18 NIV)

But my question is—and we need to ask ourselves this—are we truly shrewd as snakes and innocent as doves as Christ commanded us to be? Are we fulfilling the command to be on guard and aware of others' ill intentions? If not, life could go wrong, as I will show you in this chapter.

I've had my eyes opened recently and learned a lot of this the hard way. During my detention in the U.S. Department of Homeland Security office in Orlando, I took part in a meeting regarding my asylum case. As I entered the room, they showed me a Federal Bureau of Investigation badge. The two people in the room were a part of an FBI task force in which U.S. Immigration and Customs Enforcement, Homeland Security and the FBI worked together, as I understood it. They detained me in that place.

They took my phone, asking me to write down the numbers I needed. As I did, one of the officers looked over my shoulder and got my PIN code. Then, the day after they transferred me here to the Baker County Detention Center, I received a property list with the things I had brought with me: shoes, belt, pants, and socks. But my phone was not on the list. Which means the FBI has my phone. With my PIN number, they can easily access everything I have on it.

Knowing now that there are people who don't want good things for me, who want to find bad things on me, this reality has brought a lot of thoughts to me. Am I truly ready for someone who wants to hurt me, who wants to find something they can use against me, to go through my phone? To go through my whole life to see if they can find something. Do I have something there on my phone that cannot see the light of day? Or is there something on my phone that can easily be misinterpreted? They will also have access to anything on there: bank accounts, browsing history, email, pictures, Signal, Facebook—yes, all of it.

As I spent time thinking of what they have access to, the answer came to me: Yes, I am ready for I have nothing to hide! Peace has washed over me now. Wow! What a special moment I will never forget! Jesus' words that we should be as innocent as doves now has deeper meaning. If we are not innocent, and such incidents occur, our hidden secrets can be used against us and lead to our downfall.

Recently, I needed to give my bank information going back four years to an independent investigation because some people were investigating what I do with money. A lot of people are telling lies about me, like I have not paid taxes.

One person said he has proof that I have hundreds of thousands to even millions of dollars put away. He is calling into question my level of honesty when it comes to money.

But I have nothing to hide and willfully sent in all my bank records, and all was proven to be good on my end.

I knew there was nothing for them to come after because many years ago I experienced the fear of God in my life in a very powerful way. One day, the fear of God came over me in a deep, deep way, and I saw God as holy at a level I've never realized before. I went through deep, deep repentance. I understood that I cannot play with sin, and I understood that everything that has been done in the dark will one day come to light in front of Him; He sees it all.

After that deep repentance, and the instilling fear of God, I have tried to live in His light and have a very high standard of Biblical, moral living. This is something I am truly thankful for—it has saved me in this current trial. But even though all was good, it was still scary and I learned a lot from this and got even more fear of God in my life.

My question to you is, "Are you ready?"

Are you ready for the FBI or someone else to take your phone and go through your life? To see all your pictures, emails, bank accounts— yeah, everything?

Are you ready? If not, then repent. Change your life today.

If there is something hidden, it will be found out, and used against you. One day it will not "just be the FBI" but God Himself whom we will stand in front of and be judged by.

God used this time here to remind me of the importance of living in the light, the fear of God, being as innocent as doves, as He has commanded us to do.

But Jesus does not stop there: He also said we should be wise and shrewd—or discerning—as snakes. Jesus said that we need to be more alert of what is going on around us. I needed to be more awake here, wiser, more discerning.

For instance: what do you share on the internet? I put the picture of me with a rifle over my shoulder on Facebook, and that has been used against me. I think I have two pictures on Facebook where I stood with a weapon, and those images were misused because I was not wise in doing that. I was not discerning. It's not that we should be full of fear, because we should not be fearful, but we should be wise and alert.

Another time, a man blessed us with a delightful house we could stay in for three months. The house cost about $6,000 to $9,000 per month. I felt bad when we got to the house, but it was a gift from him, and we needed a place to stay. I took pictures of me in front of it, and people thought it was my house, paid for by money people had donated to The Last Reformation.

But it wasn't—I would never do that. I should have been wiser and not lived a life that can be misunderstood, even if it was a gift and it was only a few months we stayed there.

I should have followed my conviction or been wiser with it and with what I posted on the internet, as it can so easily be misunderstood and used against us to paint a picture of who we are and how we fail to live out the truth. In the end, it can damage the spread of the gospel.

Jesus is very clear: don't live in fear, but be on watch. It's important we do both. But sadly, we often mix the two, so we don't watch out but we give in to fear.

When Danish TV in Denmark came after me, for example, they had undercover journalists. They came with hidden cameras after me. I had no idea—in fact, I actually baptized both of them. Why? They said all the right things. I had no idea that those people were undercover journalists. They just seemed like people who loved Jesus and wanted to follow Christ.

When they came out of the water, at that moment, I knew for sure something was off. I felt it. I saw it in them; the joy was missing. However, it wasn't right away that I realized they were undercover journalists. I couldn't have imagined that journalists would do something so deceitful as faking a baptism. Where is the fear of God in doing something like that?

At that time, one of them actually took me aside and offered me a lot of money. It was all a trap to get me to do something wrong. Later, I found out that the undercover journalists were actually funded by the man who sent me the, "I will destroy you and put you in jail" email. Had I not been wise, had I not done what was right, they could have got me there.

I told the man offering me money I was thankful for the offer, but I said he should be giving the right way: through our organization. I declined his gift, and I did not fall for it. Even though he tried very hard to trick me into receiving the money, I didn't do it. We have an enemy who will do what he can to get us to sin, to fall, by not being wise and alert.

With the other journalist, a woman, she wanted to talk to me about her medicine. We did that in a café at our Jesus Center. She wanted us to be alone and talk, and I said yes to that, because it was in our café where people were walking around, going in and out, and the door was open all the time. However, they edited it in such a way that made it look really bad, suggesting that I was alone with her behind closed doors, telling her to trust me and throw away her medicine.

I could have been wiser in that situation. Even though it wasn't a sin, and I didn't say anything wrong, it's not always about sin or doing wrong. It's about how things can be twisted and used against us. I should have declined to meet with her and talk alone. I should have had someone with me, and that was my mistake. I never drive alone in a car with a woman or am alone with someone to pray for them. Not that I think I will do anything wrong, but our enemy can use it. I see now that I need to be even more vigilant. But it doesn't stop here.

This isn't limited to our actions: we also need to be careful what we listen to. So much poison is being spread, causing so much pain and destruction because we are not alert to what we listen to. We just drink the poison we hear, even from our enemies. Paul warns us like Jesus did when he wrote:

"I urge you, brothers and sisters, to watch out for those who cause divisions and put obstacles in your way that are contrary to the teaching you have learned. Keep away from them. For such people are not serving our Lord Christ, but their own appetites. By smooth talk and flattery they deceive the minds of naive people." (Romans 16:17-18 NIV)

Paul is telling us to watch out for those who cause division and put obstacles in our way when it comes to following Christ. They do this with their tongues, through flattery. They deceive the minds of naïve people through their speech. The church is full of those people.

You see this on YouTube all the time. Sadly, there are a lot of those on YouTube destroying the faith of many people. I can produce many sad examples. A few years ago, I was in contact with a young man who was so hungry for God. He wanted to be baptized, filled with the Holy Spirit, to follow Christ, and we agreed to meet to pray for him and to baptize him. I was so excited. But the day before we were to meet, I got an email from him that said, "You are a fake, you are a false prophet, God led me to this YouTube video so I did not get deceived by you. You need to repent."

He included a link to somebody who spoke very badly about me. So sad! This young man, who really truly wanted God, had his faith destroyed because he did not discern the message he saw. Too many people, sadly, believe everything they see out there. God is calling us to be more skeptical, discerning, to grow up because we are in a war. YouTube, Facebook, and the internet is destroying so many people's lives.

But they are also all over in the churches. Jesus has given us strong warnings when he says this:

"Watch out for false prophets. They come to you in sheep's clothing, but inwardly they are ferocious wolves. By their fruit you will recognize them. Do people pick grapes from thornbushes, or figs from thistles? Likewise, every good tree bears good fruit, but a bad tree bears bad fruit. A good tree cannot bear bad fruit,

and a bad tree cannot bear good fruit. Every tree that does not bear good fruit is cut down and thrown into the fire. Thus, by their fruit you will recognize them." (Matthew 7:15-19 NIV)

All of this applies to false apostles, false leaders, false pastors, and false Christians. It's also not only about wolves that come in sheep's clothing that we should watch out for. In another place, Jesus warns against those who are blind who led the blind, like the Pharisees.

Some people on YouTube are not wolves in sheep's clothing, but are more like blind people trying to lead the blind, and thereby deceiving many, as they themselves are deceived.

They won't enter into the kingdom of God and they won't allow others to enter either. That is the sad truth to see, as Jesus said:

"Woe to you, teachers of the law and Pharisees, you hypocrites! You shut the door of the kingdom of heaven in people's faces. You yourselves do not enter, nor will you let those enter who are trying to." (Matthew 23:13 NIV)

I encourage you to read all of Matthew 23, as there are some very strong words spoken by Jesus there. Again and again, He talked about how to recognize people by their fruit. Signs are not enough. Many people are known for signs—prophesying, casting out of demons and miracles—but still have bad fruit in their lives. They live like evildoers, and therefore they will not inherit the kingdom of God.

"Not everyone who says to me, 'Lord, Lord,' will enter the kingdom of heaven, but only the one who does the will of my Father who is in heaven. Many will say to me on that day, 'Lord, Lord, did we not prophesy in your name and in your name drive out demons and in your name perform many miracles?' Then I will tell them plainly, 'I never knew you. Away from me, you evildoers!'" (Matthew 7:21-23 NIV)

It is so important to understand you don't know a person by signs but by their fruit, but many don't know the difference between fruit and signs. Signs are like healing the sick and casting out demons. Those who lay hands on the sick and pray in faith will see people get healed. But you can do that while you still have unrepentant sin in your life.

If we live in continuous sin, we show the world that we never really knew Jesus. And you, as evildoers, will not inherit the kingdom of God. Paul told the church in Galatians that the acts of the flesh are evident.

> "The acts of the flesh are obvious: sexual immorality, impurity and debauchery; idolatry and witchcraft; hatred, discord, jealousy, fits of rage, selfish ambition, dissensions, factions and envy; drunkenness, orgies, and the like. I warn you, as I did before, that those who live like this will not inherit the kingdom of God." (Galatians 5:19-21 NIV)

Please note, Paul wrote this to the church. He wrote this to people who had seen the signs, spoke in tongues, healed the sick, cast out demons, and he said if you live like this, if you continue living a life of sin, you will not inherit the kingdom of God.

Then he talks about what the fruit is:

> "But the fruit of the Spirit is love, joy, peace, forbearance, kindness, goodness, faithfulness, gentleness and self-control. Against such things there is no law. Those who belong to Christ Jesus have crucified the flesh with its passions and desires." (Galatians 5:22-24 NIV)

This is why we need to repent and truly be born again. That is why we need the fear of God and to let the Holy Spirit transform our lives.

But my question to you is, do you know the fruit of the people you are listening to on YouTube? Do you know the fruit of the people you follow? Or do you only see the signs or listen to their words?

When Paul talks about elders and deacons in 1 Timothy, he says what fruit, what good character, we should look for with an elder, with a deacon, and not the signs.

> *"Here is a trustworthy saying: Whoever aspires to be an overseer desires a noble task. Now the overseer is to be above reproach, faithful to his wife, temperate, self-controlled, respectable, hospitable, able to teach, not given to drunkenness, not violent but gentle, not quarrelsome, not a lover of money. He must manage his own family well and see that his children obey him, and he must do so in a manner worthy of full respect. (If anyone does not know how to manage his own family, how can he take care of God's church?) He must not be a recent convert, or he may become conceited and fall under the same judgment as the devil. He must also have a good reputation with outsiders, so that he will not fall into disgrace and into the devil's trap.* (1 Timothy 3:1-7 NIV)

My question is, is that person you listen to on YouTube, those people you follow, are they without reproach? Are they faithful to their wife? You probably don't know if they have a wife, you don't know how their everyday lives are lived. You know almost nothing about them and that is dangerous.

It is so easy today to set up a video and make everything look good. Some of those out there on YouTube have no church family. They are just spreading the poison and creating division and destroying people, and we truly need to wake up.

And it's not only those on YouTube; this is with all of us. If we do what Paul says we should do, if we look at what we're called to look for as with elders, using the same standard for every person who is in ministry in the body of Christ, we will know who to follow or not. If they don't meet those qualifications, we don't follow them. If we do that, Satan will really lose a lot, because right now, he's destroying the souls of many through deceiving ministers.

Let me share one more important area we are being deceived in.

Jesus answered them, *"See to it that no one deceives you, because many will come in my name and say, 'I am the Messiah,' and they will deceive many people."* (Matthew 24:4-5 NIV)

We often misunderstand this verse because of the translation. I don't think we will see many deceived by people walking around saying, "Hey, I am the Messiah" or "I am Christ, follow me." No, when we see those weird people who dress up like Jesus, talk like Jesus, say they're Jesus, we know something is off. We know they are not Jesus and, therefore, are deceivers. Those kinds of people are not the ones who will deceive many as Jesus warns about. They might deceive a few people, but not many.

We need to remember the word "Christ" in Hebrew is "Messiah" and in Greek is "Christos," with the word meaning "anointed, the anointed one." If we then read it with the word "anointed," it suddenly opens the Word up in a totally different way. Try reading it again with the word "anointed":

Jesus answered them, *"See to it that no one deceives you, because many will come in my name and say, 'I am the (Anointed),' and they will deceive many people.* (Matthew 24:4-5 NIV)

Many are being deceived by people who are "anointed," and because they are anointed, others follow them blindly. Not long ago, over the phone, I heard of somebody who started to follow one of those people that Jesus warns about. This person he started to follow is new in his faith, doesn't hold onto sound doctrine, his wife just left him after a short time of marriage, but people still follow him. They listen to him like an elder in the church because of his "anointing."

When I heard my friend telling me about how many people follow this man, I asked why? Why do people follow him when there is such bad fruit in his life?

The answer I got just highlights this problem. He said, "Yeah, there is bad fruit, but he's so anointed, and therefore God must be with him."

Because of his "anointing" people don't see the rotten fruit and therefore they blindly follow him. The "anointing" is not the sign that God is with a person.

But is this not exactly what Jesus warned about?

Many will come in His name, and they will say, "I am anointed, follow me." And many will be deceived because of their "anointing," the "healings," the "miracles." I am putting quotes around "healing" and "miracles" because I am not sure about them. It can be God as God blesses faith even if people live in sin. If you have faith and pray for people, you can still see God use your faith and heal people because He loves those you pray for and He can use anyone.

But it doesn't mean all that is being done is good with that person who prays. Just look at Judas in the Bible. He did miracles together with the other apostles— he was sent out, too. He was given authority to heal the sick and cast out demons. But look at what he did in the end.

He was a deceiver and ended up getting lost.

I've heard about "miracles" and "healings" like this and I am not sure if it is not sometimes demons at work. In this case I have heard of many people he prayed for who got worse afterward. But on Facebook it all looks so good, even if the truth is something else.

This is a big problem today as people don't see the rotten fruit coming out from the lives of those people. It's truly time to wake up my friends. Be careful who you follow. Be careful who you listen to. Let's take the standard God gives for an elder in the church and apply that to everyone in ministry.

Let's be wise and discerning as snakes and innocent as doves.

Teach others around you to do the same.

Let people around you know the war we are in. It's happening right now. It's happening here. We are losing so many people in the battles because we haven't prepared them for this war. We are not alert, don't know the difference between fruits and signs, and drink the poison of the lies out there. And we are therefore so easily deceived.

There is more to share about our battle: what it is and how we fight it. I needed to learn the hard way, but if I did not have the fear of God in my life, I would have been destroyed by now.

So, start there. Start with praying to God to reveal His holiness to you. If there are things you need to repent for and clean up, then do it today—don't wait for tomorrow. Ask God to reveal the fear of Him in your life, so you're ready one day when the enemy comes your way to stand bold and firm where you have nothing to hide, nothing to fear, because you are living in the light that Jesus called you to.

Chapter Twenty-Seven
Our Battle

A new man has been moved into my cell. I loved being alone in my cell and I've been alone most of the time here. The Pod is full now so they moved a man into my cell. It's so full, they've started putting people on the cells' floors. This man in my cell doesn't speak any English, not one word, and I don't speak Spanish, and of course it just makes everything so much more difficult.

It is hard to use the toilet while somebody is in your cell with you, but there are many things in here you just need to get used to. In many areas, you die to yourself again and again. You also learn to appreciate small things. For example, when we change clothes two times a week, we often get socks with holes in them, or shirts missing the sleeves, as people love to take them off because they feel they look fantastic. But as it is freezing at night, I don't like to sleep in shirts with no sleeves. And the shorts we get are often torn or have been sewn together again, so they're often weird to wear as they are out of shape.

But last week something special happened. I got a new pair of socks. It was the first time I got a new pair, and it was like a beautiful birthday gift. Yes, it brought joy to me, when you haven't had anything like that for a long time. So, I don't want to get rid of them again: I keep them, take them with me in the shower, and wash them there when they need to be cleaned. I also now have my "own" favorite T-shirt to wear with my new socks. And I am so thankful for them. You learn to appreciate and be grateful for small things like this. And you then see how we in the Western world are so spoiled, and still, in so many ways, we always complain.

We have forgotten to be thankful and appreciate the small things in life. If we look at the Western church and compare us with the persecuted church, then we, as I said before, think we are blessed compared to them. But if we look with spiritual eyes, it is very different. Why? Because there's something persecution and suffering can do that nothing else can. A saying goes like this: "Hard times make strong people, strong people make good times, good times make weak people, weak people make hard times."

The Western church has had easy times, good times without real persecution and suffering, and therefore, we have become weak. As I said, we have also taken things for granted. But I believe that things are changing in our Western world, and I am convinced that we will see a new level of persecution shortly. As you see, it's already started, but it will grow stronger and stronger as time passes.

But as it is right now, persecution is mainly for those who really do the work of the Kingdom. You can believe in all the right things and Satan will leave you alone, but the moment you start to do it, preach the gospel, lead people to Christ, cast out demons and heal the sick, then you become a threat to Satan and his kingdom and then, welcome to the war for the battle is on, and it is real.

A radio interview a short time ago had a story about me being in jail. A Danish man called in and said that there was no persecution in Denmark. He said he didn't experience anything like I have, and therefore, I must be lying. Yes, most Christians in Denmark and around the world don't experience any persecution, and therefore, they don't understand what is happening to me and others. As I said, you are free to believe in everything in the Bible, and as long as you don't do anything about it, the devil will leave you alone.

That is the problem. Many today have faith and go to church like this Danish man but don't do anything more with it, and therefore, Satan leaves them alone. Again, you can believe that casting out demons is for today, but as long as you don't do it, as long as you don't cast out devils, Satan has no problem with you believing it. That is how it is with every truth in the word of God. We can "believe" it is the truth, as long as we don't begin to obey it. It is our obedience that Satan doesn't like and will do anything to stop.

God has used this time to teach me and Lene a lot about spiritual warfare. A prophetic word I received speaks to this:

"Remember, we are fighting the greatest and most gruesome war over the souls of mankind. Life vs. death. God vs. devils. Heaven or hell. Nations are at stake. Regions and cities are at stake. Eternity is at stake. Hell is enlarging itself, darkness is prevailing, and souls are being lost every single minute. Millions of souls are on the line. Meanwhile, the churches of God lie in ruins. More souls are being lost than are being saved at this point in time. But God is raising up true leaders to take over and lead His church into her true destiny. He is building an army. He is raising up generals that are gonna take His army of disciples into battle against devils. Leaders like yourself that won't compromise. Leaders that won't be afraid of darkness. Leaders that will forsake their entire lives for Christ and His Kingdom, and whatever commands He instructs. Leaders that are gonna bring restoration of the true Gospel, reformation to the church, and the Revelation of Jesus Christ to the entire world. Remember, we are fighting the greatest and most gruesome war over the souls of mankind.

"BECAUSE OF WHAT IS HAPPENING FREEDOM IS GOING TO EXPLODE."

There is also the strategic objective of what God is working in your own heart and mind during this time. He is building your faith and increasing your endurance for the days ahead.

You will have to lead many through some very difficult times in the future. You will have to be able to impart endurance into others for the hard things the body of Christ will have to experience in the future. God is preparing and purifying you for the coming seasons of warfare. He is making you into a more effective war leader."

When I first heard the word, I did not truly understand what it meant. How will God make me a more effective war leader?

I've only recently started to understand this more and more, and I see now how the fight was occurring on so many fronts simultaneously. The fight for my case, the fight for the truth against the lies that have labeled me a dangerous person and a national security threat, the fight in our minds involving fear, doubt, and hopelessness that suddenly comes over us. The fight is for the gospel and being bold to share the gospel—and it started with those in here with me.

The pressure here has often been so intense that it's difficult to explain, but in those moments, I know the war is on.

The twenty-four teachings I've done here, there are three primary lessons where I look at the war we are in. One lesson is called, "Satan is the god of this world," another I call, "Our battle," and the third one I call, "Our weapons," and I know our enemy really doesn't like these lessons. When I did them, we experienced attacks like we've never experienced before.

I know there are things our enemy doesn't want me to speak about. He doesn't want us to be aware of the ways he works and how this battle is fought and won because when we know how to fight it, what our weapons are, and what authority we have, then he will lose.

This is a real war, and I felt it as soon as I started working on this chapter. After an hour of writing, I went through some of the most intense, crazy, spiritual attacks ever. I am still in shock and shaking writing this.

Lene and my family have driven from California to Florida to be close to me. And even though it was a big step of faith to drive the whole way here, it went perfectly. However, as soon as they arrived in Florida, tired after three days of driving, the attacks became very hard. The battle was on the moment they entered the state. They got a phone call from our legal team.

"What are you doing, Lene," they said, "you need to turn the car around and get as far away from Florida as you can."

This call came in when they crossed the border and finally arrived in Florida. Our legal team had heard of her plans, but as they found out more information about the corruption in government agencies, they feared they would come after Lene and my girls just to get to me.

I heard this story a few hours ago when I called Lene to welcome them to Florida. They were tired and crying, sitting in the car not knowing what to do. Yes, even my girls, who have been strong through it all, were crying and could not take it anymore.

What now? They wanted to drive to a friend's house and stay there as agreed, but the legal team had said no. They knew that my phone calls were being listened to and the people in here know too much about our plans. It sounds like a movie, but this is not a movie; this is real life. And it is happening right now as I am writing to you, trying to get the words down on paper. We feel fear, fear you can cut through. But we prayed, and we still pray. We know where the war is. It is spiritual, even if it sometimes can feel like it is just physical. But behind all of this are evil spirits that are trying to get us to stop and give up. That comes with fear, doubt, or attacks in our minds.

I remember reading the book The Heavenly Man by Brother Yun. He spoke about how, in China, the attacks were mostly physical, but when he came to the West, there were more lies being spread and the attacks were mental in nature. He also said that in China it was often clear who your enemy was, as it was those who were anti-God, including people in the government. But in the West, the attacks often came from people within the church. So, the presentation is very different here. As Brother Yun says, mental attacks, and how we experience them in the West, are not easier than physical attacks and how they experience them in China; it is just different but not easier.

Satan can come in many forms like he came in the form of a snake in the garden. When Satan tried to divert Jesus away from God's plan for Him, he worked through Jesus' close friend Peter. The attack came from a close friend who spoke words that were a stumbling block to Jesus. How did Jesus handle it?

"Jesus turned and said to Peter, 'Get behind me, Satan! You are a stumbling block to me; you do not have in mind the concerns of God, but merely human concerns.'" (Matthew 16:23 NIV)

This doesn't mean that the people who are used by the enemy in this way are evil. They can love God, love us, and think they are doing what is best for us. I think this is how it was with Peter. But they don't know what God is doing, and maybe they just speak out of fear. But it can be something Satan wants to use as a stumbling block in our lives, and my family and I have experienced this many times during this season. We had to learn to be alert to prevent the words from coming in and getting us off track.

What I love about Peter is that even Satan tried to use him, and even though he at one time denied Jesus three times, God turned it all around and used him mightily. Before he denied Jesus, Jesus said this to him:

"'Simon, Simon, Satan has asked to sift all of you as wheat. But I have prayed for you, Simon, that your faith may not fail. And when you have turned back, strengthen your brothers'" *(Luke 22:31-32 NIV)*

Peter turned back to God, and God used him greatly to strengthen his brothers and sisters. Not only did he strengthen the people close to him, but Peter's first letter also helps you and me when we go through suffering and trials.

But before we look at Peter's first letter, I want to ask you, why did God allow Satan to do this against Peter? I believe there are many reasons why God let Satan do this. However, one was that this would, in the end, make Peter stronger, and God wanted to use Peter to strengthen his brothers afterward. Peter needed to go through various trials to learn and become a tool in God's hands so he could be a blessing to others.

The same thing is also seen with Jesus. Jesus went through suffering and temptations so he could feel our pain and help us in those things we now face.

> *"For we do not have a high priest who is unable to empathize with our weaknesses, but we have one who has been tempted in every way, just as we are—yet he did not sin."* (Hebrews 4:15 NIV)

Jesus can now relate to our suffering and understand us because He has been tested and tempted in all things like us. When Jesus was tempted in all things, it wasn't easy what He went through. So now He understands our weaknesses and has compassion for us as He has experienced the same things.

If we go back to Eden's garden, we read how Adam and Eve were tempted. They were tempted by the temptations of this world.

John lays out what those temptations are:

> *"For everything in the world—the lust of the flesh, the lust of the eyes, and the pride of life—comes not from the Father but from the world. The world and its desires pass away, but whoever does the will of God lives forever."* (1 John 2:16-17 NIV)

When it comes to the sins of this world, we can divide them into three areas: the lust of the flesh, the lust of the eyes, and the pride of life. These three areas are also where the enemy tempted Adam and Eve, and they fell.

> *"When the woman saw that the tree produced good food, was attractive in appearance, and was desirable for making one wise, she took some of its fruit and ate it. Then she also gave some to her husband who was with her, and he ate some, too."* (Genesis 3:6 NIV)

The woman saw the fruit was good; that was the lust of the eyes. For food; that is the lust of the flesh. And to gain wisdom or to be like God; that is the pride of life. Adam and Eve fell, so they are not a good example to follow.

But we can follow Jesus; we can look at Him. Jesus came as the new Adam to restore what was destroyed by the fall of Adam. To do that, He needed to be tempted in all things like Adam and Eve were.

Jesus started His ministry by the Holy Spirit leading Him out into the desert to be tempted. In Luke 4, you can read how Jesus encountered the same temptations Adam and Eve experienced.

At one time, Jesus was hungry, and Satan said, *"Tell this stone to become bread"* (Luke 4:3 NIV). That was the lust of the flesh.

Then he showed Him all the kingdoms of the world and said, *"All this I will give you if you will bow down and worship me"* (Matthew 4:9 NIV). That was the lust of the eye.

When Satan took Him to the highest point in Jerusalem and said, *"If you are the Son of God, throw yourself down. For it is written: 'He will command his angels concerning you, and they will lift you up in their hands, so that you will not strike your foot against a stone,'"* (Matthew 4:6 NIV), yes, prove to me who you are, that was the pride of life.

God let Jesus go through those things for a reason, and the final reason is to bring us forgiveness, as He was the Lamb without sin, slain to bring us forgiveness. But He also makes Jesus an example when it comes to testing and suffering. Jesus is our example in all areas of this life.

Peter has also been an example to us today as he went through trials and temptations and learned. Let's look more at Peter. After all his failings, Peter wrote a masterpiece about suffering, persecution, testing and trials. When you read 1 Peter, try to keep in mind that this is the same guy, the same man who failed so much.

If you keep that in mind as you read, it becomes so much more powerful. In chapter one, Peter starts to explain why suffering is so important to us. First, he says that it proves the genuineness of our faith and helps to purify it.

"In all this you greatly rejoice, though now for a little while you may have had to suffer grief in all kinds of trials. These have come so that the proven genuineness of your faith—of greater worth than gold, which perishes even though refined by fire—may result in praise, glory and honor when Jesus Christ is revealed." (1 Peter 1:6-7 NIV)

Suffering and trials are there to reveal the genuineness of our faith and to purify it. But without these tests and suffering, we don't know how genuine our faith is, how real our faith is, or how honest others' faith is.

And this is a big problem when it comes to the Western church. I sadly believe that one day, many people will deny their faith and fall away. That will happen in our Western churches as soon as real suffering and persecution come our way.

When this happens, many will fall away because the Word hasn't penetrated deep enough into their lives; the roots are not deep enough to handle this.

This is what Jesus teaches in Mark 4, with the Parable of the Sower. As we see some fall away, we will see others stand firm in their faith and testing. That will purify their faith and make them grow even more in the Lord. Yes, they will come out so much stronger on the other side.

Trials help the right people grow but also reveal those who are not sincere in their faith as they will fall away. Later in the same letter, Peter says that those who have gone through physical suffering have done away with sin and every human desire. What is left is to do God's will.

"Therefore, since Christ suffered in his body, arm yourselves also with the same attitude, because whoever suffers in the body is done with sin. As a result, they do not live the rest of their earthly lives for evil human desires, but rather for the will of God." (1 Peter 4:1-2 NIV)

I feel that it just comes to a point for me where it hurts so much that I give up and surrender all. I became so desperate and just wanted it all to stop, and you just give everything over to God, and there is nothing left of yourself; you cannot do it anymore; you genuinely die to yourself; you die to your flesh. As I said, you just give everything over but in a new way that you would have never done if you did not suffer.

It truly becomes not your will, but His will be done. Without suffering, we will never really come to the place where we are finished with ourselves, and that is also where we have overcome sin as we read in Scripture.

Suffering works in many ways and is essential to us. It is so vital for me. Yes, it has transformed me in a way that when this pain is over, I pray I will remember what I have obtained and not go back to where I was before because we so easily forget and fall back into the old ways of living again. Not that my "old" ways of living were not living for Jesus and seeing God doing extraordinary things, but there is something new I did not have before.

If we look more at 1 Peter, Peter goes on with a beautiful text in which he says how Satan goes around as a lion seeking whom he can devour. But note what he says just before and after:

> "Humble yourselves, therefore, under God's mighty hand, that he may lift you up in due time. Cast all your anxiety on him because he cares for you. Be alert and of sober mind. Your enemy the devil prowls around like a roaring lion looking for someone to devour." (1 Peter 5:6-8 NIV)

This is pure gold. This is how we overcome, how we survive our enemy's attacks in the battle we are in. The first thing we always need to do is humble ourselves; humble ourselves under God's hand, yes, humble yourself under Him. Give everything to Him, surrender it all, and let go of all control, knowing that He is the one who needs to be in control and not you. And know that this present suffering is only for a short time. As we read in the next verse, He will lift you up in due time.

"And the God of all grace, who called you to his eternal glory in Christ, after you have suffered a little while, will himself restore you and make you strong, firm and steadfast." (1 Peter 5:10 NIV)

The time of suffering is an opportunity to humble yourself under God in an extraordinary way. But that is not the only thing because we, as we read here, need to cast all anxiety on Him. All fear, all worries, let go of all of it, and I know it is so much easier said than done. But if we don't learn to do it, it will take us down, but we also need to be alert and sober-minded as we read. Why? Because the attacks from our enemy can come suddenly and from everywhere, so we need to be alert and sober.

The attacks are very often in the mind. It suddenly comes, it comes through words that are spoken, it comes through things that happen or it just comes from nowhere, and suddenly doubt comes in, fear comes in, and then it is so important that we stand firm in the truth.

When I share this with you, I can come up with many examples of how this has happened to us in the last few months. Suddenly, the attacks aren't just in our minds. Words are spoken by somebody, even a friend, and sometimes even misunderstandings, are used by our enemy to take us down.

Fear suddenly comes very strong on us. We ask ourselves the question, "What if?"

Yes, what if this and that will happen or what if God will not do this? When this happens, it is time to humble ourselves, let go of all fear and feelings, and know in faith that God is faithful. Cast all anxiety on Him and be of sober mind, do everything Peter said that we should do. And when we do that, we will resist the devil. We are called to resist him, standing firm in our faith.

I truly love these words. These have been some of my favorite words in this season. But I admit that every time I read 1 Peter 5, I stop on the words, "a little while." Let's read this verse:

"And the God of all grace, who called you to his eternal glory in Christ, after you have suffered a little while, will himself restore you and make you strong, firm and steadfast." (1 Peter 5:10 NIV)

The reason why this doesn't feel like "a little while" is because it has now been many months, but in God's eyes it is just a little while.

This will all be a minor thing if we compare it with the blessing of all eternity awaiting us. Every suffering we go through here on earth will just be a little while in the light of the age to come. What I shared here is so important, and I pray that it will encourage you and prepare you when you stand in the battle.

I encourage you to read Peter's whole first letter and remember who wrote it; then, it will be a blessing. Know that God has a plan for you, and He knows what He is doing.

When you go through trials and suffering, the battle is real. A spiritual and physical war, as I experienced, can come. Most often, the fight happens in our minds, but we can learn to stand firm in our faith and understand that this is a way to prove our faith's genuineness, which is important. It is there to purify our faith and it's there to help us to grow so God can bless us even more on the other side. When you have that understanding, these walls around me and the closed door don't mean so much.

In all you go through, remember this truth here in 1 Peter.

I will end with another important, simple truth. Lene and I remind each other of this simple truth:

> "No temptation has overtaken you except what is common to mankind. And God is faithful; he will not let you be tempted beyond what you can bear. But when you are tempted, he will also provide a way out so that you can endure it." (1 Corinthians 10:13 NIV)

This applies not only to temptations, but trials and testing too. God is faithful, and He will not let us go through things beyond our strength, or He will prepare a way out of it for us. He knows what we can handle and is with us through it all. This is a really good reminder when we go through things. Thank God for Your faithfulness.

This text I write now was added after I got released, as I could not write what I write here and record it over the phone while I was in jail. Yes, they were listening to my phone calls and I could not say where Lene and my girls were.

We prayed and felt we could not live in fear. We should not think, "What if?" So even though our legal team did not like it, and wanted my family to leave Florida and go as far away as possible, we felt it was an attack from our enemy and we should just go in faith no matter what our legal team said. We should trust in God and not in man. So Lene and the girls ended up going over to our friend's home in Florida that same evening. But we also felt we should be careful and wise in how we did it.

So, over the phone, we did not talk about where they were. We used code language, like giving people other names, and spoke in a way that if they were listening, they did not know where my family was hiding.

Yes, I know it sounds extreme, but when you know what the people here have been doing toward me and how far they have gone with lying and breaking the laws like creating false accusations against me, you know that they are not to be trusted and will go very far to stop me. This is the reality we are living in.

Chapter Twenty-Eight
God's Plan, God's Will

Today is day three hundred in jail; this will also be the last chapter I write from my cell. I am still waiting to find out if I am leaving soon. I still don't know when I will get out, but God knows. And He has spoken, and He has a plan for all of it; I am sure of that.

Last night around 12:30 a.m., just before they turned out the lights, I was lying in bed praying and thinking about the last three hundred days.

Then suddenly, I became very, very thankful to God for putting me here. It was so very special. I just became thankful for everything that has happened, and it was a special moment and a special feeling. It all came as a surprise to me because it came from deep, deep inside of me, like a joy bubbling up of thankfulness for the last three hundred days.

But the last three hundred days have also been truly hard. I have cried more than I ever have before in my life. I've felt so lost, so depressed, so abandoned, so scared, and so lonely. I've hoped, again and again, that now, I would be let out.

And when it didn't happen, I became very disappointed. I experienced this many times. I've wanted to leave this place, and I did not understand why it did not happen. Why am I still here? Why is it taking so long to get me out? And why do I need to suffer like this? And why did my family need to go through all this pain?

But lying on my bed last night, I suddenly understood things more clearly than ever before. I understood more clearly what the prophecy said: God has a plan for this. He is the one who sent me here to re-make me—to remake both Lene and I at this time—because who we were before was not enough for who He needed us to be in the next season. And therefore, we needed to go through all of this. I just saw it so clearly—God's plan. I thought I saw it before. I read the prophecy many times. I'd said God has a plan with all of it. But yesterday, in my bed, it just became different, and I was joyful. I was thankful. God has done excellent work in my life, and He is still profoundly working in me and Lene.

I've had so many experiences in the last three hundred days that I would not want to have been without. The Word has transformed my life. God has opened Scripture to me in a new way. I've seen lives changed. I've seen how amazing the Bible Discovery Groups are. Besides that, I've lost almost forty pounds (eighteen kilos). I've trained my body and am stronger now than ever. So many things have happened, especially the revival I have seen here. It's been mighty and nothing like I've ever seen. Yes, I keep discovering things I would not want to have been without.

I have cried, begged, and prayed many times, and I know many others have prayed for my release, but nothing happened. My legal team has been working hard to get me out but could not. A short time ago, they said to me that it was like they hit a spiritual wall, and nothing was happening no matter what they did. I know today that the wall they felt was God because He had a plan. He still has a plan.

He planned to bring me here, and so much has happened in these three hundred days. What would three hundred days out there have given me? Of course, three hundred days out there could have given me a lot. But here, the days have been so much more intense and compact than anything I've ever experienced. God truly has a plan for it, and we can all submit to His plan and His will because He truly knows what He is doing.

I really want to get out, but in His time, because He has a plan. I can now pray, "God, not my will be done, but Yours."

Lene is still suffering, and it's still tough. She's still not free, so it is hard for me to be here. But still, I can relax, knowing God is in control also of her life. He has spoken, and it will happen according to His will. I can also rejoice over how God will use this afterward. Because He has spoken of many things that will come out of this—many things that will happen in the future. And I am very excited about that.

We will see salvation and freedom come to many people because of what is happening right now. Yes, I genuinely believe we will see churches all over this country, all over the world, be reformed and transformed because of what God is doing. I don't say that to say, "Look at me!"—not at all. It's all about Him and what He will do. We are just a tiny part of the big picture God is putting together right now.

At one point, God spoke to me, through a prophetic word: "There are things God is accomplishing in you, things He is accomplishing in that region, and things He is accomplishing in His church by you being there. He is preparing a lot of things for the future. This is much bigger than it appears to be on the surface. Because of what is happening freedom is going to explode."

If I could talk to myself three hundred days ago, I would say, "Torben, don't fear. You don't have to be anxious. It is going to be very hard, but God is in control. And you can trust God's plan and surrender totally to His will, even though it will be the hardest thing you've ever experienced. God has a plan, and He knows exactly what He's doing. So just submit and surrender everything to Him."

Twenty years ago, I wrote a book called, Finish the Race. It was in Danish, and I never got it translated into English. But I have always shared its teachings in our Bible schools over the years. Even though I've spoken the message from that book many times—maybe over thirty times—I see it much more clearly than ever before. And it is so freeing.

The fear is leaving, just thinking about it—even when it comes to Lene and what she's going through now. I just called Lene this morning and encouraged her with these words, "It will be good because God has a plan. We just need to surrender to His will, and we can trust Him."

This morning, I was training in my cell and praying. I did some exercises—sit-ups, pushups, and back exercises. Then, I ran up and down the stairs for fifteen to twenty minutes. It's good training, but at the same time, it's a good time for praying.

But this morning, I felt God spoke to me that this should be the last chapter I write from here, and I should call it "God's Plan, God's Will." When I am finished with this chapter, I will put this book away until I am out.

My legal team has said that I could get out in a few days, but they also said that five months ago, and I am still here. Three months ago, I heard I would get out at the end of the month. They once said there was a big chance I would be released within three weeks, but that was a half-year ago.

So, this time, I will not put too much hope into that. This is not to criticize them; they try as hard as possible.

I don't know—and they don't know—but God knows. I stopped putting a date on when I will come out, but this is the last chapter from here.

When Jesus walked the earth, He said, *"My food...is to do the will of him who sent me and to finish his work. By myself I can do nothing; I judge only as I hear, and my judgment is just, for I seek not to please myself but him who sent me. For I have come down from heaven not to do my will but to do the will of him who sent me"* (John 4:34, 5:30, 6:38 NIV).

Jesus truly knew why He was here: to finish God's plan and purpose for His life. This was His mission, this was His food, this is what He lived for. And believe me when I say it was not always easy, even for Jesus. He knew He needed to die on that cross and become a curse to set us free and thereby fulfill the plan God had for Him. Others around Him did not understand that, and the enemy was doing everything to stop Him, even Jesus' closest friends.

When Jesus foretold His death, Peter tried to get Him to walk away from the crucifixion. But Jesus needed to rebuke Peter, as we have already looked at in another chapter, with the words, *"Get behind me, Satan! You are a stumbling block to me"* (Matthew 16:23 NIV). And then He continues, *"You do not have in mind the concerns of God, but merely human concerns."*

Later, the pressure on Jesus was so strong in the Garden of Gethsemane. He knew what was going to happen to Him: He would be whipped, His flesh torn apart, a crown of thorns jammed into His skull, causing great pain, humiliated by guards making fun of Him and pretending to worship Him. He also knew that, ultimately, the wrath of God would be poured out on Him. He was deeply distressed by it all. He was so overwhelmed by sorrow that He reached the point where He actually sweated blood. *"And being in agony, He was praying very fervently; and His sweat became like drops of blood, falling down upon the ground"* (Luke 22:44 NIV).

None of us have ever experienced anything like this before. We have never been close to anything like what Jesus needed to suffer. And none of us have suffered to the point where we sweat blood. That is where the blood vessels burst, and blood runs out because of stress. None of us have ever been close to that. In the last ten months, I have experienced the hardest moments in this cell. I have cried out, "My God, my God, why have you forsaken me?"

I have been lying on the cell floor and crying like never before, crying out to God in distress and deep pain. But I have never experienced anything like Jesus experienced. Out there, before the cross, Jesus fell to the ground and prayed, *""Abba, Father, everything is possible for you. Take this cup from me"* (Mark 14:36 NIV). Yes, Jesus wanted it to stop, again knowing everything that would happen to Him. Jesus did not want it to happen that way, so He prayed if there was any way for this not to happen, then let it be.

I prayed that many times also. Please let me out right now. I cannot do it anymore. I beg you to let me go right now. If there is any way, God, You can do it now, then stop this and let me go home to my family.

I have often said that if I had a special phone number I could dial, and then it would stop, I would have called it many times. But I did not have that number. Jesus did though, and He could have stopped it if He wanted to. And even though He prayed for that, He did not stop it. Why? Because He continued His prayer, *"Yet not my will, but yours be done"* (Luke 22:42 NIV).

He wanted it to stop. He wanted the cup of God's wrath and everything with it not to happen, but not if it meant He was denying the Father's will. He wanted to finish the plan God had for Him. Because that was why He was sent here. That was more important than anything else for Him. And because of this, He prayed, *"Not My will, but Yours, be done"* (Luke 22:42 NKJV). Therefore, He continued the whole way to the cross, and He said, *"It is finished"* (John 19:30 NIV).

What was finished? He did what He was sent to do, the work the Father had sent Him to do. Jesus was fully surrendered to the Father's will and plan for His life, no matter what it cost. To do the will of the Father was His food. We read in Philippians 2, Paul says we should have the same attitude and humility as was found in Christ:

> *"Who, being in very nature God,*
> *did not consider equality with God something to be used to*
> *his own advantage;*
> *rather, he made himself nothing*
> *by taking the very nature of a servant,*
> *being made in human likeness.*
> *And being found in appearance as a man,*
> *he humbled himself*
> *by becoming obedient to death—*
> *even death on a cross!"* (Philippians 2:6-8 NIV)

Why the cross here? It was God's plan—God's will for His life. The next verse starts with, therefore, because Jesus was obedient to the end, because Jesus was obedient to the cross, because He finished God's plan; therefore, we read this:

> *"Therefore God exalted him to the highest place*
> *and gave him the name that is above every name,*
> *that at the name of Jesus every knee should bow,*
> *in heaven and on earth and under the earth,*
> *and every tongue acknowledge that Jesus Christ is Lord,*
> *to the glory of God the Father."* (Philippians 2:9-11 NIV)

Woah! These are beautiful words, but it doesn't stop there. The next verses are written to you and me:

> *"Therefore, my dear friends, as you have always obeyed—not only in my presence, but now much more in my absence—continue to work out your salvation with fear and trembling, for it is God who works in you to will and to act in order to fulfill his good purpose."* (Philippians 2:12-13 NIV)

As Jesus was sent here to earth, we are now sent in His place. *"So Jesus said to them again, 'Peace be with you; as the Father has sent Me, I also send you'"* (John 20:21 NIV).

The Father has sent Me, Jesus said. Now I am sending you, and we see that clearly in Paul's life. Not only was Paul sent, but he also had the same mind as Christ. Paul knew that like Christ was sent to do His Father's work, he was now sent here by Christ to obey Him as part of His body on earth. One time, Paul was compelled by the Holy Spirit to go to Jerusalem, even though he knew that prison and hardship were waiting for him there.

> *"And now, compelled by the Spirit, I am going to Jerusalem, not knowing what will happen to me there. only know that in every city the Holy Spirit warns me that prison and hardships are facing me."* (Act 20:22-23 NIV)

Paul was not led by fear but by faith. He knew he was sent, and there was a plan and purpose for his life. He was here in Christ's place to do His will.

"However, I consider my life worth nothing to me; my only aim is to finish the race and complete the task the Lord Jesus has given me - the task of testifying to the good news of God's grace." (Acts 20:24 NIV)

May we all come to a place where we can face prison and hardship with these words in our mouths.

In the next chapter in the book of Acts, a prophet named Agabus prophesied over Paul what would happen when he was in Jerusalem:

"After we had been there a number of days, a prophet named Agabus came down from Judea. Coming over to us, he took Paul's belt, tied his own hands and feet with it and said, "The Holy Spirit says, 'In this way the Jewish leaders will bind the owner of this belt and will hand him over to the Gentiles.'" (Acts 21:10-11 NIV)

When the believers heard the word of the Lord, they said, "Oh no! Hardship is coming! Prison is coming!"

Like Peter, who tried to persuade Jesus not to give His life, they tried to persuade Paul not to go to Jerusalem.

"When we heard this, we and the people there pleaded with Paul not to go up to Jerusalem" (Acts 21:12 NIV).

But Paul responded like Christ:

Then Paul answered, "Why are you weeping and breaking my heart? I am ready not only to be bound, but also to die in Jerusalem for the name of the Lord Jesus." When he would not be dissuaded, we gave up and said, "The Lord's will be done." (Acts 21:13-14 NIV)

The Lord's will be done. God had a plan with the suffering of Christ and Peter and Paul, and He was in control through it all, so with us.

We often say that God will never let His children suffer. But just look at Jesus, and you know that statement is incorrect. When it happens, it is because He has a purpose for it and is in control the whole way.

In the middle of suffering, we can find freedom and peace by knowing there is a reward on the other side. Jesus *"endured the cross for the joy set before Him"* (Hebrews 12:2 NIV).

There was a great reward on the other side for Jesus, and in that, He found strength to endure the cross. Paul also looked forward to the reward that was before him:

> *"I consider that our present sufferings are not worth comparing with the glory that will be revealed in us."* (Romans 8:18 NIV)

God has been teaching me about the Kingdom of God, the treasure in heaven we one day will receive when we go through these things. I have learned a lot about our coming inheritance, how God is using suffering to bring us into obedience and make us look more like Jesus, and the fruit that will come out of it.

But let's move on and look more at Paul and his focus in this life. Paul, just before he died, said these words:

> *"For I am already being poured out like a drink offering, and the time for my departure is near. I have fought the good fight, I have finished the race, I have kept the faith. Now there is in store for me the crown of righteousness, which the Lord, the righteous Judge, will award to me on that day—and not only to me, but also to all who have longed for His appearing."* (2 Timothy 4:6-8 NIV)

If we have the same mind as Christ, this is the focus we will have. Try to think of the reward Paul got out of his life here on earth, the glory awaiting him, the glory awaiting all of us when we take part in serving Christ, and when we take part in the suffering of Christ!

Why not live out these words, *"Not my will, but Yours, be done"* (Luke 22:42 NKJV). God's glory can be revealed in us now in this life, but even more in the life to come.

I have often quoted and taught on the verses in this chapter. But now I have experienced them. What once was just in my mind is now my life. This truth is in my heart. I've experienced it in a deeper way than I've ever seen before. God has a plan with all of it. And it is all about believing in Him. To believe is to trust. Trusting Him with everything, even our lives. Trusting that He loves us and He knows what is best. Trusting that He's good and His plan is perfect. Trust Him and surrender to His will, not only when it is easy but also when it is painful.

I know there are areas I need to grow in here because when I read about Paul, I know I'm not there yet—not at all. But I also know I'm not the same person I was ten months ago. I'm in a very different place, and I see that very clearly now. I feel the freedom and don't need to fear the future no matter what happens, because God has a plan, even when it becomes truly hard.

As I said before, I often wish I had a phone number to call and stop it, but I'm happy I did not. If I had a number I could call, I would have called that number many times and stopped this many times. I would have missed God's plan. I would have missed the purpose He had for my life. I wanted to stop this so many times, but what amazes me, is that I did not have that number to call. But Jesus had that, and He did not use it.

When Jesus was arrested in the garden, Peter took the sword and wanted to fight for Jesus. But Jesus stopped him and asked him to put the sword away. If Peter had fought and succeeded, he would have thought that he had done a good thing and saved Jesus from being arrested. But the opposite was the truth. He would not have done a good thing but instead hindered God's plan, or at least tried to but would not have succeeded.

Another time, Jesus says He could have called twelve legions of angels right away and just stopped it. Twelve legions of angels are seventy-two thousand angels. Want to know what angels can do when God sends them? Then just read here:

> *"That night the angel of the Lord went out and put to death a hundred and eighty-five thousand in the Assyrian camp. When the people got up the next morning—there were all the dead bodies!"* (2 Kings 19:35 NIV)

Wow. Just one angel killed one hundred and eighty-five thousand soldiers. How much can seventy-two thousand angels then not do? So, Jesus, He had the power. He could have stopped it all right away, but He didn't. We often fight so hard to stop what we think the enemy is doing because we don't see the big picture and what God is about to do. I'm thankful that God is in control and that His way is so much higher than ours.

God has a plan even in the hard times. And it's all about His will. If we, like Paul, are ready to lay down our lives, then we have nothing to fear because to live is Christ, but to die is gain. I thank God for opening my eyes and letting me see these things. I thank Him for the freedom He has given me. Even more than ever, I want to surrender to His will and say, *"Not My will, but Yours, be done"* (Luke 42:22 NKJV).

God's plan for our lives is always the best, and the glory that comes out of it is nothing compared to the short suffering we are going through.

I look forward to the next season, and I truly believe we will see a church rise up and live the way God has for us. It's time for the gospel to be restored to the church, for the reformation of the church, and for the revelation of Jesus Christ to all people. And I am very excited!

Chapter Twenty-Nine
Finally Out

I am writing this chapter to you, not from my cell in Baker County Detention Center, on a piece of paper with a security pen, like in the previous chapters. No, the day finally came when I left the jail and was reunited with my family. I am writing this to you from an Airbnb house in Germany, sitting with my computer.

It has been eight days since I was released from jail, and so many things have happened this last week. There are so many new impressions to take in, so many emotions, and so many memorable moments I will never forget. The greatest of them was when I saw my wife Lene and my girls again, and when I could finally hug Lene.

A few days later, I saw our son, his wife, and our four grandkids. To hold my new grandson for the first time was so special, as you will understand later in this chapter. I've never felt anything like that before in my life, and I will come back to this in the next chapter, where I will share more of what happened that day when I finally left jail and was reunited with my family. It was a long day, and many things happened.

But here, I first want to share what happened since I wrote the last chapter. I wrote everything in this book up to this chapter in sixteen days. It was some very intense days, but it gave me so much. After I had written the chapters, I started to call my friends on the outside and read the chapters to them over the phone, while they recorded it. I was afraid someone would come and take my papers, or I would somehow lose them when I finally got released, and everything I'd been writing would be lost. To make sure I got the book out of jail, I therefore recorded it. My legal team advised me to do so, and they also suggested I take copies of everything I'd written down and mail them out because no one promised that I would get to take my papers with me, especially with everything that happened around my case.

Therefore, I started taking copies of the chapters I wrote and mailing them out a little at the time. This way, I would have a backup in case I lost my papers on the way out. I think this was very important because I felt it was gold I was sitting on and God wanted to do something special with this book. And we know we have an enemy, and he will do everything he can to destroy the work God has.

I recorded every chapter in the book, but there were things I could not say over the phone because it was on a recorded line. So, several times I needed to say, "Add later," because I could not say it over the phone. The same with the copies: there were things I needed to leave out when I mailed them out because they made a copy of everything I mailed out from the jail.

I did that during the next few weeks, and when I had finally finished getting all the chapters out over the phone or by mailing out copies, I thought, "Now, it is time. I will leave this place. The time must come. Yes, it makes so much sense to me that it is now, as I have just finished this book, and did not see anything else that needed to happen?"

Then, April arrived, and I knew I could get an answer from our appeal any day. If I won, I would get my asylum and finally be released. I hoped for and prayed for that. I had been here for over three hundred days, and my family and friends thought that was long enough, so I was so ready. But little did I know, I still had one hundred days to go. God still needed to do much more in my life, and He still had work for me here. He had another book He wanted me to write, so the journey was far from over.

A few days after I finished recording this book, my appeal case was denied. It was a big shock for me and my legal team.

I thought, "What is happening here? It's like I'm losing everything there is to lose."

We all knew I had a strong asylum case, so nothing made sense to me or my legal team.

When I heard that, I thought, "Okay, God, that means I'm still here, and that means that You have a plan for this."

It was not, "My will be done," it was God's will be done. I was now ready for what He had for me, even if it meant I would not get out. Yes, that alone shows how much I have changed since I first arrived.

I would not have been praying and thinking like this months ago. But God has done a deep work in my life, and I knew at this moment when I lost the appeal that I would be here several more weeks or even months.

"Okay, God, what now? I'm here—I will be here for at least several more weeks. What do You have for me now, God?" I prayed.

Then He spoke, which was one of those times when you just know that God spoke. This was for me one of the strongest moments I had in jail. It was here everything came together in a new way and made so much sense to me. He said very clearly:

"Now, you write the book."

When the words came, "Now, you write the book," I was like, what? "Now I write the book? But God, I just finished the book a short time ago. I just finished recording the book a few days ago."

But then He spoke again, "Now, you write THE book."

This time there was a strong emphasis on "THE" book.

When He spoke that, I was like:

"Ahhh! THE book!" I said. "Whoa. Now I understand."

In that second, I understood what God was saying. He wanted me to write "THE" book with the Kingdom teachings God had revealed to me in the last few months. Whoa! God did not just call me to write one book in jail, he wanted me to write two books.

I truly did not see this coming. And since this was not something I had been thinking about, and the way it all happened, I know this was God speaking to me and this was something very special.

In some ways, I was very sad that I did not get out because I'd hoped for it. But for the sake of the Kingdom, and getting this book with teachings about the Kingdom of God out, I was excited, and it was suddenly okay that I should stay here longer. The sorrow of losing and not getting out was suddenly turned to excitement of the call to write another book— to write the book with the Kingdom teachings—and I started immediately, which was terrific.

I loved writing this book you are holding in your hands about my testimony and what happened to me in jail, but it will be even more remarkable in some ways to write the next book, as it teaches about the Kingdom of God.

The teachings are the teaching God gave me to teach the new disciples in the Pod. That was when God called me to create a teaching series in which we go through the Bible from beginning to end, looking at Jesus and the Kingdom.

It started with God giving me many lessons about the Kingdom of God to share with the people here. Then God called me to create a teaching series to share on YouTube. I began to write down those teachings, so I would have them ready when I would be able to film again. As I revisited all the lessons, I learned so much and new things were added to them. God then prompted me to turn those teachings into a book, and I compiled all the lessons into a book. As I went through the lessons a third and later a fourth time while working on the book, it continued to grow within me, and more revelations came to me.

The first few chapters of the Kingdom book were a kind of intro-duction. Then I took every lesson from the teaching series and made it into a chapter in the book. I truly felt God helped me in all of this, and it was a very special time. This book you are reading is about 80 percent on my testimony and 20 percent on Kingdom teachings. But the Kingdom book is 90 percent teachings and only 10 percent testimony from my time in jail.

I truly love the Word of God, and I know it is so important. I know God will use the Kingdom book mainly because it is God's Word. We all love testimonies, which are significant, but in the end, we cannot build on testimonies alone and what others have experienced. Faith comes from the Word, and that is the Word of God. And this is the foundation we should build on, and nothing else.

I was all into the Kingdom book, spent so much time on it, and was very focused on writing it, and I wrote it in just twenty-three days. It was a very intense time for me. During those days, I hand wrote almost three hundred pages. The Kingdom book will be more than twice the size of the book you are holding in your hands now.

After I finished writing it down, I went through it again, made copies, sent it out, and then started to record it over the phone like I did with this one. All of this took me about a month and a half. At that time, I became very thankful that I lost my appeal because I would not have the Kingdom book if I had won and been out. And again, it was so personal to write it and to see the Word go even deeper into me.

Some might say, "Yeah, but Torben, you could have written the Kingdom book when you got out."

I could have, but not with the same focus as I did in jail. Inside there, there was not many distractions, and it was very intense and fresh in my mind. Outside, I would not have been able to write it in such a short time.

Again, I saw how it was all in God's hands and how He had a plan with everything that happened, something I learned a lot about in this season—to trust God and His plan, even though it doesn't always make sense initially. As time went on, I really started to see more and more how God had a plan, and He knew what He was doing, and that we can trust Him. We can surrender, even when it hurts and it doesn't make sense.

While I finished the Kingdom book, many other things were happening. I still had powerful experiences in jail, and people met God.

But I also had many scary experiences during that time. When we lost our appeal in the immigration court, we appealed right away to the United States Court of Appeals for the Eleventh Circuit. At the same time, we sent in a motion to stay, which would give me a chance to be released from jail and stay in America while we were waiting for our case to go before the Eleventh Circuit.

But it was clear that U.S. Immigration and Customs Enforcement didn't like me. They did not want me to do ministry in the United States. They came and intimidated me several times. They wanted me to sign papers, papers I was not allowed to talk with my lawyer about. For example, just a few weeks before I was released, they took me into a room, sat me in a chair, had a camera to film me, and then really intimidated me. They wanted me to sign some papers that if I did not work with them and give them everything they wanted, I could be federally prosecuted and go to jail for up to ten years. There were things in those papers I did not understand, so I wanted to talk with my lawyer, but they did not want me to speak with my lawyer.

That day, I even had a lawyer call in and I asked, "Can we not continue in four hours? Then I will talk with my lawyer?"

But I was not allowed. I needed to sign right then and not talk to anyone.

They also lied to me and told me things that I should have said to my lawyer, and so on. It was very, very uncomfortable and scary. Afterward, I was crying, and my whole body was shaking in shock. I have never experienced anything like that before.

At the same time, it was very hard for my family. They were living in a trailer in Florida, and as time went on, they were hoping I would get out. But I didn't, so they needed to move to another trailer and move again. They actually moved four times from trailer to trailer. There was a lot of crying and praying. All of this was happening while I was writing and finishing the Kingdom book.

On July 1, 2023, my daughter Stephanie celebrated her birthday. I called from prison to wish her a happy birthday, and Lene told me to call our son, Sonni.

I said, "But I just talked with him."

"No, you need to call him again," she said.

And then I thought, "Okay, maybe they are having a baby!" Our little family usually shares those surprises on birthdays when everyone is gathered.

So, I called Sonni and said, "What's up?"

And he said, "We are having a baby!"

When I heard that, I was like: "Yes, whoa!" and cried.

Even though I thought this could be the case, it was very emotional and I was very happy.

Then he continued, "A son!"

And I said, "Whoa, a son! Amazing!"

I thought, do they already know what gender it will be?

Then he continued and said, "On Wednesday."

"What? On Wednesday?" And I was thinking, "Are they going to adopt a son on Wednesday?"

I was confused, and nothing made sense to me. But then he told the story that when I got put in jail, a few months later, his wife Hannah got pregnant, but they wanted to wait to tell us until I got out, to tell all of us when we were together again. They waited a few more weeks, but I did not get out. They waited a month, and I was still in jail. They waited another month, but I was still locked up. And now, nine months later, they couldn't wait anymore to tell me because the time had come to give birth to the baby! So, it was very, very special!

On July 12, 2023, Caleb was born. It was special when I saw the pictures of the little boy sent to me in jail. One photo of him and his big brother Joshua spoke to me because Joshua was sitting there, so cute, looking at little Caleb. There we had Joshua and Caleb. I felt I needed to go in and read again about Joshua and Caleb in the Bible and that God would speak to me through it. This happened at the same time the ICE officer was threatening me about signing papers, wanting to federally prosecute me and put me in prison for five to ten years if I did not do what they said.

If you don't know the story about Joshua and Caleb, you can read it in Numbers 14 or at the beginning of the book of Joshua. In Numbers 14:24 (NIV), we read about the attitude of Caleb, and here it says, *"But because my servant Caleb had a different spirit, and was following Me wholeheartedly, I will bring him into the land he went to, and his descendants will inherit it."*

We need "another spirit!" Not a spirit of fear but a spirit of strength and faith. We need to follow God wholeheartedly, with everything in us. This truly spoke to me.

Yes, I did not only get a new grandson in jail, God used this blessing to speak to me in a particular place where I needed it.

So, God blessed Sonni and Hannah and the rest of their family with little Caleb. God indeed used that little boy to speak to me. And now He uses him to talk to all of us. We need to have a spirit different from that of most people today. We cannot follow Christ and be full of a spirit of fear and compromise simultaneously. We must surrender wholeheartedly like Caleb and have the strength to keep running our race.

May this be a prayer to all of us: God, give me a spirit of faith, and may I follow you wholeheartedly, holding nothing back. Amen.

I know God will use little Caleb and Joshua, their brother David, and their sister Abigail—four beautiful names for four beautiful grandchildren.

Despite the blessing, the fight just kept going and going until on August 9, 2023, my second birthday here, I got a beautiful gift. That day, our team posted a video on YouTube with a congressman talking about me in Congress.

It was Congressman Clay Higgins. He is a U.S. House of Representatives member from Louisiana's Third District. He also serves as the chairman of the Border Security and Enforcement Subcommittee & Counterterrorism, Law Enforcement, and Intelligence Subcommittee. This subcommittee has oversight over ICE.

In the video, we hear him say: "I have a letter to be entered into the record regarding the case of Mr. Torben Søndergaard, a legal immigrant from Denmark. He came to our country legally and applied for asylum properly. Had no criminal charges. He was arrested for overstay of his visa. He's been incarcerated and in solitary confinement for over one year. He has been persecuted by this administration and targeted, we believe because he's an Evangelical Christian minister. I'd like to enter this into the record without objection."

This was big. It was huge. Think of that: the chairman of the Border Security and Enforcement Subcommittee, which oversees ICE and U.S. Customs and Border Protection, the highest authority over those departments, was on my side. This chairman and congressman, along with his office, spent hundreds of hours on my case, turning over every stone, and the conclusion was clear: I am innocent. I was being persecuted by the sitting administration and targeted because I am a Christian. I was not in jail because of something wrong I did but because of my faith in Jesus. It was the greatest birthday gift I've ever gotten!

Finally, somebody took the time to turn over every stone and see that I was innocent. Finally, somebody could see that I was innocent and something was completely wrong here!

Finally, somebody stood up for me!

The video of the congressman can be seen on our website: TorbenSondergaard.com.

I will end this chapter with the last words I wrote from jail. May this speak to you, no matter where you are. When you read these few words, try to have Joshua and Caleb in your mind.

BE BRAVE.

BE DEVOTED TO GOD WHOLEHEARTEDLY.

LET'S STAY STRONG.

DO NOT FEAR THE GIANTS.

LET'S HAVE FAITH.

GOD IS WITH US, AND IT WILL BE EXACTLY AS HE HAS SAID.

Chapter Thirty
The Day Finally Came

Since I was detained, I've dreamt about that day when I would finally get out and see my wife and the rest of my family again. I did not imagine that it would take over four hundred days—four hundred and twelve days, to be precise. And I did not imagine it would happen the way it happened: in an airport in Hamburg, Germany.

As I've explained previously, my family drove from California to Florida to be closer to me and our friends and to be in the same time zone as me. This made it easier for us to call each other and say good morning and good night. It was a big step for Lene to return to Florida, as she was not feeling good, but we thought it was God, and she got different words that confirmed this as she was praying.

One day, she got a particular word, which came as she prayed, "God, shall I go back to Florida, where I feel at home and where I know more people?"

While she was praying, she suddenly got a powerful word from somebody who knew nothing about the things going on in her life or about her longing to go back to Florida. The word was from Jeremiah 50: 18-20 (NIV):

Therefore this is what the Lord Almighty, the God of Israel says:
"I will punish the king of Babylon and his land as I punished the

king of Assyria. But I will bring Israel back to their own pasture,
and they will graze on Carmel and Bashan; their appetite will
be satisfied on the hills of Ephraim and Gilead. In those days,
at that time," declares the Lord, "search will be made for Israel's
guilt, but there will be none, and for the sins of Judah, but none
will be found, for I will forgive the remnant I spare."

It could seem like a peculiar word to give to somebody, and the woman who gave us this word was also asking God, "Why should I give them this word?" because it made no sense to her.

But it made a lot of sense to us and was a great confirmation. God wanted Lene to return to Florida to her "own pasture." And when she would go there, they would "search" for my guilt, and find none.

Then, Lene left California and drove back to Florida in faith. While she was on the way, I prayed for Lene, the girls, and the trip. As I said, it was a big step for her, as she was not feeling well. But one day, as I was praying out of this verse we had gotten, thanking God for bringing Lene back to her pasture, something special suddenly happened.

As I was praying, "God, thank You for bringing Lene back to her pasture," it suddenly came to me, "Denmark." It suddenly felt like it was not Florida. Yes, her own pasture is not Florida. It is Denmark. God wants to bring Lene—and God wants to bring me—back to Denmark.

And I was like, "No! What? Stop a moment! Back to Denmark? But we are not going to go back to Denmark!"

So, it was bizarre to me, and I put it away and thought that it must have just been my own thoughts, even though I could not let it go completely.

I did not share it with Lene at first, as she arrived here, that I felt God did not only want to bring her to Florida but also wanted to bring us the whole way back to Denmark. It was still unthinkable for us at this time, but I still couldn't let that thought go.

As the months went by, I was still waiting for a federal court hearing. As I was waiting, I was seeking something called a motion to stay so I could stay here in the United States while I waited. If I got that

340

there would be a big change, I could be set free from jail, and be with my family here in the United States while we waited for the hearing.

But then I was told that we have now finally come so far in this journey that if I lost my motion to stay, I would for sure leave this place with in a very short time and sent back to Denmark where I could be with my family. And if I was sent back to Denmark, I could still win my case, and then be able to return to America.

When I heard that, suddenly, the word started to grow in me even more. And I began to think I would be deported back to Denmark. Yes, I was ready to leave.

Now, I saw an opportunity for us to return to Denmark, to be with my family and see my son, his wife, and grandkids, to see Lene's parents again, and to return to America if we won our case.

This really was something I wanted, so I started to pray, "God, if it's possible, then bring us back to Denmark, and then let us win there and be able to come back to America."

I longed so much to see our son, as well as our grandkids and Lene's parents. It could bring a lot of healing to us because the last time we left Denmark, four years ago, it was extraordinary, and it went very fast, and we didn't get the opportunity to say goodbye to many of our friends and family.

And it happened! I'm now sitting here, writing this to you from Denmark! I was first in Germany for some weeks, and then we were able to return to Denmark. We are still keeping a low profile while we wait for our case to finalize, but it's extraordinary to be here.

I know this is difficult for people on the outside to understand. But for us, it is truly a blessing to be here, even if only briefly, as we know we cannot live here anymore. It is a blessing from God, bringing us a lot of freedom and healing. We don't feel at home here like we did before. Our heart is in America or any other place God sends us. We know we have given what we could here, and with everything that has happened, we don't feel free here anymore. We are also not free to do ministry here because of the things that have happened and the new law and focus they have on me.

What is important for us is the freedom to serve Jesus and do what He has called us to do, and that is not here. I just want to be obedient. Our home here on earth is where God wants us to be. But my real home is in heaven. That is what I honestly long for.

My understanding about the Kingdom of God has grown in my heart over the last year, so even if we can return to America, I will still be like a stranger in the country, seeking the heavenly Jerusalem, where I truly belong. I've learned a lot this time about where we have our hearts, and God wants it to be in heaven, even though we can enjoy the things here on earth. But God had a reason for us to be here right now, as the prophetic word said. I also believe that one day, there will be a search for my guilt and that they will find nothing.

It was very special for me that I got released and saw Lene again. As I said, I lost my motion to stay, and therefore I knew that I could get deported any day. I was told it could take one to two weeks, but I did not know when. I was very excited but also scared at the same time. Yes, what would happen out there?

Would I really be released, or would the U.S. Department of Homeland Security be waiting for me and arrest me for something else? Yes, these were questions I asked because of all the things that had happened in the last month—the corruption that was taking place. They have identified me as a dangerous person, and they knew it was a lie. Yes, I did not trust them at all.

At the same time, I was now so used to being locked up that the world out there almost scared me. It's difficult to describe, but this last year, my "eight by thirteen feet" (2.5 by 4 meters) cell had somehow become my home, and everything inside Pod B-6 had become my life. This is what I knew. I knew the routine. I knew the daily program, and everything outside seemed so far away that I was almost scared to leave. I spent so much time with God here, and it was so special. Would I lose this when I got out? Yes, many things have been in my head over the last few weeks.

In the last few weeks, many things happened while I was waiting to come out. One thing I can share is that a man came into my cell with tears in his eyes one evening. He said, "Torben, you cannot leave us. What shall we do here without you? I cannot be here without you. You have transformed my life. You have transformed so many people in here. You have changed this place; nothing will be the same without you." Yes, he poured out his heart to me while tears ran down his cheek.

It was a man who had truly transformed his life in the last few months, and it was really special, as this came from the depths of his heart. It was so beautiful to hear and see what God had been doing. Everyone was excited about me and talked about that day when I would finally leave.

I was the guy who had brought so much to this Pod. I was also the old guy in the Pod. I had been there twice as long as anyone else. I was the missionary, pastor, and preacher, as some guards called me, and now it was my time to leave. So, everyone was excited and talking about it.

A few days later, when I was going to call Lene, my PIN number suddenly did not work. "Whoa! What is happening here?"

I tried another phone, and my PIN number still did not work. Then, I tried the vending machine with my code, which also did not work. This could only mean one thing—I had just been locked out of their system—and that meant it was time for me to leave.

They normally lock people out of their system up to twenty-four hours before they leave, as this gives them time to get all the papers ready and to get the money we might have in our accounts when we leave. And that is our way of understanding we are soon leaving. So, I understood the time was now. I was shaking all over and cried a little. I am really leaving this place.

I used a friend's PIN number to call Lene, and I remember it so clearly; she answered the phone, and right away, it came out of me, "It is happening. It is happening now. I'm leaving this place," and I broke down, crying. It was so unreal—"It is finally happening!"

Lene was crying too and she called the girls and told them it was time. And it happened the following day.

I was on the phone with a good friend, Kim. He has been such a blessing to me during this time. As Lene got sick, he took over much of the communication between me and the legal team. While I spoke with him at 9 a.m., I heard my name over the loudspeaker: "Torben Sondergaard, pack up!"

I said, "Kim, Kim, they are calling my name, and I am leaving."

Right after, an officer called my name, and it went really fast.

I hurried to call Lene, "I'm leaving right now!"

In five minutes, I was out the door with all my things—my mattress, papers, Bible, and everything else I'd had in there.

It was exceptional to say goodbye to everyone and go through those doors. I entered the check-in area for the first time since I got here four hundred and eleven days ago after spending one night at an Orange County jail before arriving at the Baker County Detention Center.

I was there again, leaving this place as a new person, so much richer in so many ways, with so many experiences. I felt so blessed.

But I was also broken in many ways and hoped never to see this place again, as this had been the most challenging time in my life, and in many ways something I never wish to experience again.

My family had sent me some clothes, as I needed something a few sizes smaller. I also needed a new belt, as the one I came in with did not have enough holes to be used, and I'd lost so much weight.

There were two others with me that day who also got deported. One was a man from England who had been imprisoned for twenty-two years. Yes, for twenty-two years he had been locked up in another prison, and then he came here for a short time before he was deported home to England. I had never talked with him before, as he was from another Pod, but we had a good talk on the way to the airport, where six officers were awaiting us—two officers per person. It was extraordinary to talk with this man.

I felt my one year was a long time, but twenty-two years locked up is incredible.

He looked out the window, and looked at the cars, and said, "Whoa! Is that how cars look today?"

He told me that he had never held a smartphone in his hand and was afraid to come out into this world but also was very excited.

When we arrived at the Jacksonville International Airport, he was very nervous about stepping out of the car, but I encouraged him to go out, and after taking a deep breath, he did. He was now standing outside looking around at everything; the world had just changed so much in those twenty-two years.

Then we got separated as we flew to different places. I flew from the Jacksonville airport to John F. Kennedy International Airport in New York. The two officers who escorted me were very friendly. They asked me if I preferred handcuffs and the hard way or if I would be nice, behave, do everything they told me, and always walk between them, and then I could avoid the handcuffs. So, we took the easy way.

Lene needed to fly out of the United States the same day together with the girls, as they needed to be out the country the same day that I left so they wouldn't be put in the system as having overstayed their visas. They had been standing by for several weeks, waiting for the day I would leave. So, they flew from the Orlando International Airport to the Frankfurt Airport in Germany, and then to the Hamburg Airport, where I was supposed to meet them later.

I flew from Jacksonville to New York. When we arrived at JFK, we were met by an airport policeman who followed us around. It was new for the U.S. Immigration and Customs Enforcement officers to need a policeman to follow us around, but the rules had been changed. So, he needed to be with us the whole time we were there. It was not enough to have two ICE officers at my side; there also had to be a policeman, as I am a very dangerous person.

But because he did not want to wait the five hours until we boarded the next plane, they ended up putting me in a holding cell at the JFK airport. So there, I waited three or four hours to board the plane.

I boarded the plane before everyone else, and it was an exceptional experience to be guided like that by two officers, one on each side. Finally, the plane took off, and I was leaving America. It was remarkable to be free, and the airplane food was terrific. Whoa, I've never enjoyed airplane food like this before in my life. It was so hot—steaming hot—like the coffee, it was hot! I had been drinking lukewarm, shower-water coffee for a year.

For a year, I'd been eating lukewarm food, and now, on the airplane, I got the hottest coffee I'd ever gotten, and the food was like five-star restaurant food! It tasted so good!

Ten hours later, I landed in Copenhagen, Denmark, where the ICE officer handed me over to the police. The police scanned my passport and said, "You are free to enter," as there were no charges against me. We knew that, as we had already contacted the police chief in Copenhagen before I landed. But we also knew my enemies were still there and busy working to get me, so I needed to stay low.

I briefly met with a good friend, a guy from my legal team who had also flown in from America, and then a Danish lawyer. After a few hours there, I boarded a plane from Copenhagen with my friend Lebo, as they did not want me to fly alone to Hamburg, Germany, where Lene and the girls were waiting. It was weird to be out, but at the same time, so natural to just see people again, to see Lebo and his wife again and their little boy. It was the first time I saw him, and just to walk around the airport.

It felt so good, so relaxed. I was happy. I was free. But at the same time, I was thinking about Lene the whole time and that I would soon see her, and I felt the emotions rising in me. But I could now hold back on the way to Hamburg where they were. I knew they were waiting for me when I landed, and I would soon see them. All the emotion just rose up in me, and I cried most of the way from Copenhagen to Hamburg.

I was, at the same time, exhausted. I hadn't slept that whole night. I had a painful headache, as it was all so much for me. The stewardess in that small plane to Hamburg noticed me and how I was crying off and on, and we started to talk. I told her the story of how I'd just been detained in America for more than a year for things I hadn't done. I explained how I'd been married for twenty-seven years, and I'd only been away from my wife for a few weeks, but now I haven't seen her for more than four hundred days, and now she's waiting for me when we land.

As she heard the story, the stewardess had tears in her eyes, and she asked if she could hug me, as it had touched her very, very deeply. She also told me she wanted to leave the plane with me and meet my wife if she could, but she needed to stay back. I gave her the website, and I know she will go in and see our movies there. Yes, it was good to share Jesus again outside in the free world.

When I left the airplane, she and the other stewardesses stood in the doorway, waving at me and making hearts with their hands. It touched her deeply, and she took the time to share my story with the other stewardesses.

Lene and the girls stood just outside where we picked up the luggage. I couldn't hold back as I left the airplane and came close to them. So many emotions—I'd never experienced anything like this before in my life. I'd been waiting for this day—I'd been dreaming about this day—almost every day for over a year, and now, in a few minutes, it would happen.

There, just behind the next door, I would see Lene and hug her, and I would see the girls again. Walking toward that door where they were on the other side, it came to me that it would be Jesus one day. It would be Him I would see, and that day, my pain would finally be over, and everything would be so good forever.

What a day!

God used this to get me to experience how it might feel that day. I got a little taste of it because that day will be so much stronger. But for me, this was a moment I will never forget, and it truly gave me a special connection to the revelation I had in jail about the day of the Lord. The longing, the joy, the end of the separation, would soon all be over! Yes, this was all a small shadow of what one day will be waiting for me and everyone looking for our Lord's return.

On the other side of the door now I will meet Lene, but one day, I will see Him face to face. And this is how it will be for everyone who has prepared themselves and longed for His appearing. It will be a wonderful, indescribable moment—a moment when God will wipe away every tear from our eyes, and we will finally see Him face to face.

"He will wipe every tear from their eyes. There will be no more death or mourning or crying or pain, for the old order of things has passed away." (Revelation 21:4 NIV)

They will see his face, and his name will be on their foreheads. There will be no more night. They will not need the light of a lamp or the light of the sun, for the Lord God will give them light. And they will reign for ever and ever. (Revelation 22:4-5 NIV)

It is truly unique and beautiful, and I could spend so much time just dreaming and thinking of that day. But as unique as it will be for some of us who are born again, it will be terrifying for most people. Those who have not lived for that day and have not prepared themselves will know what awaits them on the other side of that door, and there is no way to escape it.

Try to think of that. They know what awaits them on the other side, and there is no escape. They know that it's too late to repent, too late to receive forgiveness, and too late to change the outcome. Think of that feeling. It's so terrifying, but that is a reality for many people.

I know that I will live and die for that day because there are only two outcomes. I will live for Jesus and prepare myself as His holy bride, ready to meet her Groom. I will run the race of faith and obedience with endurance, as He has called us all to.

Then I went through the door, and Lene came forward to me. I threw my bag to the ground and hugged her, and we cried. It was as if the whole airport just stopped. I felt everyone was looking at us. Simone and Stephanie then came to us, and we all stood there, hugged each other, and cried. It was a very, very special moment.

Afterward, I asked Lene how it felt. At first, she said it was so weird to see me again, now with a long beard, and when she gave me a hug it felt so different, as I'd lost so much weight since the last time she'd hugged me, but it was so good.

Conclustion
The Road Less Traveled

As I write this last chapter to you, it has been eight months since I was released, and I am now writing this last chapter to you from Mexico, where we are currently located.

After spending some time in Europe, we felt the call to return to the mission field again. Mexico was something that God had already placed on our hearts while we were in the United States, and we knew it was just a question of time before we came here.

The idea of coming to Mexico started to grow in us some years ago while still in the United States. However, as we were waiting for our asylum papers in America, we could not leave. But as I said, we knew we would be here one day. I'm not saying that because I believe the United States is finally over for us. I still hold on to the idea of returning there, even if everything looks impossible. There is still work there that I feel God wants us to do in the United States, and part of my heart is there with my amazing family in Christ and my vision to help the church there.

Regarding my asylum case, I lost the case on February 6, 2024, two months ago. It was not a big surprise when it happened. With everything that was happening regarding my case, the lies, the corruption, and all the false accusations against me, even from some people inside the government, I knew it was not a question of whether I had a good case or not. As time went on and I understood more of who was behind this, I somehow knew that they would not let me win no matter what.

But even though I somehow was prepared that the answer would be a no to my asylum case, it was still difficult to hear that they had denied me. Some of the arguments presented as to why they denied me also revealed that I had lost from the very beginning, and they would not give me asylum no matter what.

In regard to some of the reasons why they denied me, they started saying again that I had overstayed my visa, which was not true. Another argument for denial was that my son, Sonni, was in Denmark, which meant he was not persecuted, and therefore, I would not be either. However, that argument is so far out. It was not my son Sonni who was persecuted and referred to the Danish government. It was not my son Sonni who was the target of false accusations, or had his U.S. Department of Homeland Security ESTA (Electronic System for Travel Authorization) application denied, or was identified as a national security threat by DHS, or was brought up by a member of Congress as someone who was being persecuted by the sitting administration because of his faith.

No, all of this involved me. So, when I read the reasons why I was denied asylum, it just confirmed what I have seen the last year. Persecution is real, also in America.

When we consider how there is an open border to the United States right now and that millions of illegal immigrants are crossing those borders illegally, yes, then it all becomes so much clearer what this is all about.

My case has truly become a modern example of how Christian persecution is happening in our Western countries. And I know this book is here to help prepare you for what is coming, as we are only at the beginning of this.

But as I have said again and again, God is faithful, and even if we need to wake up and understand what is happening, we should not live in fear. I still trust that God has the final say.

But as I said, it was hard to hear the denial, but it was also a release as we felt so stuck waiting and not knowing what would happen and when it would happen. We have lived out of our suitcases during this whole time because most of our things are still in California. But this gave me the freedom to move on, and we will now try to ship some of our belongings down here to Mexico where we know God has a work for us right now.

It doesn't mean we have given up on the United States in the future, but we are where we should be now, and the future is, as always, in God's hands.

The journey to Mexico has also been powerful, and it aligns with God's plan from the beginning, even though we thought it would happen in another way. Yes, we never had the fantasy to imagine all of this would happen like it did. When God first spoke about Mexico, we thought we would have a base in the United States and then travel to Mexico. But events often don't happen the exact way we imagine them.

We first experienced how God put Mexico and Latin America in our hearts in a very unique way back in July 2021, a year before my detention.

During a camp we had in Georgia, a pastor and his family from a very small Spanish-speaking church nearby came to our meetings and powerfully experienced God. Everyone in his family got healed, set free, and filled with the Holy Spirit.

After the first evening at our camp, he wanted to bring his whole church to the camp as he wanted them to experience the same thing. But I thought that instead of bringing them all to our camp, we should instead send a team to minister to them where they are in their church. That way, we could ensure everyone got the same training and connect with them more personally. I then talked to several Spanish-speaking people on our team as they were ready to go there instead. But then I suddenly felt very strongly how God wanted me to go myself. Yes, I just suddenly knew that I needed to be there myself. When that happened, I still remember what I prayed:

"But God, we have a camp here with a few hundred people; I cannot just leave them. Some have been driving far to come here and also to hear me speak."

But no, I know I needed to go there no matter what.

I said that we needed to change the program because I was leaving to speak in a small Spanish-speaking church. We changed the plans by having me speak in the afternoon at our camp instead of the evening, where I was on the program. So just after I spoke during the afternoon meeting, my family and I left the camp with a few other Spanish-speaking members from our team.

On the way there, it didn't make sense to me, but I prayed to God: God, why did I leave a few hundred people at our camp to drive forty-five minutes to speak to twenty to thirty people at a small Spanish-speaking church? Yes, it truly did not make much sense to me. But we knew it was God. But then suddenly, it came to me very clearly: "I will show you what your future will look like."

Wow. I did not see that coming. I told Lene: "God just spoke to me. Tonight, we will see what our future will look like," and we were both amazed. We were very excited about what was going to happen. I will never forget that moment in the car and how this came to be so powerful to me. So, we arrived with great expectation and excitement.

It was an extraordinary evening. As we stood in that small church with not more than twenty-five to thirty people, singing Spanish worship songs, I did not understand; it was so special. I could not stop thinking of what God had just spoken and everything that led up to that meeting, and that this is what our future would look like.

And now, sitting here in Mexico, writing this to you is truly special. I love it here and what God is doing. The last few months have been so special.

Yesterday, I spoke in a local church, which was truly powerful. They were so hungry, and to be honest, it was one of the strongest meetings I've ever experienced. So many got healed, set free, and filled with the Holy Spirit, and suddenly, we had a spontaneous baptism in the middle of the church as they brought a baptismal pool in. And when we left the church meeting four hours after we arrived, I was exhausted and amazed at the same time. So, this is our future now, and this is just the beginning.

But back to the meeting in the small Spanish-speaking church in the United States. That evening was so special, and we also experienced a spiritual hunger and so many things happened, even though there were only around twenty-five to thirty people there.

On the way home from that meeting in the car, we first talked about how good it was and what God had for us in the future, and then, after talking a little, we suddenly all became quiet, just reflecting on everything that had happened and that this would be our future and what it would mean.

As we arrived home, I said to Lene: "We need to go back tomorrow. I need to be there tomorrow also."

The following day, we met with our team at the camp and explained everything that had happened the day before and that we needed to change our plans again, as we knew God wanted us to go back there again.

So that day we changed the plans again. I spoke briefly at the beginning of our Sunday meeting, and then we left the meeting, where they had worship, and another person from the team shared the Word. Then we drove back to the same little Spanish-speaking church.

I was excited to come back and see what God would do. But what I encountered when we arrived was something I did not expect.

When we arrived at the little church, some members of our team had already been there the whole day. They had been out on the streets sharing Jesus with people, and they were now standing there waiting for me, eager to share what God had done.

They had been at the local Walmart where they met a woman named Krista who was sitting in a wheelchair with a sign that read "HELP." She was homeless, asking for money. But not only that. She had a brain tumor, was blind in one eye, had difficulty walking, and had lost her two kids due to her situation and lifestyle. But then God intervened.

They prayed for her, her eye opened, she gained strength in her legs and could walk again. She followed them home to the church, and on the way to the church, they found some water, and she was baptized, received the Holy Spirit, and started a new life in every way. She stood there with them, sharing her testimony, crying and smiling at the same time. I was amazed. We held a meeting, and everyone was excited about what had happened that same day. We collected an offering for Krista and found a place for her to stay for a few days. Later, we set up a GoFundMe page to help her rebuild her life and reunite with her kids. Today, she has her kids back, is healed, and has a brand-new life. It's a beautiful testimony.

And that was just a glimpse of what God did that day with that little church. They have never been the same since, and as we left the church to drive back to the camp, I was once again amazed, thinking that this is what our future would look like.

Yes, that was just a part of the experiences we had when God called us to Mexico and Latin America. We knew it was only a matter of time. However, we couldn't leave the country as we were still waiting for our asylum interview, which never came.

Now free from jail and back in Europe, we felt it was time to go to Mexico. We also had an invitation to Australia, a place we knew well and where many friends were eager to see us. As we prayed about whether to go to Australia first and postpone Mexico, God gave us a clear confirmation about Mexico. Personally, I was more excited about Australia at the time, as I loved the country and had not been to Mexico before.

So, we were praying and seeking God: God, shall we travel to Australia or Mexico?

Then, a few days later, we received a prophetic word saying, "Take the road less traveled because it leads to righteousness." When a friend suddenly sent us that word, we knew this was God speaking and that it referred to Mexico and Latin America, places less familiar to us. We had been to Australia before, but Mexico and Latin America were uncharted territory for me, except for a visit to Brazil.

So, we understood it was time to venture into the unknown and head to Mexico and Latin America.

When we arrived in Mexico, we stayed at a home owned by an American missionary from Florida whom we had known for years. He had been working in Mexico for a long time and had a house for missionaries to stay in when they were visiting.

As we entered the house, we experienced another powerful confirmation of God's plan. The house was on a property with a church he had built years ago. The sign outside the church said, "Fuente de Vida," which means "fountain of life." Seeing the sign outside the church and seeing the house where we would stay was a powerful experience that brought it all together.

It right away brought me back to the small Spanish-speaking church in Georgia where God had said He would show me what our future would look like. The name of that small church was also "Fuente de Vida." It was a special moment to see the connection between the two places.

As we stepped inside the house at "Fuente de Vida," there was a picture on the wall of trees in a forest with a quote that read, "Two roads diverged in a wood, and I took the one less traveled by, and that has made all the difference."

Wow. I just stood there and looked at it. It took all my breath away from me. This was the word we got coming here.

I called the missionary who owns the house and asked about the picture. He shared that it was a word God had given him twenty-eight years ago when he first was called to Mexico. Wow. What a profound moment of confirmation.

Being in Mexico at the house named "Fuente de Vida," with the picture symbolizing the road less traveled, with the inspirational quote on it, we felt strongly that this was all set up by God in a very special way. Many pastors in the city also knew the story behind the picture, and hearing my testimony, they all took it as a confirmation that God had sent us there. This opened many new doors for us, and we have already witnessed amazing things happening in this city. The experiences we have had here in Mexico have truly been amazing. And we see God's hand guiding us every step of the way.

We are certain that we are where God wants us to be, and we are excited about the future in Mexico and Latin America. But we still acknowledge that there is work for us in the United States in the future.

What God is doing here has to do with the whole body of Christ all over the world. It is time for the churches to come back to the real and simple life that we see in the Bible, time to not only read about this life, but to live it.

If you recall, in chapter five, titled "A Shift is Coming," I shared how God, a short time before I was put in jail, started speaking to me about the churches and how a shift is coming. God wants to bring the churches back to discipleship in a fresh new way. We have been doing schools and training people for years, mostly outside the churches, but it was time for us to bring it into the churches and train them where they are.

During that time, I connected with Josiah, a pastor in San Diego as I shared about. I talked about how I did some training with him and his team, and it was amazing, the best I have seen, marking the beginning of something new. I made some videos about it. The first one was called, "BEST VIDEO EVER! - POWERFUL DISCIPLESHIP & MULTIPLICATION - A SHIFT HAS COME!"

The next was called, "NEXT BEST VIDEO EVER! - "CASTING A DEMON OUT OF MY MOM" - Don't Complicate It!" And the third was called, "THIRD BEST VIDEO EVER 'THE HOLY SPIRIT CAME OVER MY DAUGHTER' - THE FRUIT CONTINUES!"

I said in these videos, "God this is so good, but this is not just for them, it is for the whole church," and few days later I was detained.

What has happened since then with me being in jail and us now being in Mexico has been a continuation of God started doing there. It is a shift, and it is time for the churches.

After spending a few weeks in jail, one day, I spoke with Josiah, who suddenly said, "Torben, it looks like there may be an opening for the senior pastor position in our church and how amazing would it be if you come out the same week I'm put in as senior pastor?"

When I first met him, he was an assistant pastor and wanted to bring this new approach to the whole church, but it was not easy, as he was not the senior pastor, but then a short time later an opportunity arose for him to become the senior pastor, so he applied for the position.

However, when he mentioned this to me, saying, "How amazing would it be if you come out the same week I'm put in as senior pastor?" I was like, "No, I really don't hope so," because I couldn't imagine being in jail for three to four more days, and this could take several weeks or even a few months.

But those words, "How amazing would it be if you come out the same week I'm put in as a senior pastor," became very prophetic for us and something we often talked about.

And then it happened. It did not happen in just a few weeks or a few months. He went through his own crazy journey, and instead, it took almost a year before he finally became the senior pastor.

What was special is that he was appointed as senior pastor on Sunday, August 13, 2023. He informed me the next day, Monday, and when I heard that, I said to him, "Finally, now I can come out and leave this place."

The next day, Tuesday, August 15, I was told I would be released, and on Wednesday, August 16, 2023, I was finally set free, just as he had said. But it wasn't just a few weeks later, as he said, but almost a year later. And during that time, God had done a great work in both of us and many others out there.

I wanted to share this as it was very special to me. Throughout that year, I often spoke with Josiah about how I would come out the same week he would become the senior pastor, and how God had a plan with all of this.

I therefore often got frustrated over why it was so difficult for him and why it should take so long, as I felt I would not be released before he took on his new role as God had indicated. Yes, it was very special, and now looking back, we see God's hand all over it. It took so long because God needed to do a work in me, him and many others out there.

This was also what the prophetic word I received in the beginning said:

"Your situation is happening in order that true SALVATION and FREEDOM can come to so many who live in complete darkness—even the sleeping church. There are pieces that God is working behind the scenes that you are unaware of. There are things God is accomplishing in you, things He is accomplishing in that region, and things He is accomplishing in His church by you being there. He is preparing a lot of things for the future."

Yes, God has been working behind the scenes in so many people and places, and I truly believe in this shift that is coming to the church. It has to do with preparing the church for what is coming and making strong disciples, obeying Jesus, and focusing on the Gospel of the Kingdom, as I also wrote about being one of the main reasons God allowed this to happen.

I could share much more about this, but you can find additional details in videos on a new website we have created: TorbenSondergaard. com/412days.

Now, this shift has begun to be visible in his church, where many new things are happening. The fruit continues to grow, and we see that also in Mexico, where I work with many different churches. One pastor said to me a few days ago, "We have seen more people baptized in the last month than we have in our church in the last five years." Another pastor said, "Our church is transformed, and now everyone is living as disciples and seeing fruit in their everyday lives."

Yes, the shift is coming, and it has begun. It's time to take Jesus' words, obey them, and live authentically because of what is written.

As we close this chapter and this book, I want my incredible wife, Lene, to share some words with you. She has faced her own challenges and struggles, and her journey is also a testimony to God's faithfulness and grace, even if it has been extremely hard for her. She has been in her own type of jail, gone through her own tests, and has had her own moments with God.

Lene Sondergaard:

When Torben first got arrested, it was hard. But I became very busy talking to people, handling emails, and being the link between Torben and everything out there. It kept me very busy and somehow it helped me in the beginning.

I did not have time to think too much about everything that was happening. But as time went it became very hard on my body, and in the end, my body couldn't take it anymore. That was when I got sick, and suddenly I couldn't do anything as Torben has shared here. But that was when God started to work on me in a new way. He began to speak to me more and show me things. We have been through different desert times before in our journey, when God was teaching me things, like to let go of control and trust Him. Yes, I have learned to be dependent on Him.

Having gone through these challenging times in our lives has really helped me through the years. It also helped me this time. But this time was different. I was even more stretched this time than I had ever been before, as this time Torben was not here, so everything landed on me.

We often talked many times a day over the phone, and that helped me a great deal. But it was still not the same as if he was here. It was then I really started to see how we had a great need for each other and a need for the body of Christ. Before, I often stayed close to my family because it was easier, especially when we, as a family, traveled so much, as we often did, moving from place to place.

But now I didn't have him, and I, in a new way, suddenly needed the body of Christ. I needed to come closer to the body and let them come closer to me. It was there that God began to send different people to help us. And I saw how God used all these different people to show us many things, both in my life and in Torben's life.

God did not only send people we had been close to and know very well, but also people we did not know, and some that we in ways disagreed with in terms of their beliefs. Yes, God sent them and used them in this way to humble us, to encourage us to examine our hearts. God is preparing His people for the end times, preparing us for a time of persecution, and then we will need the body of Christ even more. Even though we may disagree in some areas we will need to stand together in the time to come.

When I started to get sick, my prayer to God was that when all of this was over, I would come back with a testimony that God was faithful. Yes, He has always been faithful, but that should also be our testimony after this. I know that people who know me knew I often say, "God is in control; God is faithful." Yes, that has somehow been my statement, and it was really important to me after this experience that I would still be able to say that I saw that every day.

Yes, we saw God's faithfulness every day, even though it often seemed like it was more than what we could bear. The cup often overflowed. But even though every day was a struggle for us, we still received manna every day—a word of encouragement or something that helped us make it through that day. Yes, we took it one day at a time.

At one point, I felt that God wanted us to travel to Florida to be closer to Torben. So, we traveled in faith, all of us, because I was not feeling well, and I really needed God's help to manage that trip across America. And there, God gave me just enough to manage the journey, even though it was a very special experience, where we needed to go underground, as Torben has shared.

When we arrived in Florida, we first stayed with some friends, and then we moved to a campsite where we rented a recreational vehicle to stay in. The time in Florida was a really difficult time for the four of us—me, our two daughters Stephanie and Simone, and Joshua, Simone's boyfriend.

We ended up staying at the campsite for several months, the four of us. Another family we know was also staying there at the campground, and that was a big help for all of us.

At the campsite, I struggled a lot, but I was able to go for some walks and seek God. I took many walks at the campground and prayed, even though I didn't have a lot of energy for praying or anything else. God led me to a very special place at the campground, a spot that meant a lot to me. It was by a huge tree near water, reminding me of Psalm 1:1-6 (NIV), and the tree mentioned there:

> "Blessed is the one who does not walk in step with the wicked or stand in the way that sinners take or sit in the company of mockers, but whose delight is in the law of the Lord, and who meditates on his law day and night. That person is like a tree planted by streams of water, which yields its fruit in season and whose leaf does not wither— whatever they do prospers. Not so the wicked! They are like chaff that the wind blows away. Therefore the wicked will not stand in the judgment, nor sinners in the assembly of the righteous. For the Lord watches over the way of the righteous, but the way of the wicked leads to destruction."

In the end, almost every morning, I started the day by walking to that tree to ask God to help me manage the day. I truly needed His help like never before. It was there that He reminded me of a word I had received, that God wanted to make me stronger. I prayed that word, thanking God for His faithfulness and His strengthening.

At the end of the day, I often went back to the same spot and thanked God for helping me through the day, acknowledging that He had been there for me that day.

It was really tough, and every day was survival. I needed to pray. It was almost the only thing I could do—take short walks, pray, and have brief conversations with Torben.

But every day I saw how God was faithful throughout this season. In the end, that day came when Torben would be released, and we needed to fly back to Europe, and that also was a huge step for me but God was faithful. He had arranged everything. The family that stayed with us at the camp had parents living in Germany and they were more than willing to join us on the trip. They went with us and took care of all the practical details, so everything went smoothly. We saw how God had planned it all. It was a true blessing for us.

So, I will still say today that God is faithful and God is in control, as we have truly witnessed that, even though it has been one of the hardest tests we have ever gone through.

Torben Sondergaard:

I will end this book by encouraging you to run with Jesus and serve Him wholeheartedly, holding nothing back.

May we all one day be able to say the same thing the Apostle Paul said at the end of his journey before he got to lay down his life for Christ:

> *I have fought the good fight, I have finished the race, I have kept the faith. Now there is in store for me the crown of righteousness, which the Lord, the righteous Judge, will award to me on that day—and not only to me, but also to all who have longed for his appearing.* (2 Timothy 4:7-8 NIV)

Yes, I pray you hold nothing back from serving Him and finish your race strong in faith and one day receive the crown of righteousness that the Lord has for all of us who are longing for Him to return.

Jesus is real, and each of us are called to serve Him with our whole being. Just as He laid down His life for us, we are called to take up our cross and live sacrificially for Him. One day, He will return and reward us for our actions in this life, whether good or evil.

Live with that day in mind, and it will not catch you by surprise when you suddenly stand there in front of Him on that day. Let us all have the right focus and store up treasures in heaven, as Jesus said, and not focus too much on this short life here:

> *"Do not store up for yourselves treasures on earth, where moths and vermin destroy, and where thieves break in and steal. But store up for yourselves treasures in heaven, where moths and vermin do not destroy, and where thieves do not break in and steal. For where your treasure is, there your heart will be also."* (Matthew 6:19-21 NIV)

Yes, I have much more I want to share. But as you know, I have written another book in jail—The Kingdom Book. In that book, I share the teachings God revealed to me in jail, the teachings that finally set me free behind bars.

On my new website, TorbenSondergaard.com, we will keep you up to date about my case, The Kingdom Book, and about the word we are now standing in, preparing the churches.

Maranatha: Come, Lord Jesus, come.

With love and faith in Christ, and a big thanks to all of you who stood together with us on this journey. We will always be grateful for your love, prayers, and support toward us.

- **Torben Sondergaard,**
A disciple of Christ

Appendix
Learn More

On the website, TorbenSondergaard.com, there is a dedicated page at TorbenSondergaard.com/412days. You can access on the website links to the videos and teachings referenced in this book. You will also find images from Torben's jail, additional information about his journey, and more details about this book.

We highly recommend viewing the mini documentary, "Revealing," and the "Timeline," which gives great insights into Torben's legal case and who was behind the persecution.

This mini documentary and the "Timeline" showcase the deposition with one of Torben's persecutors in which he disclosed his communication with the U.S. Immigration and Customs Enforcement officer responsible for Torben's detention, and how this officer instructed him to falsely accuse Torben of human trafficking, resulting in his unjust classification as a national security threat.

We also reveal how they produced videos specifically targeting Torben and monitored his phone conversations in an attempt to find evidence against him. These new revelations will astonish you and shed light on the ongoing battle we are engaged in—a fight for the gospel.

Notes

Chapter Ten

1. Brother Yun, Living Water: Powerful Teachings from the International Bestselling Author of The Heavenly Man, (Nashville, Tennessee: Thomas Nelson), 204.

2. Brother Yung, Living Water, (Nashville, Tennessee: Thomas Nelson), 205.

Chapter Twenty

1. Brother Yung, Living Water, (Nashville, Tennessee: Thomas Nelson), 204.

Chapter Twenty-Two

1. Steve Addison and Dave Ferguson, Pioneering Movements: Leadership That Multiplies Disciples and Churches,(Lisle, Illinois: InterVarsity Press),22.

Chapter Twenty-Nine

1. U.S. Rep. Clay Higgins, "The Real Cost of an Open Border: How Americans are Paying the Price," Border Security and Enforcement Subcommittee & Counterterrorism, Law Enforcement, and Intelligence Subcommittee Hearing, July 26, 2023, https://www.youtube.com/live/ q2n1h6lIbMg?t=10429s.

About the Author

Torben Søndergaard, born in 1976 in Denmark, grew up with little exposure to faith. Though baptized as an infant in the Lutheran Church, it was more of a cultural tradition than a reflection of personal belief. His home lacked a Bible, and prayer was absent from family life. However, everything changed on April 5, 1995, when Torben heard the gospel, repented, and committed his life to Christ. Not long afterward, Torben started on a 40-day fast that transformed his life. He began to understand how lukewarm and far away from the truth Christians had become. He saw that God had called him to speak His Word without compromise. Since then, Torben has seen thousands of people saved, healed, and set free from demons. For over 27 years, Torben has been married to Lene, with whom he has three children and four grandchildren. He is the founder of The Last Reformation, a global movement aimed at restoring the church to the vibrant, disciple-making community described in the Book of Acts. Through his ministry, Torben has traveled to 47 nations, authored eight books, and produced three impactful movies, reaching countless lives around the world. Torben is known for his "kickstart weekends," intensive training sessions designed to equip believers in discipleship, spiritual rebirth, and obedience to the teachings of Jesus, especially those in Luke 10. These weekends have trained tens of thousands, and his YouTube channel, with over 30 million views and 160,000 subscribers, continues to spread his message far and wide. A man of unwavering faith, Torben's primary focus is to lead others to a transformative encounter with Jesus Christ. His direct approach to the Bible and deep personal relationship with God have made him a well-known figure in Christian circles, in Denmark, America and internationally.

For more information about Torben and his ministry, visit TheLastReformation.com or TorbenSondergaard.com

Other books by Torben Søndergaard

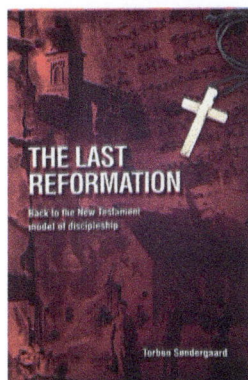

The Last Reformation

Much of what we see happening in the church today is built on more than just the New Testament. It's built, instead, mostly on the Old Testament, church culture, and paganism. In his book, Torben Søndergaard shares some of his journey out from more traditional church life to seeing a movement of disciples grow all over the world. This book emerged from his first desert period, a time he often thought about while he was in jail and that aided him during this time. The book has been translated into over twenty languages and has blessed many all over the world.

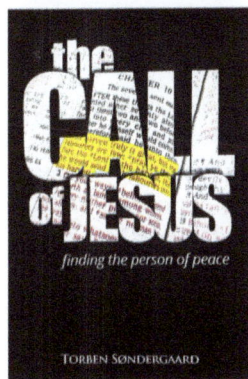

The Call of Jesus

This is an easy-to-understand "instruction manual" pulled from Scripture to help us effectively live the life to which Jesus has called us. This is based on Jesus' call to us in Luke 10. This teaching helps in becoming obedient disciples—seeing daily fruits—as you receive not only teaching but also practical tools that will make you and your church soul winners in your everyday lives.

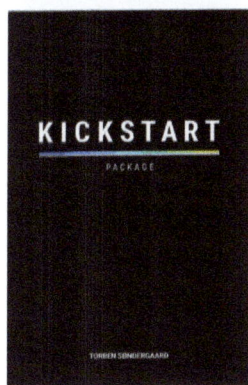

Kickstart Package

For years, Torben have been hosting life-changing kickstart weekends all over the world. Now, we bring the kickstart to you! This book helps you understand the basics of what a disciple of Christ is, what the gospel is, how to heal the sick and cast out demons, and make disciples as Jesus calls us all to do. Let The Kickstart Package help transform you and make an impact in your own church and network!

More books by Torben Sondergaard are The Sound Doctrine, Christian, Disciple, or Slave?

"The Kingdom Book," Torben's second book written in jail, will be published at the beginning of 2025.

For further information, visit TheLastReformation.com or TorbenSondergaard.com.

Free movies by Torben Søndergaard

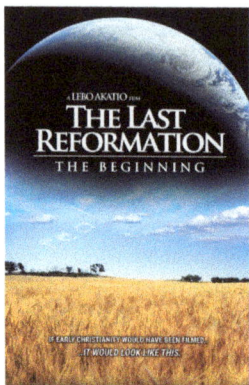

The Beginning

This documentary has changed the lives of many people all over the world, marking the beginning of their journey as disciples of Christ. The film shows what a Christian's life should look like—not just sitting in church dreaming about something more, but actively following Jesus and obeying His commands. This is a life where the gospel truly transforms a person from the inside out, where signs and wonders follow us as we obey our Lord's commands.

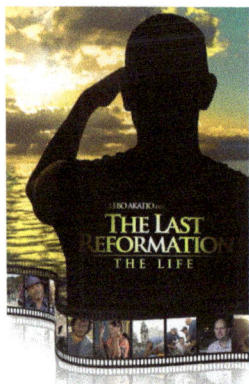

The Life

If the early apostles had a camera, it should look something like what you see here. A life following Jesus full of the Holy Spirit. From the living room of a pop-star to a homeless man on the streets in Brazil, this movie shows extraordinary and authentic moments of lives surrendered to Jesus, both the hardships and victories. Viewers are invited to experience the movement that is growing all around the world as people discover what it truly means to become disciples of Jesus.

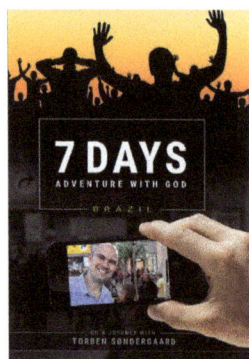

7 Days Adventure

Join Torben Søndergaard on a seven-day trip to Brazil that turns into a true adventure! You will witness things you've never seen before. God is showing us how real He is and what an amazing life He has for each and every one of us. Our lives should be very different from those who don't know Christ, as we follow a different Spirit, the Holy Spirit. This is a supernatural life with everything that follows. Watch the movie today and join the adventure.

Watch for free on www.TLRmovie.com

Other books by Torben Søndergaard

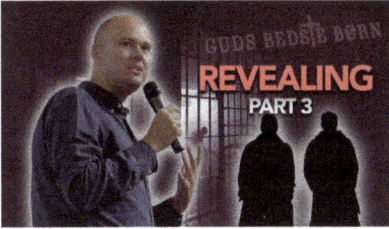

Revealing the Truth Series

Watch these four episodes in the "Fighting for the Gospel Revealing" series that show things are not as they seem.

The first episode focuses on the documentary that was broadcast on Danish TV. It shows the connection between this broadcast and a bill that was being passed at the same time in the Danish government and why Torben ended up leaving Denmark for the US.

In the second episode, they continue analyzing the documentary that was broadcast on Danish TV and address the false rumors that have been spread on social media.

In the third episode, the attention turns toward two specific individuals who have emerged as significant adversaries to Torben and his ministry. Their actions involve coordinating a campaign against Torben and his work both in Denmark and the United States.

The last episode in the "Revealing" series shows vital evidence around the persecution of Torben in the United States and the terrible effects of slander. The episode identifies the main source of this slander, which eventually led to Torben's detention.

This series will shed light on what happened and help us understand the fight we are in—a fight for the gospel.

You can watch the series on TorbenSondergaard.com or scan the QR code

Milton Keynes UK
Ingram Content Group UK Ltd.
UKHW020639041224
3391UKWH00002B/3